P9-EMO-879

Sunset

ANNUALS AND PERENNIALS

BY PHILIP EDINGER, JANET H. SANCHEZ,
AND THE EDITORS OF SUNSET BOOKS

SUNSET BOOKS • MENLO PARK, CALIFORNIA

INFINITE VARIETY

Like a tapestry that changes its color and pattern with the seasons, annuals and perennials bring endless beauty and variety to your garden. Their spectrum covers every possible hue, shade, and tint, and some have blossoms (or even leaves) in color combinations a textile designer might envy. Flower forms are likewise limitless—from the tidy simplicity of a daisy to the exotic beauty of salpiglossis, from the stately, sculptural elegance of iris to the delicacy of columbine. And the plants themselves run from gigantic to petite, in a range of habits and textures to suit any artistic desire and fill any garden need.

In this book, you will first learn how gardeners define annuals, perennials, and their in-between kin—the biennials. You'll then explore the opportunities for using these plants in the garden, finding design tips and plant lists that will help you come up with effective combinations. The next section presents sample garden designs to inspire your planning. These are followed by a thorough discussion of how to grow annuals and perennials and, finally, an encyclopedia of favorite plants.

The information in this book is distilled from experience—the trials, errors, and triumphs of generations of dedicated gardeners. Use it as a guide to creating your own wonderful garden of annuals and perennials.

SUNSET BOOKS

Vice President, General Manager: Richard A. Smeby
Vice President, Editorial Director: Bob Doyle
Production Director: Lory Day
Director of Operations: Rosann Sutherland
Art Director: Vasken Guiragossian

Staff for this book:
Managing Editor: Joan Beth Erickson
Sunset Books Senior Editor: Marianne Lipanovich
Copy Editor: Rebecca LaBrum
Contributing Editor: Tom Wilhite
Indexer and proofreader: Barbara J. Braasch
Photo Editor: Cynthia Del Fava
Production Coordinator: Eligio Hernandez

Art Director: Alice Rogers
Designer: Kathy Barone
Illustrators: Gwendolyn Babbitt, Erin O'Toole
Additional Illustrations: Jane McCreary, Lucy Sargeant, Elayne Sears, Jenny Speckels
Computer Production: Linda M. Bouchard

Cover: Assorted perennials and annuals, dominated by stately foxglove *(Digitalis purpurea)*. Photograph by Roger Foley. Border photograph of hosta foliage by Jerry Pavia.

10 9 8 7 6 5 4 3 2
First printing January 2002

Copyright © 2002 Sunset Publishing Corp., Menlo Park, CA 94025. Second edition. All rights reserved, including the right of reproduction in whole or in part in any form. Hardcover edition: Library of Congress Catalog Card Number: 2001096667. ISBN 0-376-03065-8. Softcover edition: Library of Congress Catalog Card Number: 2001094606. ISBN 0-376-03067-4.

Printed in the United States.
For additional copies of *Annuals and Perennials* or any other Sunset Book, call 1-800-526-5111 or visit our website at *www.sunsetbooks.com*

Contents

ANNUALS AND PERENNIALS

ON STAGE

Whether you stage your garden show in grand beds and borders or in a modest collection of containers on the patio, annuals and perennials can make each season's performance beautiful. These plants offer a wealth of colorful choices—so many, in fact, that narrowing the field down to just those that are right for you can be quite a challenge. In the next chapter (pages 10–43), we offer advice on matching plants to your garden conditions—soil type, exposure, available water, and so on. Before you begin that process, though, you'll find it useful to know just what the words "annual" and "perennial" mean to botanists (and to gardeners). We'll start by defining those terms—and discussing the less familiar category of biennials, as well. We'll then focus on the many ways to present these plants, using the photos at left and on the next four pages to illustrate the possibilities. You'll see traditional beds of annuals and perennials, cottage gardens featuring a charming jumble of all sorts of plants, and plots of brilliant flowers just right for showy bouquets. There are graceful ornamental grasses, fast-growing annual vines ideal for decorating trellises, and even lush gardens grown entirely in containers.

Photographed in autumn, this garden features a striking mix of late-flowering annuals and perennials, including asters, sedums, and nicotiana. A variety of plants with handsome foliage make the scene even brighter.

WHAT ARE ANNUALS AND PERENNIALS?

"Annual," "perennial," and "biennial" all have fairly straightforward botanical definitions. In gardening usage, though, the category lines can become somewhat blurred. For example, some plants a botanist would categorize as perennials can be grown most successfully as annuals.

ANNUALS

Botanically, an annual is a plant that completes its life cycle in a year or less. In the course of a single growing season, the seed germinates and the plant grows, blooms, goes to seed, and dies. Because they must complete their life cycle in such a short time, annuals grow and bloom quickly in their rush to set seed, bringing their joyous color to the garden in only a few months from sowing. They are reliable bloomers: if spent blossoms are removed, most kinds flower for a long period, persisting in their quest to produce seed.

Depending on the varieties you choose, annuals can decorate your garden for much of the year. Cool-season types (calendula and viola, for example) prosper in cool soils and mild temperatures—from fall through spring in mild-winter climates, from early to late spring elsewhere. Following the cool-season show are warm-season annuals such as cosmos and zinnia, which are typically planted after the year's last frost and, in most climates, bloom generously throughout summer and fall.

TOP: This bright group of warm-season annuals includes gloriosa daisies *(Rudbeckia hirta),* marigolds *(Tagetes),* and zinnias.

MIDDLE: Pansies *(Viola × wittrockiana)* grow and bloom best in cool weather.

BOTTOM: Though they're perennial in mild climates, garden geraniums *(Pelargonium × hortorum)* are treated as annuals in colder regions.

PERENNIALS

In botanical terms, perennials are nonwoody plants that live for more than 2 years. Unlike annuals, they return to grace the landscape year after year, requiring no replanting—though many grow at a somewhat relaxed pace and may require a season or two to settle in and reach their full potential.

Paeonia
'Festiva Maxima'

Among perennials, you'll find plants with various growth habits. Some, such as hosta and peony *(Paeonia),* die down to the ground at the end of each growing season, then reappear at the start of the next; these are often referred to as "herbaceous" plants. Others, including Shasta daisy *(Chrysanthemum maximum)* and coral bells *(Heuchera),* go through winter as low tufts of leaves, ready to grow when spring arrives. A third type of perennial is truly evergreen, with foliage that persists almost unchanged throughout the winter months. New Zealand flax *(Phormium),* some daylilies *(Hemerocallis),* and perennial pinks *(Dianthus)* are familiar examples.

A few plants, though technically perennials, may be grown as annuals. Examples include certain tender plants (those that cannot survive freezing temperatures) such as common geranium *(Pelargonium),* fibrous begonia, marguerite *(Chrysanthemum*

Surrounded by smoothly mowed lawn, this perennial island bed can be viewed from all sides.

In this mixed border, low-growing moss pink *(Phlox subulata)* and white evergreen candytuft *(Iberis sempervirens)* enhance the springtime blossoms of a dogwood tree.

frutescens), and some kinds of salvia and verbena. These flower year after year in mild-winter climates, but where winters are cold they're typically treated like annuals and discarded at the end of the growing season. Others, such as snapdragon *(Antirrhinum),* are hardy enough to live through frost—but because older plants don't perform as well as young ones, such hardier types too are usually grown as annuals.

BIENNIALS

By definition, these are plants that complete their life cycle in 2 years. During their first year, they grow from seed to form a foliage rosette, but they do not bloom. They live through the winter, experiencing the period of cold temperatures that many require to induce flowering; then, in the following spring or summer, they bloom, set seed, and die. Familiar biennials include foxglove *(Digitalis),* Canterbury bells *(Campanula medium),* hollyhock *(Alcea),* and sweet William *(Dianthus barbatus).* Note that for some biennials, breeders have developed strains that behave like annuals; that is, they bloom the first year from seed sown early in spring. Such plants are noted in the encyclopedia beginning on page 84.

Usually grown as biennials, tall hollyhocks *(Alcea)* are standouts in a sunny garden.

This cottage-style garden features an eclectic assortment of annuals, perennials, and ornamental grasses, as well as shrubs and small trees.

TOP: Salvia, spider flower *(Cleome),* petunias, and impatiens mingle in this pink-and-blue design. White-flowered phlox adds a refreshing accent.

RIGHT: Annuals such as larkspur *(Consolida)* and cosmos are ideal for bouquets.

ABOVE: Glowing orange and gold marigolds *(Tagetes)* in bright blue pots line a path.

LEFT: Intense purple petunias, red verbena, and red garden geraniums *(Pelargonium × hortorum)* bring summertime interest to container-grown evergreens and ornamental grasses.

RIGHT: Built on a raised bed, a cedar trellis cloaked in vining sweet peas *(Lathyrus)* offers a beautiful way to divide a large garden into smaller spaces.

BELOW: Featuring colorful annuals such as sunflowers *(Helianthus),* salvia, and coleus, this cheerful cottage garden looks great all summer.

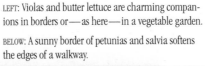

LEFT: Violas and butter lettuce are charming companions in borders or—as here—in a vegetable garden.

BELOW: A sunny border of petunias and salvia softens the edges of a walkway.

ABOVE: Impatiens is a popular choice for bringing bright color to areas in dappled sunlight or shade. Here, the vivid blooms are set off by a tidy edging of annual lobelia.

LEFT: Ornamental grasses, including blue oat grass *(Helictotrichon),* feather reed grass *(Calamagrostis),* and red Japanese blood grass *(Imperata)* bring this border alive with their texture, color, and movement.

Inch for inch, pound for pound, planting bed for planting bed—by any measure, annuals and perennials give you the greatest volume of beauty for your effort. For lavish production in a hurry, nothing compares with many annuals; and for year-after-year performance with minimal fussing,

ANNUALS AND PERENNIALS IN THE GARDEN

nothing touches perennials. And in all climates, you can find annuals and perennials that will deliver the goods, annually.

In the following pages, you'll first learn how to choose the plants best suited to your particular garden. Next, we discuss how to combine them effectively, reviewing elements such as size, shape, texture, and color. Throughout, we provide lists of annuals and perennials with specific characteristics. You'll find plants that prefer shade, tolerate dry soil, and enjoy life in boggy spots; you'll learn which ones provide flower color in each season. Other lists group plants by growth habit and foliage type—you'll see which ones are tall or short or bulky, which ones have bold or lacy or brightly colored leaves. We've also noted some "special-purpose" plants: those with enticing fragrance, flowers ideal for cutting, and blossoms that are magnets for butterflies and birds.

As varied as a Dutch still life, this artful combination of annuals and perennials features a white Siberian iris attended by *Geranium* 'Johnson's Blue', gray-leafed lamb's ears *(Stachys byzantina)*, purple pansies *(Viola × wittrockiana);* and pink snapdragon *(Antirrhinum).* Design by Kristin Home.

CHOOSING FOR SUCCESS

Some gardeners don't spend much time selecting plants: they already know which ones they want to grow, and devote their efforts to choosing spots where those plants are likely to flourish. Just as often, however, a gardener—particularly one confronting bare patches of earth!—focuses on location first, then seeks out plants that might thrive there. Either way, success hinges on matching the plants to the site. As you build your garden, start by thinking about your climate; then consider exposure, soil type, and the amount of water available.

If you're utterly determined to grow plants not suited to the native conditions, you can go to great lengths to modify the environment. But for lovely results with the least amount of struggle, choose plants that are likely to prosper with what your garden naturally offers.

To create a luxuriant garden in a shady spot, choose shade lovers such as hosta and yellow-flowered lady's-mantle *(Alchemilla)*.

CLIMATE

Summer heat, winter cold, degree of humidity—these are just a few basic features of climate. Add to these the amount and timing of rainfall, length of growing season, presence or absence of wind—and you begin to see the countless combinations that result in vastly different gardening conditions as you move from one region to another. In the encyclopedia beginning on page 84, each annual and perennial is zoned according to *Sunset's* climate zones, which cover Alaska, Hawaii, and the contiguous 48 states, including adjacent areas of Canada and Mexico. Mapped and described on pages 184–188, these zones are unique entities, each combining a wide variety of climatic factors that affect gardening. Find your zone, then choose plants suited to it.

EXPOSURE

Every plant has a preferred exposure. A plant that needs a full day of sun will languish or fail if planted in a shaded place; conversely, one needing shelter from direct sun will certainly disappoint if given a sunny spot. In some cases, exposure needs vary according to climate: certain plants thrive in full sun where summers are cool or overcast but must have partial shade in hot-summer regions. In the encyclopedia, we note the best exposure for each plant. Observe your garden carefully, noting its sun and shade patterns; then choose plants accordingly. Remember, too,

ABOVE: Containers give you control over soil and exposure. Featured here are white impatiens and pink-flowered annual phlox *(Phlox drummondii)*.

LEFT: Blazing with color, these summer-flowering perennials adapt well to the wind and cold of the eastern Rockies. Pink Mexican evening primrose *(Oenothera speciosa* 'Rosea') fronts carmine Jupiter's beard *(Centranthus)*, orange penstemon, and purple *Salvia × sylvestris* 'Blauhügel'.

that exposure can change with the seasons. A patch receiving afternoon shade in early spring may be considerably sunnier during the summer, while one getting plenty of sun in the warmer months may be too shaded early in the year for sun-loving spring annuals and perennials.

SOIL

Some soils retain water so well they're likely to be on the soggy side. Others drain relatively quickly, while still others are so porous they dry out in no time. Knowing just what type your garden holds is important when you're choosing plants, since some demand fast drainage and others prefer a really retentive soil. Another factor to consider is soil pH: if your soil is notably acid or alkaline, it's likely to be unsatisfactory for many plants.

Of course, soil can be modified to some degree to accommodate a broader range of plants—and if it's truly inhospitable, you can do an end-run around it by filling raised beds, planters, or containers with good, plant-friendly soil. For the simplest path to success, though, choose plants that appreciate your native soil, either "as is" or with only minor modifications. For more on soils and soil preparation, see pages 62–65.

WATER

All plants require water for survival—some more, some less. Whether you need to water frequently, occasionally, or never depends in part on soil type (moisture-retentive soils let you go longer between waterings than sandy ones do), in part on the usual rainfall pattern in your region and the needs of the plants in your garden. Where summer rainfall is the norm (and the rainfall is well timed), even plants requiring regular moisture may get through a growing season with little or no supplemental watering. However, many regions typically experience long dry periods during spring, summer, and early fall. In these areas, you have two choices. You can plant annuals and perennials that need regular water, then make sure you give them enough to grow well; or you can choose low-water-use plants and save yourself considerable trouble. Do be sure, though, that you don't locate plants with differing water requirements side by side; this makes it virtually impossible to give each one what it prefers.

A lightly shaded spot with constantly moist to boggy soil brings out the best in perennial cardinal flower *(Lobelia cardinalis)*.

COLD HARDINESS

In order to live up to their name, perennials must be able to survive the expected winter low temperatures in your area. The climate zones noted for each plant let you know the degree of cold tolerance you can expect. However, certain factors can moderate winter cold and lessen the chance of damage to plants, especially marginally hardy ones. A good snow cover provides an insulating blanket, keeping the ground—and thus plant roots—a bit warmer than the air above. And every garden has its warm spots, such as wind-sheltered locations and planting beds near surfaces that absorb and radiate heat (such as south-facing walls).

Plantings near a lake, river, or ocean must be able to endure the winds that sweep unimpeded across the water. This sturdy planting contains yellow cosmos and African marigolds *(Tagetes erecta)*, coral zinnias, red petunias, and rosy purple coneflower *(Echinacea)*.

PLANTS FOR SHADE

Pale, delicate blossoms are suspended beneath the elegant leaves of Solomon's seal (*Polygonatum odoratum* 'Variegatum').

Helleborus orientalis

ANNUALS

Ageratum houstonianum. Zones 1–45
Cerinthe major. Zones 1–24, 32, 34–45
Cleome bassleriana. Zones 1–45
*Coleus × hybridus. All zones
Gomphrena. Zones 1–45; H1, H2
*Impatiens. All zones
Lobelia erinus. All zones
Matthiola. Zones 1–45
Myosotis sylvatica. A1–A3; 1–24, 32–45
Nicotiana. All zones
Nigella damascena. All zones
Tropaeolum majus. All zones
*Viola. Zones vary

* = grows as perennial in warmest zones (see encyclopedia)

PERENNIALS

Acanthus. Zones vary
Aconitum. Zones A1–A3; 1–9, 14–21, 34–45
Adenophora. Zones A2, A3; 1–10, 14–24, 30–43
Agapanthus. Zones vary
Agastache. Zones vary
Alchemilla mollis. Zones A2, A3; 1–9, 14–24, 31–43
Alstroemeria. Zones 5–9, 14–24, 26, 28, 31, 32 (warmer parts), 34; H1
Amsonia. Zones vary
Anemone. Zones vary
Aquilegia. Zones vary
Aruncus. Zones vary
Astilbe. Zones 1–7, 14–17, 32–43
Begonia, Semperflorens group. Zones 14–28; H1, H2
Bergenia. Zones vary

Brunnera macrophylla. Zones 1–24, 31–45
Calibrachoa. Zones 2–43
Campanula. Zones vary
Cimicifuga. Zones 1–7, 17, 32–45
Corydalis. Zones 2–9, 14–24, 32–35, 37, 39–43
Dicentra. Zones vary
Dictamnus albus. 1–9, 31–45
Digitalis. Zones vary
Erigeron. Zones vary
Eupatorium. Zones vary
Filipendula. Zones vary
Geranium (some). Zones vary
Helleborus. Zones vary
Heuchera, × *Heucherella.* Zones vary
Hosta. Zones vary
Ligularia. Zones vary
Lobelia (most). Zones vary
Myosotis scorpioides. Zones A1–A3; 1–24, 32–45
Nepeta. Zones 1–24, 30, 32–43
Oenothera (some). Zones vary
Ornamental grasses (some). See pages 126–129
Phlox (some). Zones vary
Phormium. Zones 5–9, 14–28; H1, H2
Physostegia virginiana. Zones A3; 1–9, 14–24, 26–45
Polygonatum. Zones A1–A3; 1–9, 14–17, 28–45
Primula. Zones vary
Pulmonaria. Zones 1–9, 14–17, 32–43
Rodgersia. Zones 2–9, 14–17, 32–41
Solidago. Zones 1–11, 14–23, 28–45
Stachys. Zones vary
Thalictrum. Zones vary
Viola odorata. Zones vary

Shady spots may be a bit dark—but that's no reason for shaded plantings to be dull or colorless. In the planting above, warm pink plumes of astilbe are complemented by the bold leaves of two hostas ('Janet Craig' and 'Ginko Craig') and the bright green, paddle-like foliage of *Bergenia cordifolia*.

Winsome violets *(Viola odorata)* carpet a shaded garden in early spring.

In another color-sparked shade garden, 'Rheinland' astilbe and fringed bleeding heart *(Dicentra eximia)* combine with contrasting leaves of *Hosta* 'Gold Standard' and *Hosta sieboldiana* 'Elegans'.

PLANTS THAT NEED LITTLE WATER

ANNUALS

Eschscholzia californica. Zones 1–45; H1

PERENNIALS

Achillea. Zones A1–A3; 1–24, 26, 28–45

Agapanthus. Zones vary

Artemisia. Zones vary

Baptisia. Zones 1–24, 28–45

Centranthus ruber. Zones 2–9, 12–24, 28–43; H1

Coreopsis (some). Zones vary

Erigeron karvinskianus. Zones 8, 9, 12–28; H1, H2

Euphorbia (many). Zones vary

Gaura lindheimeri. Zones 2b–35, 37, 38 (coastal), 39

Lobelia laxiflora. Zones 7–9, 12–24

Oenothera. Zones vary

Ornamental grasses (some). See pages 126–129

Penstemon (some). Zones vary

Perovskia. Zones 2–24, 28–43

Phlomis. Zones vary

Phormium. Zones 5–9, 14–28; H1, H2

Verbena (some). Zones vary

Zauschneria (most). Zones vary

Western native California fuchsia *(Zauschneria californica latifolia)* takes heat in stride and can survive on rainfall alone.

ABOVE: California poppy *(Eschscholzia),* the state's signature flower, offers silken beauty in orange as well as yellow, white, and assorted pastel colors.

RIGHT: Choose the right plants, and you'll get maximum color for just moderate amounts of water. Fluorescent purple *Verbena rigida* and red *Penstemon* × *gloxinioides* 'Firebird' steal this scene.

PLANTS FOR CONSTANTLY MOIST SOIL

ANNUALS

Myosotis sylvatica. Zones A1–A3; 1–24, 32–45

PERENNIALS

Aconitum. Zones A1–A3; 1–9, 14–21, 31–45

Aruncus. Zones vary

Chelone. Zones 1–9, 14–24, 28–43

Eupatorium. Zones vary

Filipendula (some). Zones vary

Hosta. Zones vary

Iris, Japanese. Zones 1–10, 14–24, 32–45

Ligularia. Zones vary

Lobelia (many). Zones vary

Monarda. Zones vary

Myosotis scorpioides. Zones A1–A3; 1–24, 32–45

Ornamental grasses (some). See pages 126–129

Primula (some). Zones vary

Rodgersia. Zones 2–9, 14–17, 32–41

For beautifying a damp swale, you can't go wrong with indestructible annual forget-me-nots *(Myosotis sylvatica).* These plants require little maintenance after the initial planting, and volunteer seedlings keep new plants coming along year after year.

Hosta sieboldiana

Japanese iris 'Caprician Butterfly' (above left) revels in pondside soil, even shallow water. Bee balm *(Monarda)* cultivars also perform best where the soil never dries out; shown above right is 'Cambridge Scarlet'.

DESIGNING WITH PLANTS

Whether you envision a garden that's all annuals, exclusively perennials, or a combination of both, a few basic principles of design will help you compose an attractive floral "painting." One simple statement sums it up: rather than focusing on color alone, consider the entire plant. Though color may be the most obvious component of a planting (see pages 28–31), other features work with it to create a pleasing, interesting, and memorable whole.

Complete with brick-wall backdrop, this classic English-style perennial border exemplifies artful plant combination, with flower colors, plant sizes and shapes, foliage textures, and bloom seasons all taken into consideration.

PLANT SIZE

Annuals and perennials vary enormously in size. In both categories, you'll find plants that grow just ankle high, giants that overtop all but the exceptional basketball player, and individuals at every possible height in between.

Size matters in several ways. The standard advice is to locate tall plants at the back of a bed, short ones in front. This rule is a foolproof one, but nonetheless, it can be broken to great effect. Placing a tall plant in the foreground can provide a telling accent, perking up the surrounding flatness—an especially effective tactic if the accent plant differs markedly in shape or texture from its companions.

In addition to considering sizes of plants relative to each other, think about plant size relative to planting-area size. In a relatively narrow bed (3 to 5 feet deep) or a small area, you won't want to use the very tallest, largest individuals—such as hollyhock *(Alcea)* and rose-mallow *(Hibiscus)*. Instead, scale down the heights and widths of the plants you use to keep them in proportion to the space. Reserve the true colossi for large planting areas, where they'll contribute to the design rather than overwhelming it.

Contemporary, pocket-size perennial border shows the classic attention to colors, shapes, and textures, forming a garden that presents an harmonious overall picture yet showcases each plant.

Lavish sweep of mixed perennials gains distinction from its striking complementary colors (yellow and violet), contrasting leaf and flower shapes, and use of vertical-growing plants as accents among spreading and billowy individuals.

Bear in mind that some perennials, in particular, grow dramatically higher at bloom time, sending up tall flowering stems from relatively low foliage masses. In these cases, height is a seasonal accent, not a permanent design element; if the plants are fairly wispy looking (as are *Verbena bonariensis* and *Anemone × hybrida,* for example), they can be used even in smaller beds, since their overall bulk is slight.

PLANT SHAPE

Spreading, rounded, vertical, fountainlike, vaselike—annuals and perennials come in as many shapes as they do sizes. And to spice up any planting, aim for variety in shape as well as size. Letting just one shape dominate will lead to monotony, whereas choosing contrasting ones automatically calls attention to the individuality of each plant or group of plants.

As noted under "Plant Size" (facing page), many plants become taller when in bloom. This increased height is accompanied by a change in form. In some cases, the entire foliage mass rises, making the plant taller and bulkier; in others, stems simply shoot up from leafy clumps that remain low. When you use these plants, think about how their changes will affect the garden's design over the course of the growing season.

PLANT DENSITY

Some plants look solid, opaque, and weighty; others are airier, with an openness to their structure that lets you see into or right through the foliage mass. A planting composed entirely of dense plants looks lumpy and impenetrable, while one using exclusively see-through plants seems insubstantial. It's a balance between the two types that makes for a dynamic composition. Some plants present a combination of density and openness, particularly those that send up flowering stems high above a thick foliage mass. Many ornamental grasses and clumping plants with narrow or swordlike leaves—New Zealand flax *(Phormium),* for example—are solid looking near the base but much less so toward the leaf tips.

Ligularia stenocephala 'The Rocket'

FOLIAGE SIZE AND TEXTURE

Though all leaves serve the same function, they are far from uniform in appearance. Just compare *Hosta* 'Sum and Substance' with threadleaf coreopsis *(Coreopsis verticillata)*—the former has broad, plate-sized leaves, while the latter's fine, feathery foliage is reminiscent of green threads. Adding to the variety is the fact that leaf size and texture don't necessarily correspond to plant size and shape. There are big plants with small, fine leaves, small plants with big, coarse leaves, bulky plants with filmy foliage, and open-looking ones with large leaves.

In designing a planting area, make use of the vast array of leaf widths, lengths, shapes, and textures. Remember that large, bold leaves are attention-getters, regardless of plant size; use them carefully, as accents. Small- and filmy-leafed plants are more subtle and retiring, fine choices for buffering and highlighting bolder-leafed individuals.

FOLIAGE COLOR

Green is the color we automatically associate with leaves. But there are hundreds of different greens—some lighter, some darker, some blended with varying amounts of yellow, blue, or gray. And some plants depart quite markedly from the usual, offering leaves in "unconventional" colors: gray (sometimes so pale as to be near-white), blue, yellow, red, bronze, purple, and variegated combinations. Such colored-leaf plants (listed on pages 26–27) are first-rate accents, adding sparkle to the garden's greenness and working in concert with floral color.

FOLIAGE SURFACE QUALITY

Combining elements of both texture and color, the quality of a leaf's surface is a subtle design feature that can be used to great advantage, particularly in plantings that emphasize foliage rather than flowers. Some leaves look polished, shiny enough to reflect light; others have a matte finish, like slate, or have a whitish bloom like that on the skin of a plum. Still others are covered with silky hairs that give them a silvery sheen. And some leaves are thickly furred and totally nonreflective.

ABOVE: Brilliant 'Sunrise' coleus is highlighted by the slim foliage of ornamental grass and the spent flower heads of lily-of-the-Nile *(Agapanthus)*.

RIGHT: Vividly striped leaves of 'Pretoria' canna (right) have a bold shape that contrasts with adjacent perennials—but their colors harmonize with orange Mexican sunflower *(Tithonia)* and blue floss flower *(Ageratum)*.

LEFT: More than color catches the eye in this varied composition. The flowers differ markedly in shape, too, blooming in tall spires, loose clusters, tight bunches, and flat-topped heads.

TOP: Pleasant mixed planting of annuals and perennials is accented by a fountainlike clump of eulalia grass (*Miscanthus sinensis* 'Variegatus').

BOTTOM: Varied colors and shapes of leaves and blossoms provide nonstop interest. Design by Landcraft Environments.

FLOWER SIZE AND PRESENTATION

Though color plays an important role in defining floral impact, it's only one part of the picture. A flower's size and shape, the way it is carried on the plant—these too are features to consider.

Viewed individually, a large flower attracts more attention than a small one. But floral abundance can tip the scale the other way: a plant smothered in small blossoms can be showier than one with just a scattering of large blooms. Likewise, a smaller cluster of packed-together flowers may carry more visual weight than a larger but looser cluster.

Besides thinking about abundance and density, consider just how the blossoms are presented on the plant. Some, such as peony *(Paeonia),* are borne singly, each at the tip of an individual stem. Others, like hollyhock *(Alcea),* are carried in upright, many-flowered spikes, with the blooms set so close to the stem they look almost pasted on. Still others come in clusters that may be round, dome shaped, or flat topped. You'll find flowers in open sprays, blossoms arrayed like bursting fireworks, and some—like baby's breath *(Gypsophila)*—that are sprinkled over the plant like a shower of confetti. All these variations let you produce textural effects quite independent of color.

PLANT CHARACTER

A dynamic planting relies on variety in plant habit as much as it does on creative use of color. On these two pages, we list plants that depart from the typical rounded, well-foliaged shape—tall types good for accents, large, bulky sorts, and see-through kinds with an airy, open look.

VERTICAL PLANTS

Though their heights vary, the following plants all provide strongly vertical effects. In some cases, the entire plant is spire-like; in others, only the flowering stems are tall and slim.

ANNUALS

Alcea rosea. Zones 1–45

Antirrhinum majus. Zones A3; 1–45

Celosia, plume kinds. Zones A3; 1–45; H1, H2

Consolida ajacis. Zones 1–45

Moluccella laevis. Zones 1–45; H1, H2

PERENNIALS

Acanthus. Zones vary

Aconitum. Zones A1–A3; 1–9, 14–21, 34–45

Adenophora. Zones A2, A3; 1–10, 14–24, 30–43

Astilbe (some). Zones 1–7, 14–17, 32–43

Baptisia. Zones 1–24, 28–45

Campanula (some). Zones vary

Delphinium. Zones vary

Digitalis. Zones vary

Liatris. Zones A2, A3; 1–10, 14–24, 26, 28–45

Ligularia (some). Zones vary

Lobelia (some). Zones vary

Lupinus. Zones A1–A3; 1–7, 14–17, 34, 36–45

Ornamental grasses (some). See pages 126–129

Penstemon (many). Zones vary

Physostegia virginiana. Zones A3; 1–9, 14–24, 26–45

Salvia (some). Zones vary

Verbascum. Zones vary

Veronica (some). Zones vary

For a stunning vertical accent in an easy-to-grow plant, nothing touches stately foxgloves. Shown here are blossom spires of *Digitalis purpurea*, Excelsior strain.

Aconitum napellus

Given the conditions they need, hybrid lupines *(Lupinus)* bloom lavishly, bearing spikes of sweet pea–shaped blossoms in a wide range of colors.

Verbena bonariensis sends sprays of violet flowers skyward on a network of needle-thin branches.

Though they differ in form, eulalia grass (*Miscanthus sinensis* 'Variegatus') and purple-flowered spotted Joe Pye weed *(Eupatorium purpureum maculatum)* both contribute mass to this planting.

LARGE, BULKY PLANTS

Their shapes vary—some are upright growing, others broader and more rounded—but all these plants contribute solidity and mass to a planting. You can consider them the annual and perennial equivalents of shrubs.

ANNUALS

Cleome hassleriana. Zones 1–45
Helianthus annuus. All zones
Lavatera trimestris. All zones
Ricinus communis. Zones 1–45; H1, H2
Tithonia rotundifolia. All zones

PERENNIALS

Aruncus dioicus. Zones A2, A3; 1–9, 14–17, 31–43
Baptisia. Zones 1–24, 28–45
Canna. Zones 6–9, 12–31, warmer parts of 32; H1, H2

Eupatorium (most). Zones vary
Filipendula rubra. Zones A1–A3; 1–9, 14–17, 31–45
Hibiscus moscheutos. Zones 2–24, 26–41; H1
Ornamental grasses (many). See pages 126–129
Phormium. Zones 5–9, 14–28; H1, H2
Rodgersia (most). Zones 2–9, 14–17, 32–41

Big, bold, and beautiful—this hybrid New Zealand flax *(Phormium)* is a real traffic stopper.

FILMY, SEE-THROUGH PLANTS

In contrast to the bulky-looking plants listed at left, the following individuals have a see-through structure. In a few cases, the entire plant has an open look; in the rest, intricate or wispy flower stems rise above the main foliage mass, giving the impression of floral lace.

PERENNIALS

Anemone. Zones vary
Aster (some). Zones vary
Cimicifuga. Zones 1–7, 17, 32–45
Eryngium. Zones vary
Filipendula. Zones vary
Foeniculum vulgare 'Purpurascens'. Zones 2b–11, 14–24, 29–41; H1, H2
Gaura lindheimeri. Zones 2b–35, 37, 38 (coastal), 39
Gypsophila paniculata. Zones A2, A3; 1–10, 14–16, 18–21, 31–45; H1
Heuchera (many). Zones vary
Kniphofia. Zones 2–9, 14–24, 28–41
Limonium. Zones vary
Ornamental grasses (some). See pages 126–129
Perovskia. Zones 2–24, 28–43
Thalictrum. Zones vary
Verbena bonariensis. Zones 8–24, 26 (northern), 28
Verbena bonariensis. Zones 8–24, 28–31, warmer parts of 32

FOLIAGE CHARACTER

Flowers typically put on a show for just part of the growing season—but foliage enhances your garden from spring until frost, if not beyond. Use leaves of various shapes, sizes, and textures to add long-lasting appeal to your plantings.

FERNLIKE FOLIAGE

Like maidenhair fern, the plants listed below have leaves composed of numerous small leaflets that are more or less rounded or oval.

PERENNIALS

Aquilegia. Zones vary

Aruncus. Zones vary

Astilbe. Zones 1–7, 14–17, 32–43

Cimicifuga. Zones 1–7, 17, 32–45

Corydalis. Zones 2–9, 14–24, 32–35, 37, 39–43

Delphinium. Zones vary

Dicentra. Zones vary

Filipendula. Zones vary

Thalictrum. Zones vary

NARROW, GRASSLIKE, OR SWORDLIKE LEAVES

Varying from fountainlike to stiffly upright, these clumping perennials have leaves that contrast sharply in form with all other foliage shapes.

PERENNIALS

Agapanthus. Zones vary

Dianthus. Zones vary

Hemerocallis. Zones 1–45; H1, H2

Iris. Zones vary

Kniphofia. Zones 2–9, 14–24, 28–41

Liatris. Zones A2, A3; 1–10, 14–24, 26, 28–45

Ornamental grasses. See pages 126–129

Phormium. Zones 5–9, 14–28; H1, H2

Swordlike leaves of 'Yellow Wave' New Zealand flax *(Phormium)* rise above a riotous mix of coleus. Design by David Culp.

Demure pink flowers of fringed bleeding heart *(Dicentra eximia)* are beautifully set off by the finely divided, fernlike foliage.

Arching leaves of zebra grass *(Miscanthus sinensis* 'Zebrinus') almost seem to embrace the sweet William *(Dianthus barbatus)* and gloriosa daisies *(Rudbeckia hirta)* planted below.

Hostas are classic foliage plants, including a world of choices in an incredible array of leaf shapes, sizes, and colors.

LARGE LEAVES

The sheer size of their leaves gives these plants a real garden presence. The plants vary in overall size and shape, but any one of them makes a dramatic statement in the landscape.

ANNUALS

Ricinus communis. Zones 1–45; H1, H2

PERENNIALS

Acanthus. Zones vary

Bergenia. Zones vary

Canna. Zones 6–9, 12–31, warmer parts of 32; H1, H2

Helleborus. Zones vary

Hosta (some). Zones vary

Ligularia. Zones vary

Phlomis. Zones vary

Rodgersia. Zones 2–9, 14–17, 32–41

Salvia sclarea. Zones 2–24, 27–41

Verbascum (many). Zones vary

FILIGREE FOLIAGE

Threadlike leaves or leaf segments give these plants a soft, filmy look. In mixed plantings, they provide a nice contrast to large-leafed plants.

ANNUALS

Consolida ajacis. Zones 1–45

Cosmos. Zones A3; 1–45

Eschscholzia californica. Zones 1–45; H1

Nigella damascena. All zones

Tagetes. All zones

PERENNIALS

Achillea. Zones A1–A3; 1–24, 26, 28–45

Aconitum (some). Zones A1–A3; 1–9, 14–21, 34–45

Artemisia. Zones vary

Chrysanthemum (some). Zones vary

Coreopsis verticillata. Zones 1–24, 26, 28–45

Foeniculum vulgare 'Purpurascens'. Zones 2b–11, 14–24, 29–41; H1, H2

Perovskia. Zones 2–24, 28–43

Verbena (some). Zones vary

LEFT: Leaves of open, airy love-in-a-mist *(Nigella)* resemble delicate netting.

RIGHT: Threadleaf coreopsis *(Coreopsis verticillata)* is a more compact plant with threadlike foliage.

FOLIAGE COLOR

Flowers don't have a monopoly on color! As you design your garden beds, don't overlook the contributions that plants with colored foliage can make to any composition. Though leaves are typically green, there are plenty of plants with foliage in other colors: near-blue, yellow, red, pink, bronze, purple, gray, even white. In addition to these, you'll find variegated combinations that range from subtle to vividly showy. Colored-leaf plants are perfect accents for a green background, and gray-foliaged types also make lovely companions for bright or pastel flowers.

'Halcyon' hosta creates a startling patch of blue.

BLUE LEAVES

ANNUALS

Cerinthe major 'Pupurascens'.
 Zones 1–24, 32, 34–45

PERENNIALS

Dicentra (several). Zones vary
Eryngium. Zones vary
Hosta (some). Zones vary
Ornamental grasses (some).
 See pages 126–129

YELLOW LEAVES

ANNUALS

Coleus × *hybridus.* All zones

PERENNIALS

Chrysanthemum parthenium 'Aureum'.
 Zones 2–24, 28–45
Helichrysum petiolare 'Limelight'.
 Zones 16, 17, 22–24
Hosta (some). Zones vary
Phormium (some). Zones 5–9, 14–28;
 H1, H2
Stachys byzantina 'Primrose Heron'.
 Zones 1–24, 29–43

GRAY LEAVES

PERENNIALS

Achillea (some). Zones A1–A3; 1–24,
 26, 28–45
Artemisia. Zones vary
Centaurea cineraria. Zones 8–30
Cerastium tomentosum. Zones A1,
 A2; 1–24, 32–45
Dianthus (some). Zones vary
Nepeta. Zones 1–24, 30, 32–43
Ornamental grasses (some).
 See pages 126–129
Perovskia. Zones 2–24, 28–43
Salvia argentea. Zones 1–24, 26,
 28–45
Stachys byzantina. Zones 1–24,
 29–43
Verbascum (some). Zones vary
Zauschneria (most). Zones vary

LEFT: Among colored-leaf plants, coleus offers some of the brightest choices. These varieties sport foliage in shades of yellow to chartreuse.

RIGHT: Gray-leafed plants such as this *Artemisia schmidtiana* 'Silver Mound' add a soft, cool touch to the garden.

Colored foliage can be subtle—but 'Tropicana' canna is downright gaudy, with leaves striped in purple, green, yellow, pink, and red.

VARIEGATED LEAVES

ANNUALS

Coleus × hybridus. All zones
Euphorbia marginata. Zones 1–45
Impatiens, New Guinea Hybrids (some). All zones
Tropaeolum majus (some). All zones

PERENNIALS

Agapanthus (some). Zones vary
Aquilegia (some). Zones vary
Aurinia saxatilis 'Dudley Nevill Variegated'. Zones 1–24, 32–43
Begonia, Semperflorens group (some). Zones 14–28; H1, H2
Brunnera macrophylla (several). Zones 1–24, 31–45
Canna (some). Zones 6–9, 12–31, warmer parts of 32; H1, H2
Filipendula ulmaria 'Variegata'. Zones 1–9, 14–17, 31–45
Gaura lindheimeri 'Corrie's Gold'. Zones 2b–35, 37, 38 (coastal), 39
Helichrysum petiolare 'Variegata'. Zones 16, 17, 22–24
Heuchera (several). Zones vary
Hosta (many). Zones vary
Pelargonium (some). Zones 8, 9, 12–24
Phormium (some). Zones 5–9, 14–28; H1, H2

Physostegia virginiana 'Variegata'. Zones A3; 1–9, 14–24, 26–45
Polygonatum odoratum 'Variegatum'. Zones A1–A3; 1–9, 14–17, 28–43
Pulmonaria. Zones 1–9, 14–17, 32–43
Sedum (several). Zones vary

BRONZE, RED, PURPLE, PINK LEAVES

ANNUALS

Celosia (some). Zones A3; 1–45; H1, H2
Coleus × hybridus. All zones
Eschscholzia californica, Thai Silk strain. Zones 1–45; H1
Impatiens, New Guinea Hybrids (some). All zones
Perilla frutescens purpurascens. All zones
Ricinus communis (some). Zones 1–45; H1, H2

PERENNIALS

Begonia, Semperflorens group (some). Zones 14–28; H1, H2
Bergenia (some). Zones vary
Canna (some). Zones 6–9, 12–31, warmer parts of 32; H1, H2
Cimicifuga simplex (several). Zones 1–7, 17, 32–45
Eupatorium rugosum 'Chocolate'. Zones 1–10, 14–17, 28–45

Euphorbia (some). Zones vary
Foeniculum vulgare 'Purpurascens'. Zones 2b–11, 14–24, 29–41; H1, H2
Gaura lindheimeri 'Siskiyou Pink'. Zones 2b–35, 37, 38 (coastal), 39
Heuchera (several). Zones vary
Ligularia dentata 'Dark Beauty'. Zones 1–9, 14–17, 32, 34, 36–43
Lobelia (some). Zones vary
Ornamental grasses (some). See pages 126–129
Penstemon digitalis 'Husker Red'. Zones 1–9, 14–24, 29–43
Phormium (some). Zones 5–9, 14–28; H1, H2
Sedum telephium (some). Zones 1–24, 29–43

TOP: Glowing burgundy leaves of 'Dark Star' coleus
BOTTOM: 'Yellow Wave' New Zealand flax *(Phormium)*

This assortment of warm colors features bicolored gloriosa daisies *(Rudbeckia hirta)* surrounded by petite orange zinnias and yellow celosia and calendulas.

DESIGNING WITH COLOR

Annuals and perennials are a reliable and tremendously varied source of garden color—probably the main reason for their immense popularity. To guarantee color groupings that are sure to please, take time to study the basics outlined here before you finalize your design. When you're ready to make your choices, take a look at the charts on pages 32–37, where every flowering annual and perennial described in the plant encyclopedia is listed according to the colors it offers and the time of year it blooms.

THE COLOR WHEEL

The color display shown at left arranges the spectrum in a wheel, making it easy to see the relationships between colors. Refer to it as you review the discussion below.

HUE. A pure hue is an undiluted color, with no addition of white, gray, or black. Three hues are *primary colors*: red, yellow, and blue. No mixture of colors can produce them. Three other hues, each resulting from mixing two primary colors, are *secondary colors*: violet (red plus blue), green (yellow plus blue), and orange (yellow plus red).

VALUE. As the color wheel shows, each pure hue can become lighter (as you go toward the wheel's center) or darker (as you approach the perimeter). These gradations are called *values*. Adding white to a hue produces the lighter values referred to as *tints*; the addition of black results in darker *shades*.

SATURATION. Hues can be bright or dull, a condition described as degree of *saturation* (also called *intensity*). Differences in saturation result from the amount of gray added to a hue: the more gray you add, the duller and less saturated the color. Gray values are called *tones*.

WARM VERSUS COOL COLORS. When you draw a line across the color wheel between green and yellow-green on one side, between red and red-violet on the other, you divide the colors into two groups: one *warm*, the other *cool*. The warm colors are yellow, orange, and red; the cool ones are violet, blue, and green.

Shade
Hue
Tint
Tone

COLOR COMBINATIONS

The color wheel lets you view all sorts of color combinations at a glance. Three possible schemes are described on the following two pages: monochromatic, harmonious, and contrasting. Also discussed are white and gray, two "colors" not

Their colors are harmonious—but the red-violet lobelia and warm red scarlet sage *(Salvia splendens)* shown here are so rich and intense they almost seem to contrast with each other.

A horticultural heat wave, this landscape sizzles with shimmering, summery shades of yellow, orange, and red from African marigolds *(Tagetes erecta),* zinnias, and bedding begonias.

TOP: Featuring lighter, softer values of the red-and-violet combination shown on the facing page, this planting of pink bee balm *(Monarda)* and blue-violet speedwell *(Veronica)* is purely harmonious.

BOTTOM: Leaves of 'Palace Purple' coral bells *(Heuchera)* and blue blossoms of catmint *(Nepeta × faassenii)* are another harmonious pairing.

represented on the wheel but widely found in flowers and foliage. Both can be used in virtually any color combination.

MONOCHROMATIC. The simplest color scheme is centered on a single hue—blue, for example—and includes flowers in all that hue's tints, shades, and various saturations. The result is almost automatically pleasant, though monochromatic schemes based on warm colors run the risk of being overassertive. To avoid monotony, select plants with different forms and a variety of foliage colors, textures, and shapes.

The all-white garden is another application of the monochromatic idea, though white, strictly speaking, is not a color (see page 31).

HARMONIOUS. On the color wheel, harmonious colors are those that lie between any two primary hues. Moving from yellow to red, for example, you'll find yellow-

ABOVE: Pairing primary colors with similar values creates an effective contrast — as here, where yellow coneflower (*Rudbeckia fulgida sullivantii* 'Goldsturm') combines with 'Blue Fortune' agastache.

RIGHT: Coleus foliage in red and near-yellow offers another example of contrasting primary colors. Orange-red impatiens makes the picture even brighter.

Full-strength yellow gloriosa daisies *(Rudbeckia hirta)* complement lavender-blue penstemon and purple coneflowers *(Echinacea)* in rosy violet.

orange, orange, and orange-red. A broadly harmonious composition includes the full range of colors between the two primaries as well as one of those two hues; the most limited harmonious scheme encompasses just two adjacent colors on the wheel (yellow and yellow-orange, for example). Thanks to the close relationship between the colors used, harmonious combinations are pleasing to the eye. And because two hues are involved rather than just one, they're a bit livelier than monochromatic schemes.

CONTRASTING. Color contrasts occur between two totally unrelated colors. The primary hues provide an obvious example of vivid contrasts. Another contrast is formed by *complementary* colors — those opposite each other on the color wheel, such as blue and orange or yellow and violet. In most cases, you'll be aiming for contrasting flower colors; but note that the complement to red is green. Vivid red scarlet sage *(Salvia splendens)* against a backdrop of green foliage creates as true a contrast as blue delphiniums behind orange daylilies *(Hemerocallis)*.

Contrasts involving fully saturated colors are most effective when used in moderation, as accents or foils for quieter, more harmonious schemes. Used in large quantity, these vivid contrasts both jar the eye and lose their impact. Also keep in mind that contrasting colors are typically more effective if used in unequal amounts: rather than composing a planting bed of half yellow iris and half violet ones, use one color sparingly, as an accent to greater amounts of the other.

Contrasting colors need not be bright. For a softer look, use tints: cream and lavender, for example, instead of yellow and violet. You can also mix values when you create contrast, combining a fully saturated color with a softer, paler one—intense blue with pale peach, for instance, or bright green foliage as a foil for soft pink flowers.

WHITE. Gardeners think of white as a color, but to color theorists, it's atonal—the complete lack of color. As white is added to a color, it produces lighter and lighter tints, until—at the center of the color wheel—only white remains. White, then, can assort with all colors, light or dark. Combined with lighter values, it is harmonious; its lack of color seems closely related to the paleness around it. Used with fully saturated colors or darker shades, it offers a sharp contrast. (Use it sparingly in this role—overuse of contrast will give the planting a discordant, uneasy feel.)

GRAY. Though you won't find truly gray flowers, there are plenty of gray-leafed plants. Usually thought of as a cool color, gray actually results from mixing any two complementary colors. This explains its unique ability to fit into virtually any scheme, warm or cool. Gray is the great moderator: its soft neutrality tones down brilliance, highlights every color, and imparts softness to the overall picture.

ABOVE, LEFT: Used in combination with fully saturated colors, white creates an effective contrast.

ABOVE: Paired with green foliage alone, white looks bright yet cool.

Yellow marigolds *(Tagetes)* and red verbena look cooler and less assertive when separated by a drift of gray dusty miller *(Centaurea cineraria)*.

FLOWER COLOR BY SEASON

Many annuals and some perennials have notably long flowering periods, but none blooms for the entire growing season. The charts on these six pages give bloom seasons and flower colors for all the annuals and perennials described in the encyclopedia beginning on page 84. Use them to find the plants that will give you flowers when you need them, in the colors you want.

The exact onset and end of flowering depends somewhat on climate. Cold-winter regions (other than parts of Alaska) have shorter bloom seasons; in hot-summer climates, flowering usually starts earlier in the season and comes to an end more quickly. In mild-winter and Southwest desert regions, some spring flowers reliably bloom in winter. Be sure to read the encyclopedia descriptions and heed the zone recommendations.

ANNUAL NAME	BLOOM SEASON				ZONES
	SP	SU	F	W	
Ageratum houstonianum ✿ ✿ ✿		■	■		1–45
Anchusa capensis ✿		■			All zones
Antirrhinum majus ✿ ✿ ✿ ✿ ✿	■				A3; 1–45
Asarina (see page 180) ✿ ✿ ✿		■			1–45
Calendula officinalis ✿ ✿ ✿	■				1–45; H1
Calibrachoa ✿ ✿ ✿ ✿ ✿ ✿		■	■		2–43
Callistephus chinensis ✿ ✿ ✿ ✿ ✿		■			1–45
Catharanthus roseus ✿ ✿ ✿ ✿		■	■		1–45; H1, H2
Celosia ✿ ✿ ✿ ✿ ✿		■			A3; 1–45; H1, H2
Centaurea (some) ✿ ✿ ✿ ✿ ✿	■				Zones vary
Cerinthe major ✿ ✿	■				1–24, 32, 34–45
Chrysanthemum (some) ✿ ✿ ✿ ✿ ✿	■				Zones vary
Clarkia ✿ ✿ ✿ ✿ ✿	■				1–45
Cleome hassleriana ✿ ✿ ✿ ✿		■	■		1–45
Cobaea scandens (see page 180) ✿ ✿		■			3–41
Consolida ajacis ✿ ✿ ✿ ✿	■				1–45
Convolvulus tricolor ✿ ✿ ✿ ✿ ✿	■				1–45
Coreopsis tinctoria ✿ ✿		■			1–45; H1, H2
Cosmos ✿ ✿ ✿ ✿ ✿		■			A3; 1–45
Dianthus (some) ✿ ✿ ✿ ✿	■				A2, A3; 1–24, 30–45
Dolichos lablab (see page 180) ✿		■			All zones
Eschscholzia californica ✿ ✿ ✿ ✿ ✿	■			■	1–45; H1
Euphorbia marginata ✿		■			1–45
Gaillardia pulchella ✿ ✿ ✿ ✿		■			1–45; H1, H2
Gomphrena ✿ ✿ ✿ ✿		■			1–45; H1, H2
Helianthus annuus ✿ ✿ ✿ ✿		■	■		All zones
Helichrysum bracteatum ✿ ✿ ✿ ✿ ✿ ✿		■			All zones
Iberis (some) ✿ ✿ ✿ ✿		■			1–45

Annual Name	Bloom Season				Zones
	SP	SU	F	W	
Impatiens ✿ ✿ ✿ ✿	▓	▓		▓	All zones
Ipomoea (see page 180) ✿ ✿ ✿ ✿		▓			All zones
Lathyrus odoratus ✿ ✿ ✿ ✿	▓			▓	All zones
Lavatera trimestris ✿ ✿		▓			All zones
Limonium sinuatum ✿ ✿ ✿ ✿ ✿		▓			All zones
Lobelia erinus ✿ ✿ ✿	▓	▓	▓		All zones
Lobularia maritima ✿ ✿ ✿	▓	▓	▓		All zones
Matthiola ✿ ✿ ✿ ✿				▓	1–45
Moluccella laevis ✿		▓			1–45; H1, H2
Myosotis sylvatica ✿ ✿ ✿	▓			▓	A1–A3; 1–24, 32–45
Nicotiana ✿ ✿ ✿ ✿	▓	▓			All zones
Nigella damascena ✿ ✿ ✿ ✿	▓				All zones
Papaver ✿ ✿ ✿ ✿ ✿ ✿	▓	▓			Zones vary
Petunia × hybrida ✿ ✿ ✿ ✿ ✿	▓	▓	▓		All zones
Phlox drummondii ✿ ✿ ✿ ✿ ✿ ✿	▓	▓	▓		A2, A3; 1–45; H1
Portulaca ✿ ✿ ✿ ✿ ✿		▓			All zones
Rudbeckia hirta ✿ ✿ ✿		▓	▓		1–24, 28–43
Salpiglossis sinuata ✿ ✿ ✿ ✿		▓			1–45
Salvia (some) ✿ ✿ ✿ ✿ ✿		▓	▓		All zones
Sanvitalia procumbens ✿ ✿		▓	▓		1–45
Scabiosa atropurpurea ✿ ✿ ✿ ✿		▓			1–45; H1, H2
Tagetes ✿ ✿ ✿ ✿	▓	▓	▓		All zones
Thunbergia alata (see page 181) ✿ ✿ ✿		▓			All zones
Tithonia rotundifolia ✿ ✿		▓	▓		All zones
Tropaeolum ✿ ✿ ✿ ✿		▓	▓		All zones
Verbena (some) ✿ ✿ ✿ ✿ ✿		▓	▓		All zones
Viola (some) ✿ ✿ ✿ ✿ ✿ ✿	▓	▓		▓	Zones vary
Zinnia ✿ ✿ ✿ ✿ ✿		▓			1–45; H1, H2

TOP: *Petunia × hybrida,* Primetime series
BOTTOM: *Antirrhinum majus*

Matthiola incana

Flower Color by Season **33**

TOP: *Tagetes patula*
BOTTOM: *Calendula officinalis*

Amsonia tabernaemontana

PERENNIAL NAME	BLOOM SEASON				ZONES
	SP	SU	F	W	
Acanthus ✿ ✿ ✿		■			Zones vary
Achillea ✿ ✿ ✿ ✿ ✿ ✿		■	■		A1–A3; 1–24, 26, 28–45
Aconitum ✿ ✿ ✿ ✿		■	■		A1–A3; 1–9, 14–21, 34–45
Adenophora ✿ ✿		■			A2, A3; 1–10, 14–24, 30–43
Agapanthus ✿ ✿		■			Zones vary
Agastache ✿ ✿ ✿ ✿ ✿ ✿		■	■		Zones vary
Alcea rosea ✿ ✿ ✿ ✿ ✿ ✿		■			1–45
Alchemilla mollis ✿		■			A2, A3; 1–9, 14–24, 31–43
Alstroemeria ✿ ✿ ✿ ✿ ✿ ✿		■			5–9, 14–24, 26, 28, 31, warmer parts of 32, 34; H1
Amsonia ✿		■			Zones vary
Anchusa ✿		■			Zones vary
Anemone ✿ ✿		■			Zones vary
Aquilegia ✿ ✿ ✿ ✿ ✿ ✿	■	■			Zones vary
Artemisia lactiflora ✿		■			1–9, 14–21, 29–41
Aruncus ✿		■			Zones vary
Asclepias tuberosa ✿ ✿ ✿ ✿		■			Zones 1–45
Aster ✿ ✿ ✿ ✿ ✿			■		Zones vary
Astilbe ✿ ✿ ✿ ✿		■			1–7, 14–17, 32–43
Aurinia saxatilis ✿ ✿	■				1–24, 32–43
Baptisia ✿ ✿ ✿		■			1–24, 28–45
Begonia, Semperflorens group ✿ ✿ ✿		■	■		14–28; H1, H2
Bergenia ✿ ✿ ✿ ✿	■			■	Zones vary
Brunnera macrophylla ✿	■				1–24, 31–45
Campanula ✿ ✿ ✿ ✿ ✿		■			Zones vary
Canna ✿ ✿ ✿ ✿ ✿		■			6–9, 12–31, warmer parts of 32; H1, H2
Centaurea ✿ ✿ ✿	■	■			Zones vary
Centranthus ruber ✿ ✿ ✿	■	■			2–9, 12–24, 28–43; H1

Perennial Name	Bloom Season				Zones
	SP	SU	F	W	
Cerastium tomentosum ❀					A1, A2; 1–24, 32–45
Chelone ❀ ❀ ❀ ❀					1–9, 14–24, 28–43
Chrysanthemum ❀ ❀ ❀ ❀ ❀ ❀					Zones vary
Cimicifuga ❀					1–7, 17, 32–45
Coreopsis ❀ ❀ ❀					Zones vary
Corydalis ❀ ❀ ❀					2–9, 14–24, 32–35, 37, 39–43
Delphinium ❀ ❀ ❀ ❀					Zones vary
Dianthus ❀ ❀ ❀ ❀					Zones vary
Dicentra ❀ ❀ ❀					Zones vary
Dictamnus albus ❀ ❀ ❀					1–9, 31–45
Digitalis ❀ ❀ ❀ ❀					Zones vary
Echinacea purpurea ❀ ❀ ❀ ❀					A2, A3; 1–24, 26–45
Echinops ❀					A2, A3; 1–24, 31–45
Erigeron ❀ ❀ ❀ ❀					Zones vary
Eryngium ❀ ❀ ❀ ❀					Zones vary
Eupatorium ❀ ❀ ❀ ❀					Zones vary
Euphorbia ❀ ❀ ❀ ❀					Zones vary
Filipendula ❀ ❀					Zones vary
Gaillardia × grandiflora ❀ ❀ ❀					1–45; H1, H2
Gaura lindheimeri ❀ ❀					2b–35, 37, 38 (coastal), 39
Geranium ❀ ❀ ❀ ❀					Zones vary
Gypsophila paniculata ❀ ❀					A2, A3; 1–10, 14–16, 18–21, 31–45; H1
Helenium ❀ ❀ ❀					1–45
Helianthus ❀					1–24, 28–43
Helleborus ❀ ❀ ❀ ❀ ❀ ❀ ❀					Zones vary
Hemerocallis ❀ ❀ ❀ ❀ ❀ ❀					1–45; H1, H2
Heuchera, × Heucherella ❀ ❀ ❀					Zones vary
Hibiscus moscheutos ❀ ❀ ❀					2–24, 26–41; H1

Bergenia cordifolia

Chrysanthemum × morifolium

Heuchera sanguinea

PERENNIAL NAME	BLOOM SEASON				ZONES
	SP	SU	F	W	
Hosta ✿ ✿		■			Zones vary
Iberis sempervirens ✿	■				1–24, 31–45
Iris ✿ ✿ ✿ ✿ ✿ ✿	■				Zones vary
Kniphofia ✿ ✿ ✿ ✿ ✿ ✿		■			2–9, 14–24, 28–41
Liatris ✿ ✿ ✿		■			A2, A3; 1–10, 14–24, 26, 28–45
Ligularia ✿ ✿		■			Zones vary
Limonium ✿ ✿		■			Zones vary
Lobelia ✿ ✿ ✿ ✿ ✿		■			Zones vary
Lupinus ✿ ✿ ✿ ✿ ✿ ✿		■			A1–A3; 1–7, 14–17, 34, 36–45
Malva ✿ ✿ ✿ ✿		■	■		1–9, 14–24, 31–45
Monarda ✿ ✿ ✿ ✿		■			A1–A3; 1–11, 14–17, 30–43
Myosotis scorpioides ✿ ✿	■				A1–A3; 1–24, 32–45
Nepeta ✿ ✿ ✿ ✿		■			1–24, 30, 32–43
Oenothera ✿ ✿ ✿		■			Zones vary
Paeonia ✿ ✿ ✿ ✿	■				A1–A3; 1–11, 14–20, 30–45
Papaver ✿ ✿ ✿ ✿ ✿ ✿ ✿		■			Zones vary
Pelargonium ✿ ✿ ✿ ✿ ✿		■			8, 9, 12–24
Penstemon ✿ ✿ ✿ ✿ ✿ ✿		■			Zones vary
Perovskia ✿		■			2–24, 28–43

Hemerocallis 'Oodnadatta'

RIGHT: *Kniphofia* hybrid
FAR RIGHT: *Liatris spicata* 'Kobold'

Perennial Name	Bloom Season				Zones
	SP	SU	F	W	
Phlomis	▓	▓			Zones vary
Phlox	▓	▓			Zones vary
Phormium	▓	▓			5–9, 14–28; H1, H2
Physostegia virginiana		▓			A3; 1–9, 14–24, 26–45
Platycodon grandiflorus		▓			1–10, 14–24, 26, 28–45
Polygonatum	▓				A1–A3; 1–9, 14–17, 28–45
Primula	▓			▓	Zones vary
Pulmonaria	▓				1–9, 14–17, 32–43
Rodgersia		▓			2–9, 14–17, 32–41
Rudbeckia		▓			Zones vary
Salvia	▓	▓			Zones vary
Scabiosa	▓	▓			Zones vary
Sedum		▓			Zones vary
Solidago, × Solidaster		▓			1–11, 14–23, 28–45
Stachys		▓			Zones vary
Thalictrum		▓			Zones vary
Verbascum		▓			Zones vary
Verbena		▓			Zones vary
Veronica		▓			Zones vary
Viola odorata	▓			▓	Zones vary
Zauschneria		▓			Zones vary

Papaver orientale

Scabiosa columbaria 'Pink Mist'

FAR LEFT: *Rudbeckia fulgida sullivantii* 'Goldsturm'
LEFT: *Stachys byzantina* 'Silver Carpet'

SPECIAL-PURPOSE PLANTS

Many annuals and perennials have appealing blooms—and quite a few have a little something extra. Some bear flowers ideal for displaying in bouquets; others are sweetly fragrant; still others are irresistible lures for birds and butterflies. And many bloom happily in containers as well as in the garden.

CUT-FLOWER PLANTS

ANNUALS

Ageratum houstonianum. Zones 1–45

Antirrhinum majus. Zones A3; 1–45

Calendula officinalis. Zones 1–45; H1

Callistephus chinensis. Zones 1–45

Celosia. Zones A3; 1–45; H1, H2

Centaurea (some). Zones vary

Chrysanthemum (some). Zones vary

Clarkia. Zones 1–45

Cleome hassleriana. Zones 1–45

Consolida ajacis. Zones 1–45

Coreopsis tinctoria. Zones 1–45; H1, H2

Cosmos. Zones A3; 1–45

Dianthus (some). Zones A2, A3; 1–24, 30–45

Gaillardia pulchella. Zones 1–45; H1, H2

Gomphrena. Zones 1–45; H1, H2

Helianthus annuus. All zones

Helichrysum bracteatum. All zones

Iberis (some). Zones 1–45

Lathyrus odoratus. All zones

Limonium sinuatum. All zones

Matthiola. Zones 1–45

Moluccella laevis. Zones 1–45; H1, H2

Nicotiana. All zones

Nigella damascena. All zones

Papaver. Zones vary

Scabiosa atropurpurea. Zones 1–45; H1, H2

Tagetes. All zones

Tithonia rotundifolia. All zones

Tropaeolum majus. All zones

Viola (some). All zones

Zinnia. Zones 1–45; H1, H2

PERENNIALS

Achillea. Zones A1–A3; 1–24, 26, 28–45

Alcea rosea. Zones 1–45

Alstroemeria. Zones 5–9, 14–24, 26, 28, 31, warmer parts of 32, 34; H1

Anemone. Zones vary

Aquilegia. Zones vary

Asclepias tuberosa. Zones 1–45

Aster. Zones vary

Astilbe. Zones 1–7, 14–17, 32–43

Baptisia. Zones 1–24, 28–45

Campanula (some). Zones vary

Cosmos bipinnatus

Centranthus ruber. Zones 2–9, 12–24, 28–43; H1

Chrysanthemum. Zones vary

Cimicifuga. Zones 1–7, 17, 32–45

Coreopsis (some). Zones vary

Delphinium. Zones vary

Dianthus. Zones vary

Digitalis. Zones vary

Dictamnus albus. Zones 1–9, 31–45

Campanula medium

Helianthus annuus

Echinacea purpurea. Zones A2, A3; 1–24, 26–45

Echinops. Zones A2, A3; 1–24, 31–45

Eryngium. Zones vary

Euphorbia (some). Zones vary

Gaillardia × *grandiflora.* Zones 1–45; H1, H2

Gypsophila paniculata. Zones A2, A3; 1–10, 14–16, 18–21, 31–45; H1

Helenium. Zones 1–45

Helianthus. Zones 1–24, 28–43

Helleborus. Zones vary

Heuchera, × *Heucherella.* Zones vary

Iberis sempervirens. Zones 1–24, 31–45

Iris. Zones vary

Liatris. Zones A2, A3; 1–10, 14–24, 26, 28–45

Limonium. Zones vary

Lupinus. Zones A1–A3; 1–7, 14–17, 34, 36–45

Monarda. Zones A1–A3; 1–11, 14–17, 30–43

*Ornamental grasses (many). See pages 126–129

Paeonia. Zones A1–A3; 1–11, 14–20, 30–45

Papaver. Zones vary

Penstemon. Zones vary

Phlomis. Zones vary

Phlox (some). Zones vary

Physostegia virginiana. Zones A3; 1–9, 14–24, 26–45

Platycodon grandiflorus. Zones 1–10, 14–24, 26, 28–45

Primula. Zones vary

Rudbeckia. Zones vary

Scabiosa. Zones vary

Sedum (some). Zones vary

Solidago, × *Solidaster.* Zones 1–11, 14–23, 28–45

Veronica (some). Zones vary

Viola odorata. Zones vary

* = flowers and/or seed heads can be dried

Single-flowered herbaceous peony *(Paeonia)* with petals surrounding a cluster of stamens.

FRAGRANT FLOWERS

ANNUALS

Dianthus (some). Zones A2, A3; 1–24, 30–45

Iberis amara. Zones 1–45

Lathyrus odoratus. All zones

Lobularia maritima. All zones

Matthiola. Zones 1–45

Nicotiana. All zones

Phlox drummondii. Zones A2, A3; 1–45; H1

Two old-fashioned cultivars of sweet pea *(Lathyrus):* 'Cupani' (left) and 'Painted Lady' (right).

PERENNIALS

Dianthus (some). Zones vary

Hemerocallis lilioasphodelus. Zones 1–45; H1, H2

Hosta plantaginea. Zones 1–10, 14–21, 28, 31–45

Iris, bearded. Zones 1–24, 30–45

Paeonia. Zones A1–A3; 1–11, 14–20, 30–45

Phlox paniculata. Zones 1–14, 18–21, 27–43

Viola odorata. Zones vary

Early-blooming lemon daylily, *Hemerocallis lilioasphodelus,* is one of the few daylilies renowned for its fragrance.

TO ATTRACT BIRDS

ANNUALS

Calendula officinalis (seeds). Zones
  1–45; H1

Centaurea cyanus (seeds). Zones
  1–45; H1, H2

Clarkia (nectar). Zones 1–45

Cleome hassleriana (nectar). Zones
  1–45

Coreopsis tinctoria (seeds). Zones
  1–45; H1, H2

Cosmos (seeds). Zones A3; 1–45

Eschscholzia californica (seeds).
  Zones 1–45; H1

Gaillardia pulchella (seeds). Zones
  1–45; H1, H2

Helianthus annuus (seeds). All zones

Impatiens (nectar). All zones

Lobularia maritima (seeds). All zones

Nicotiana (nectar). All zones

Nigella damascena (seeds). All zones

A female broad-tailed hummingbird arrives to enjoy blossoms of a violet delphinium.

Petunia × *hybrida* (nectar). All zones

Phlox drummondii (nectar). Zones A2,
  A3; 1–45; H1

Salvia (nectar). Zones vary

Scabiosa atropurpurea (seeds). Zones
  1–45; H1, H2

Tagetes (seeds). All zones

Tithonia rotundifolia (seeds). All zones

Tropaeolum majus (nectar). All zones

Zinnia (nectar, seeds). Zones 1–45;
  H1, H2

PERENNIALS

Agastache (nectar). Zones vary

Alcea rosea (nectar). Zones 1–45

Alstroemeria (nectar). Zones 5–9,
  14–24, 26, 28, 31, warmer parts of 32,
  34; H1

Aquilegia (nectar, seeds). Zones vary

Asclepias tuberosa (nectar). Zones
  1–45

Coreopsis (seeds). Zones vary

Delphinium (nectar). Zones vary

Dicentra (nectar). Zones vary

Digitalis (nectar, seeds). Zones vary

Echinacea purpurea (seeds). Zones A2,
  A3; 1–24, 26–45

Eupatorium (seeds). Zones vary

Heuchera, × *Heucherella* (nectar).
  Zones vary

Kniphofia (nectar). Zones 2–9, 14–24,
  28–41

Lobelia, red-flowered (nectar).
  Zones vary

Lupinus (nectar). Zones A1–A3; 1–7,
  14–17, 34, 36–45

Monarda (nectar). Zones A1–A3; 1–11,
  14–17, 30–43

Pelargonium (nectar). Zones 8, 9,
  12–24

Penstemon (nectar). Zones vary

Phlox (nectar). Zones vary

Phormium (nectar). Zones 5–9,
  14–28; H1, H2

Rudbeckia (seeds). Zones vary

Salvia (nectar). Zones vary

Solidago (seeds). Zones 1–11, 14–23,
  28–45

Veronica (nectar). Zones vary

Zauschneria (nectar). Zones vary

Wide-open penstemon flowers offer an irresistible invitation to hummers.

Farewell-to-spring *(Clarkia amoena)* is a flashy nectar source for hummingbirds.

TO ATTRACT BUTTERFLIES

ANNUALS

Antirrhinum majus. Zones A3; 1–45

Consolida ajacis. Zones 1–45

Dianthus (some). Zones A2, A3; 1–24, 30–45

Gaillardia pulchella. Zones 1–45; H1, H2

Iberis (some). Zones 1–45

Lathyrus odoratus. All zones

Lobularia maritima. All zones

Phlox drummondii. Zones A2, A3; 1–45; H1

Salvia. Zones vary

Scabiosa atropurpurea. Zones 1–45; H1, H2

Tagetes. All zones

Tithonia rotundifolia. All zones

PERENNIALS

Achillea. Zones A1–A3; 1–24, 26, 28–45

Agapanthus. Zones vary

Aquilegia. Zones vary

Asclepias tuberosa. Zones 1–45

Aster. Zones vary

Astilbe. Zones 1–7, 14–17, 32–43

Centranthus ruber. Zones 2–9, 12–24, 28–43; H1

Chrysanthemum maximum. Zones A1–A3; 1–24, 26 (northern part), 28–43; H1

Coreopsis. Zones vary

Delphinium. Zones vary

Dianthus. Zones vary

Echinacea purpurea. A2, A3; 1–24, 26–45

Echinops. A2, A3; 1–24, 31–45

Erigeron. Zones vary

Eryngium. Zones vary

Eupatorium. Zones vary

Daisy flowers have special appeal for butterflies. At left, a tiger swallowtail drinks from a purple coneflower *(Echinacea);* below, Mexican sunflower *(Tithonia)* hosts a painted lady.

Gaillardia × grandiflora. Zones 1–45; H1, H2

Iberis sempervirens. Zones 1–24, 31–45

Liatris. Zones A2, A3; 1–10, 14–24, 26, 28–45

Lobelia. Zones vary

Monarda. Zones A1–A3; 1–11, 14–17, 30–43

Penstemon. Zones vary

Phlox. Zones vary

Rudbeckia. Zones vary

Salvia. Zones vary

Scabiosa. Zones vary

Sedum. Zones vary

Solidago, × Solidaster. Zones 1–11, 14–23, 28–45

Verbena. Zones vary

Late-summer flower heads of *Sedum* 'Autumn Joy' are convenient landing strips for butterflies.

ANNUALS AND PERENNIALS FOR CONTAINERS

A great many annuals and perennials are well suited to life in containers. Annuals are unsurpassed for container color in a hurry, while numerous perennials feature season-long attractive foliage in addition to lovely flowers. You can create stunning displays from annuals or perennials alone—and imaginative combinations of the two can be just as impressive.

Among containers, traditional terra-cotta is still a favorite; the standard design is available everywhere, and designer pots in European and Asian styles are becoming widely available. Other options include glazed ceramic, lightweight plastic (some of these mimic terra-cotta), and decay-resistant wood. For more on growing annuals and perennials in containers, see pages 68–69.

TOP: Ornamental grasses assort with blanket flowers *(Gaillardia × grandiflora),* purple coneflowers *(Echinacea),* and gloriosa daisies *(Rudbeckia hirta).*

BOTTOM: Silvery *Artemisia* 'Powis Castle' joins *Zinnia angustifolia* 'Crystal White'.

ANNUALS

Ageratum houstonianum. Zones 1–45
Anchusa capensis. All zones
Antirrhinum majus. Zones A3; 1–45
Calendula officinalis. Zones 1–45; H1
Calibrachoa. Zones 2–43
Catharanthus roseus. Zones 1–45; H1, H2
Celosia. Zones A3; 1–45; H1, H2
Cerinthe major. Zones 1–24, 32, 34–45
Cleome hassleriana. Zones 1–45
Coleus × hybridus. All zones
Convolvulus tricolor. Zones 1–45
Cosmos. Zones A3; 1–45
Dianthus. Zones vary
Gomphrena. Zones 1–45; H1, H2
Iberis. Zones 1–45
Impatiens. All zones
Lathyrus odoratus (bush kinds). All zones
Lobelia erinus. All zones
Lobularia maritima. All zones
Matthiola. Zones 1–45
Myosotis sylvatica. Zones A1–A3; 1–24, 31–45

Nicotiana alata (shorter kinds). All zones
Nigella damascena. All zones
Petunia × hybrida. All zones
Phlox drummondii. Zones A2, A3; 1–45; H1
Portulaca. All zones
Primula malacoides. Zones 1–9, 12–24, 31–41
Rudbeckia hirta. Zones 1–24, 28–43
Salpiglossis sinuata. Zones 1–45
Salvia splendens. All zones
Sanvitalia procumbens. Zones 1–45
Tagetes. All zones
Tropaeolum majus. All zones
Verbena (some). All zones
Viola (some). Zones vary
Zinnia. Zones 1–45, H1, H2

PERENNIALS

Acanthus. Zones vary
Agapanthus. Zones vary
Alchemilla mollis. Zones A2, A3; 1–9, 14–24, 31–43
Alstroemeria. Zones 5–9, 14–24, 26, 28, 31, warmer parts of 32, 34; H1

LEFT: Impatiens teams with sweet alyssum and licorice plant *(Helichrysum petiolare* 'Limelight').

BELOW: Versatile impatiens—the all-purpose container annual—dominates a window box; sweet alyssum *(Lobularia)* shows beneath. Design by Jonathan Plant.

Astilbe. Zones 1–7, 14–17, 32–43

Aurinia saxatilis. Zones 1–24, 32–43

Begonia, Semperflorens group. Zones 14–28; H1, H2

Brunnera macrophylla. Zones 1–24, 31–45

Campanula (some). Zones vary

Canna. Zones 6–9, 12–31, warmer parts of 32; H1, H2

Centaurea cineraria. Zones 8–30

Chrysanthemum (some). Zones vary

Coreopsis. Zones vary

Corydalis. Zones 2–9, 14–24, 32–35, 37, 39–43

Delphinium (shorter kinds). Zones vary

Erigeron. Zones vary

Gaillardia × *grandiflora.* Zones 1–45; H1, H2

Geranium. Zones vary.

Helichrysum petiolare. Zones 16, 17, 22–24

Hemerocallis (smaller kinds). Zones 1–45; H1, H2

Heuchera. Zones vary

Hosta. Zones vary

Iberis sempervirens. Zones 1–24, 31–45

Wire hanging basket is covered with pansies *(Viola* × *wittrockiana),* stock *(Matthiola),* and sweet alyssum *(Lobularia).* Design by Roger's Garden.

Limonium. Zones vary

Lupinus. Zones A1–A3; 1–7, 14–17, 34, 36–45

Nepeta. Zones 1–24, 30, 32–43

Ornamental grasses (smaller kinds). See pages 126–129

Papaver nudicaule. Zones A2, A3; 1–6, 10, 32–45

Pelargonium. Zones 8, 9, 12–24

Penstemon. Zones vary

Phormium. Zones 5–9, 14–28; H1, H2

Polygonatum. A1–A3; 1–9, 14–17, 28–45

Primula (many). Zones vary

Salvia (some). Zones vary

Scabiosa. Zones vary

Verbena. Zones vary

Lovely when viewed individually, annuals and perennials are perhaps even more beautiful in combination. A mixed planting delights the eye with its complements and contrasts in color and texture—

GARDEN
DESIGNS

and the best features of each plant are emphasized. A stately hollyhock looks still more imposing when fronted by a frothy mound of baby's breath or fernleaf yarrow; a blue aster is startlingly brilliant when set amid blossoms in gold and orange.

The preceding chapter covers factors to consider when you combine plants: their flower color, foliage character, and overall shape and size. In the following pages, you'll see those principles put into practice. The 12 garden designs presented here all use a wide variety of annuals and perennials, and their themes are just as varied. Some focus on particular colors or plants, others on seasonal beauty; still others are designed for "trouble spots" such as shady or dry areas. There's even a garden intended to draw butterflies and birds to your home—and one planted exclusively in containers. Use the plans as blueprints, or just let them inspire you to create similar designs perfectly suited to your own garden.

With not a square inch left unplanted, this summer garden offers a brilliant show that invites close appreciation from the garden path. Design by Kristin Home.

CREATING A
GARDEN PLAN

Young nursery-grown perennials, ready to be set out according to plan

Some gardeners compose beautiful plantings without ever putting pencil to paper. They take small plants still in their containers, shuffle them around in the planting bed until the arrangement looks "right," and plant them then and there. More often than not, though, successful gardens—even the most casual-looking ones—begin on paper.

This sort of planning can begin during the drear winter months, effectively starting the gardening year a season early (if only in the mind!). Blocking out a design also lets you make unlimited changes before you actually dig the first hole, thus minimizing mistakes that might require hours of tedious transplanting later on.

Start by gathering a tape measure, graph paper (a ¼-inch grid is convenient), a ruler or T-square, and pencils (both ordinary lead and colored). Then measure the intended planting site, noting the location of shrubs and trees as well as any hardscape elements such as paths and fences. Transfer these measurements to your graph paper, letting one ¼-inch square equal 1 foot (if the garden is very large, you may want to double the scale). Keep this plot outline as your master sheet; make photocopies of it to use for your design ideas.

Once you have a scale drawing of the plot, you can start the creative work. With a plain lead pencil, sketch in the placements of the plants you want to include, using circles, ovals, or elongated drifts. As you plan, think about the plant combination tips in the preceding chapter and the ultimate size of each plant (see the encyclopedia beginning on page 84). To work out pleasing color schemes, use colored pencils to shade in the hues of flowers and leaves.

READING THE PLANS

For each of the following 12 planting designs, we provide a watercolor illustration showing the garden at its peak. Accompanying the illustration is a plot plan, with each plant shaded in the basic color of its flowers or foliage and labeled by a letter. These letters identify the plants for you: just find the corresponding letter in the plant list provided. For every plant in the list, we give botanical name and common name (if there is one); the number in parentheses indicates the total number of that plant used in the garden shown. For details on how to read these plans, review the example below (taken from page 52).

PLAN ILLUSTRATION AND DESCRIPTION

PLANT LIST

Botanical name — Common name

A. Artemisia lactiflora. White mugwort (1)

B. Echinacea purpurea 'White Swan'. Purple coneflower (7+)

C. Achillea millefolium, Summer Pastels strain. Common yarrow (3+)

D. Coreopsis verticillata 'Moonbeam'. Threadleaf coreopsis (1)

E. Verbena 'Homestead Purple' (4)

F. Dianthus × allwoodii 'Doris' (or other dark pink selection). Pink (3)

G. Liatris spicata 'Kobold'. Gayfeather (4)

H. Cerastium tomentosum. Snow-in-summer (7) — Cultivar name

I. Coreopsis auriculata 'Nana' (3)

J. Limonium platyphyllum. Statice (3)

K. Achillea 'Moonshine'. Yarrow (4)

Number of plants used in plan

Letter corresponds to plant location in plot plan

SUMMER OPULENCE

Spring may usher in the flowering year, but summer's show is no less dazzling—and many summer bloomers mount a longer-lasting display than the spring crowd. In keeping with the season's balmy temperatures, many of these blossoms come in distinctly warm colors. In this planting, sunny hues of yellow and rosy red are balanced by cooling blue, purple, and white. Give the garden a place in the sun (of course) and a climate with at least some winter chill.

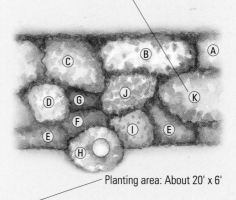

Planting area: About 20' x 6'

Dimensions of planting

PLANT LIST

A. **Hibiscus moscheutos 'Blue River'.**
Rose-mallow (1)

B. **Centranthus ruber 'Albus'.**
Jupiter's beard (3)

C. **Panicum virgatum 'Heavy Metal'.**
Switch grass (1)

D. **Gaura lindheimeri** (1)

E. **Echinops 'Taplow Blue'.** Globe thistle (2)

F. **Chrysanthemum maximum 'Esther Read'.**
Shasta daisy (4)

G. **Liatris spicata 'Silvertips'.** Gayfeather (1)

H. **Gypsophila paniculata 'Bristol Fairy'.**
Baby's breath (1)

I. **Geranium phaeum.** Mourning widow (1)

J. **Aster × frikartii 'Mönch'** (3)

K. **Scabiosa caucasica.**
Pincushion flower (6)

L. **Stachys byzantina 'Silver Carpet'.**
Lamb's ears (5)

M. **Salvia × sylvestris 'Blauhügel'** (7)

N. **Dianthus deltoides 'Albus'.**
Maiden pink (3)

O. **Iberis sempervirens 'Snowflake'.**
Evergreen candytuft (4)

P. **Limonium platyphyllum.** Statice (2)

Q. **Veronica austriaca teucrium**
'Crater Lake Blue'. Speedwell (1)

R. **Veronica spicata 'Icicle'.** Speedwell (2)

S. **Verbena 'Homestead Purple'** (1)

T. **Festuca amethystina.**
Large blue fescue (4)

U. **Lobularia maritima.** Sweet alyssum (8)

COOL SUMMER ISLAND

In the heat of the summer, this oasis of cool, fresh color invites you to spend a bit of time on the chaise longue with an iced drink and a good book. The planting is anchored by a tall, white-blossomed rose-mallow (A) and an upright clump of switch grass (C). Weaving around and between these two foundations are blue and white flowers in variety, and leaves in gray, silver, and green. Flowering starts in spring with the evergreen candytuft (O), Jupiter's beard (B), and sweet alyssum (U), reaches a crescendo in midsummer—and continues into fall, weather permitting. You'll have the best success with this island in a full-sun location receiving regular water.

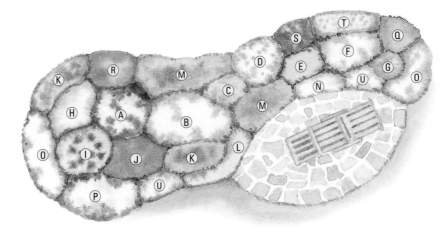

Planting area: About 20' × 8'

A WHITE GARDEN

White has an uplifting sparkle, a clean, pure look that's soothing to both eyes and spirit. What better place to relax, then, than a garden bearing only white flowers? Most of these plants are green foliaged, but the lamb's ears (S) has distinctive woolly white leaves that echo the planting's pristine blossoms. Floral offerings start in spring with the climbing rose (U), Siberian iris (K), peony (E), and dianthus (R); the remaining plants carry the show on into summer. This garden is best with at least some winter chill; the rose will need protection if winter temperatures drop below 10°F/−12°C.

PLANT LIST

A. Hibiscus moscheutos 'Blue River'.
Rose-mallow (1)

B. Digitalis purpurea 'Alba'. Foxglove (4)

C. Phlox maculata 'Miss Lingard'.
Thick-leaf phlox (5)

D. Delphinium elatum 'Galahad' (4)

E. Paeonia (herbaceous), white cultivar.
Peony (1)

F. Artemisia lactiflora. White mugwort (1)

G. Liatris spicata 'Floristan White'.
Gayfeather (2)

H. Baptisia alba. White false indigo (1)

I. Centranthus ruber 'Albus'.
Jupiter's beard (2)

J. Chrysanthemum maximum
'Esther Read'.
Shasta daisy (9)

K. Iris, Siberian, 'White Swirl' (4)

L. Filipendula vulgaris 'Flore Pleno'.
Dropwort (3)

M. Physostegia virginiana 'Summer Snow'.
False dragonhead (2)

N. Limonium platyphyllum, white form.
Statice (1)

O. Salvia × sylvestris 'Schneehügel' (5)

P. Geranium sanguineum 'Album'.
Bloody cranesbill (2)

Q. Iberis sempervirens 'Snowflake'.
Evergreen candytuft (2)

R. Dianthus × allwoodii 'Aqua'.
Pink (4)

S. Stachys byzantina 'Silver Carpet'.
Lamb's ears (6)

T. Cerastium tomentosum.
Snow-in-summer (3)

U. Rosa 'Climbing Iceberg'.
Climbing rose (1)

V. Buxus microphylla koreana.
Korean boxwood

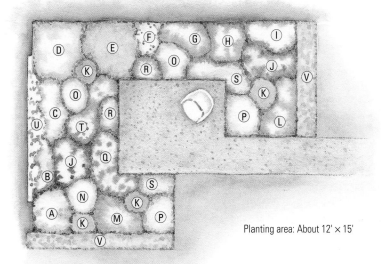

Planting area: About 12' × 15'

WARM-SEASON SIZZLER

The warmest time of year comes from late spring through summer—and this planting features a palette to suit the season, with flowers in yellow, orange, red, and mahogany. Foliage gets in on the act, too, in the reddish bronze leaves of shiso (R). Moderating the heat are a hollyhock (E), daylily (I), and sunflower (W) in pale yellow and cream, plus verbena (K) in cool, contrasting purple. A tranquil pool of water, inspired by Moorish gardens in Spain, is another soothing feature. Nearly two-thirds of the plants are perennials, giving the planting a permanent structure. The remaining annuals grow quickly and easily, amply repaying the effort required to plant them anew each year.

PLANT LIST

A. **Achillea filipendulina 'Coronation Gold'**. Fernleaf yarrow (3)

B. **Gaillardia × grandiflora 'Mandarin'**. Blanket flower (3)

C. **Asclepias tuberosa**. Butterfly weed (3)

D. **Achillea millefolium 'Fireland' (or other red cultivar)**. Common yarrow (1)

E. **Alcea rosea, light yellow selection**. Hollyhock (3)

F. **Chrysanthemum frutescens, yellow cultivar**. Marguerite (2)

G. **Coreopsis verticillata 'Moonbeam'**. Threadleaf coreopsis (2)

H. **Hemerocallis, red cultivar**. Daylily (1)

I. **Hemerocallis, cream cultivar**. Daylily (1)

J. **Canna 'Wyoming'** (1)

K. **Verbena, Tapien hybrid, purple selection** (1)

L. **Coreopsis grandiflora 'Sunray'** (3)

M. **Oenothera macrocarpa**. Ozark sundrops (1)

N. **Gaillardia × grandiflora 'Goblin'**. Blanket flower (3)

O. **Phlomis russeliana** (1)

P. **Gaillardia × grandiflora 'Baby Cole'**. Blanket flower (3)

Q. **Tithonia rotundifolia**. Mexican sunflower (2)

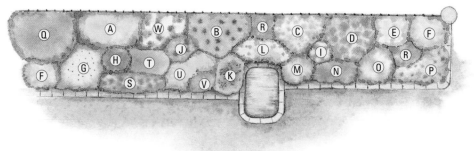

Planting area: About 24' × 5'

R. **Perilla frutescens purpurascens**. Shiso (4)

S. **Tagetes patula, Aurora strain**. French marigold (5)

T. **Celosia 'Apricot Brandy'**. Plume cockscomb (5)

U. **Tagetes erecta, Galore strain, yellow selection**. African marigold (4)

V. **Portulaca grandiflora, orange selection**. Rose moss (2)

W. **Helianthus annuus 'Moonshadow'**. Annual sunflower (4)

BREATH OF SPRING

As the chill and gloom of winter slowly give way to brighter days, nothing is more heartening than flowers. At first, blossoms appear in scattered bursts; but as spring settles in for good, the garden is soon awash in waves of color. The cheery (and cheering) assortment of perennials shown here captures the spirit and bounty of spring in all its colors—compressed into one simple cottage-garden planting. This plan works best in a climate with some winter chill; site it in a sunny location.

All of these plants blossom in spring, and at least half of them are likely to continue to bloom into the summer months.

Kniphofia 'Shining Scepter'

PLANT LIST

A. **Kniphofia, yellow cultivar.**
Red-hot poker (1)

B. **Baptisia australis.** Blue false indigo (1)

C. **Paeonia (herbaceous), white cultivar.**
Peony (2)

D. **Centranthus ruber 'Albus.'**
Jupiter's beard (4)

E. **Penstemon barbatus 'Rose Elf'** (3)

F. **Aster × frikartii 'Mönch'** (4)

G. **Chrysanthemum coccineum.**
Painted daisy (3)

H. **Iris, Siberian, 'Caesar's Brother'** (1)

I. **Hemerocallis, cream cultivar.** Daylily (2)

J. **Hemerocallis 'Stella de Oro'.**
Daylily (4)

K. **Gaura lindheimeri 'Siskiyou Pink'** (1)

L. **Geranium 'Johnson's Blue'** (4)

M. **Papaver orientale, pink cultivar.**
Oriental poppy (1)

N. **Coreopsis grandiflora 'Early Sunrise'** (2)

O. **Heuchera 'Palace Purple'. Coral bells** (6)

P. **Iberis sempervirens 'Snowflake'.**
Evergreen candytuft (2)

Q. **Campanula portenschlagiana.**
Dalmatian bellflower (2)

R. **Aurinia saxatilis.** Basket-of-gold (3)

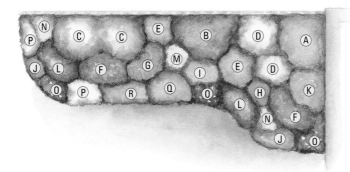

Planting area: About 20' × 8'

PLANT LIST

A. **Artemisia lactiflora.** White mugwort (1)

B. **Echinacea purpurea 'White Swan'.** Purple coneflower (7+)

C. **Achillea millefolium, Summer Pastels strain.** Common yarrow (3+)

D. **Coreopsis verticillata 'Moonbeam'.** Threadleaf coreopsis (1)

E. **Verbena 'Homestead Purple'** (4)

F. **Dianthus × allwoodii 'Doris' (or other dark pink selection).** Pink (3)

G. **Liatris spicata 'Kobold'.** Gayfeather (4)

H. **Cerastium tomentosum.** Snow-in-summer (7)

I. **Coreopsis auriculata 'Nana'** (3)

J. **Limonium platyphyllum.** Statice (3)

K. **Achillea 'Moonshine'.** Yarrow (4)

L. **Hemerocallis, cream cultivar.** Daylily (2)

M. **Dictamnus albus 'Albiflorus'.** Gas plant (2)

N. **Chrysanthemum maximum 'Aglaya'.** Shasta daisy (5+)

O. **Veronica 'Goodness Grows'.** Speedwell (4+)

SUMMER OPULENCE

Spring may usher in the flowering year, but summer's show is no less dazzling—and many summer bloomers mount a longer-lasting display than the spring crowd. In keeping with the season's balmy temperatures, many of these blossoms come in distinctly warm colors. In this planting, sunny hues of yellow and rosy red are balanced by cooling blue, purple, and white. Give the garden a place in the sun (of course) and a climate with at least some winter chill.

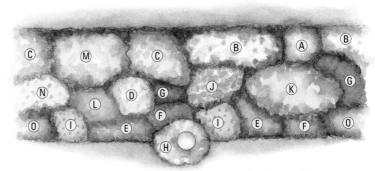

Planting area: About 20' × 6'

AUTUMN ASSEMBLY

Designed for fall—the last act of the gardening year, in many regions—this planting features the warm hues typical of the harvest season. Prominent is an assortment of daisy-flowered plants with wide-open, circular blossoms that offer a striking contrast in form to the fine foliage and filmy seed heads of the four featured ornamental grasses (A through D). Two of these daisies, both of them New York asters (F and L), bring lovely touches of autumn-sky blue to the composition.

There's no need to tidy up the planting before winter; let the daisies and grasses go to seed, providing tempting fare for birds.

Calamagrostis × acutiflora 'Karl Foerster'

PLANT LIST

A. Calamagrostis × acutiflora 'Karl Foerster'. Feather reed grass (1)

B. Miscanthus sinensis 'Malepartus'. Eulalia grass (1)

C. Muhlenbergia rigida. Purple muhly (2)

D. Festuca glauca 'Blausilber'. Common blue fescue (4)

E. Phormium tenax 'Bronze Baby'. New Zealand flax (1)

F. Aster novi-belgii 'Climax'. New York aster (4)

G. Solidago 'Goldenmosa'. Goldenrod (4)

H. Helenium 'Crimson Beauty'. Sneezeweed (2)

I. Achillea filipendulina 'Coronation Gold'. Fernleaf yarrow (3)

J. Gaillardia × grandiflora 'Burgundy'. Blanket flower (4)

K. Sedum 'Autumn Joy' (4)

L. Aster novi-belgii 'Professor Anton Kippenburg'. New York aster (4)

M. Hemerocallis 'Stella de Oro'. Daylily (1)

N. Chrysanthemum × morifolium, light yellow pompom type. Florists' chrysanthemum (3)

O. Tithonia rotundifolia. Mexican sunflower (3)

P. Helianthus annuus 'Italian White'. Annual sunflower (3)

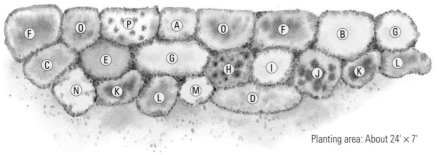

Planting area: About 24' × 7'

A COTTAGE-GARDEN BORDER

The original cottage garden was a riotous plot where "one of everything"—flowers, vegetables, even fruit trees—mingled in an apparently artless jumble. In Edwardian times, this humble garden was elevated to an actual landscape style, formalized in the English border. Variety is still paramount, and the look is still casual, but the sizes, colors, textures, and bloom periods of the plants are carefully calculated to keep things looking good from spring straight through fall. This candy cane–shaped border brings the spirit of cottage garden to a bed that will fit easily into most contemporary gardens.

PLANT LIST

A. Digitalis purpurea, Foxy strain. Foxglove (4)

B. Gypsophila paniculata 'Bristol Fairy'. Baby's breath (1)

C. Alcea rosea, Chater's Double strain. Hollyhock (6)

D. Foeniculum vulgare 'Purpurascens'. Bronze fennel (1)

E. Paeonia (herbaceous). Peony (1)

F. Aster × frikartii 'Mönch' (2)

G. Geranium endressii (1)

H. Iris, Siberian, white cultivar (1)

I. Physostegia virginiana 'Variegata'. False dragonhead (1)

J. Kniphofia 'Little Maid'. Red-hot poker (1)

K. Sedum 'Autumn Joy' (1)

L. Achillea 'Moonshine'. Yarrow (2)

M. Chrysanthemum maximum 'Alaska'. Shasta daisy (4)

N. Scabiosa caucasica. Pincushion flower (2)

O. Dianthus plumarius. Cottage pink (3)

P. Heuchera 'Palace Purple'. Coral bells (3)

Q. Phlox subulata, lavender cultivar. Moss pink (2)

R. Hemerocallis 'Stella de Oro'. Daylily (2)

S. Coreopsis rosea (2)

T. Iberis sempervirens. Evergreen candytuft (3)

U. Stachys byzantina 'Silver Carpet'. Lamb's ears (3)

V. Aquilegia, McKana Giants strain. Columbine (1)

W. Heuchera sanguinea. Coral bells (4)

X. Hemerocallis lilioasphodelus. Lemon daylily (1)

Y. Aurinia saxatilis. Basket-of-gold (3)

Z. Nepeta × faassenii. Catmint (2)

AA. Cosmos bipinnatus, Sonata series (6)

BB. Lobularia maritima. Sweet alyssum (6)

CC. Cleome hassleriana. Spider flower (1)

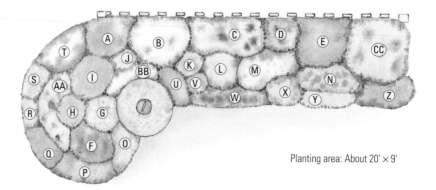

Planting area: About 20' × 9'

A SHADY GARDEN OF PERENNIALS

There's no shortage of choices for that tree-shaded patch of your domain. It's true that shade-loving plants aren't as numerous as those that like sun, but they still offer plenty of variety—both in foliage and in flower. In this planting, blossoms are spread out over a period that runs from late winter (in milder regions) clear into summer, and foliage is a constant source of beauty from spring through fall. Most of these plants can remain in place for many years, requiring only an annual late-winter cleanup. For best success, use this plan in regions with at least some winter chill.

Helleborus orientalis

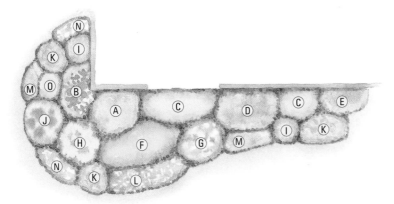

Planting area: About 24' × 12'

PLANT LIST

A. **Thalictrum rochebrunianum.** Meadow rue (1)

B. **Campanula persicifolia.** Peach-leafed bluebell (3)

C. **Alchemilla mollis.** Lady's-mantle (3)

D. **Digitalis × mertonensis.** Foxglove (6)

E. **Adenophora confusa.** Lady bells (3)

F. **Helleborus orientalis.** Lenten rose (4)

G. **Hosta 'Francee'** (1)

H. **Hosta 'Gold Standard'** (1)

I. **Hosta 'Blue Wedgwood'** (2)

J. **Brunnera macrophylla** (2)

K. **Bergenia 'Abendglut'** (4)

L. **Pulmonaria saccharata 'Janet Fisk'.** Lungwort (3)

M. **Heuchera americana 'Pewter Veil'.** Coral bells (5)

N. **Carex morrowii 'Variegata'.** Variegated Japanese sedge (5)

O. **Polygonatum odoratum 'Variegatum'.** Solomon's seal (1)

Eschscholzia californica

UNTHIRSTY ISLAND

As originally conceived, the "island bed" was a sizable group of plants rising from a sea of turf. In semiarid regions, seas of turf are a troublesome extravagance—but even there, the island concept still works. Just make it an oasis of flowers and foliage in an otherwise dry expanse (such as gravel or raked bare earth). With its colorful blossoms, foliage in gray and silver as well as green, and wide assortment of leaf sizes and shapes, this unthirsty island looks interesting throughout the growing season. The plants used here do best in the West and Southwest.

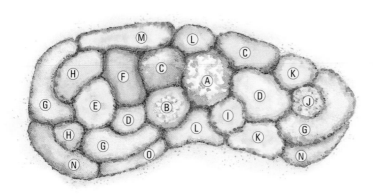

Planting area: About 20' × 9'

PLANT LIST

A. **Centranthus ruber 'Albus'.** Jupiter's beard (2)

B. **Gaura lindheimeri 'Whirling Butterflies'** (1)

C. **Phlomis russeliana** (4)

D. **Panicum virgatum 'Heavy Metal'.** Switch grass (3)

E. **Euphorbia characias wulfenii** (2)

F. **Artemisia absinthium.** Common wormwood (2)

G. **Artemisia 'Powis Castle'** (5)

H. **Muhlenbergia emersleyi.** Bull grass (3)

I. **Achillea filipendulina 'Coronation Gold'.** Fernleaf yarrow (2)

J. **Gaura lindheimeri 'Corrie's Gold'** (1)

K. **Oenothera macrocarpa.** Ozark sundrops (5)

L. **Verbena bipinnatifida** (5)

M. **Coreopsis grandiflora 'Sunray'** (5)

N. **Zauschneria californica 'Etteri'.** California fuchsia (5)

O. **Eschscholzia californica.** California poppy (from seed scattered over the area)

FOR BIRDS AND BUTTERFLIES

Plant it and they will come! Birds and butterflies are drawn to plants that supply them with food: nectar for butterflies and hummingbirds, seeds for seed-eating birds. This colorful group of late-spring and summer bloomers offers treats for all comers, with some plants providing both nectar and seeds. While the garden won't guarantee you a swallowtail or an oriole—that depends on where you live—you can still be assured of an array of winged visitors. This is a widely adapted planting, suitable for much of the country (steamy-summer Deep South excepted).

Achillea millefolium

PLANT LIST

A. **Agastache rugosa.**
   Korean hummingbird mint (1)

B. **Alcea rosea.** Hollyhock (6)

C. **Centranthus ruber 'Albus'.**
   Jupiter's beard (1)

D. **Asclepias tuberosa.** Butterfly weed (3)

E. **Achillea filipendulina 'Coronation Gold'.** Fernleaf yarrow (2)

F. **Achillea millefolium, Summer Pastels strain.** Common yarrow (4)

G. **Echinacea purpurea 'Bravado'.**
   Purple coneflower (3)

H. **Chrysanthemum maximum 'Alaska'.**
   Shasta daisy (7)

I. **Coreopsis grandiflora 'Early Sunrise' or 'Sunburst'** (12)

J. **Liatris spicata.** Gayfeather (1)

K. **Sedum 'Autumn Joy'** (3)

L. **Salvia nemorosa 'Ostfriesland'** (3)

M. **Heuchera sanguinea.** Coral bells (9)

N. **Cleome hassleriana.** Spider flower (1)

O. **Dianthus gratianopolitanus.**
   Cheddar pink (4)

P. **Iberis sempervirens 'Purity' or 'Snowflake'.** Evergreen candytuft (4)

Q. **Antirrhinum majus, Rocket strain.**
   Snapdragon (6)

R. **Tagetes erecta, Sweet Cream strain.**
   African marigold (4)

S. **Tagetes patula, Aurora or Sophia strain.**
   French marigold (6)

T. **Nicotiana alata, Nicki strain.**
   Flowering tobacco (10)

U. **Salvia splendens.** Scarlet sage (4)

V. **Cosmos bipinnatus, Sonata series** (4)

W. **Petunia × hybrida** (5)

X. **Lobularia maritima.** Sweet alyssum (8)

Planting area: About 15' × 18'

PLANT LIST

A. **Miscanthus sinensis 'Strictus'.**
   Porcupine grass (2)

B. **Calamagrostis × acutiflora**
   'Karl Foerster'. Feather reed grass (2)

C. **Panicum virgatum 'Haense Herms'.**
   Switch grass (2)

D. **Pennisetum orientale.**
   Oriental fountain grass (2)

E. **Miscanthus sinensis 'Yaku Jima'.**
   Eulalia grass (1)

F. **Helictotrichon sempervirens.**
   Blue oat grass (1)

G. **Pennisetum alopecuroides 'Hameln'.**
   Fountain grass (1)

H. **Imperata cylindrica 'Red Baron'.**
   Japanese blood grass (3)

I. **Deschampsia cespitosa.**
   Tufted hair grass (2)

J. **Festuca glauca 'Elijah Blue'.**
   Common blue fescue (5)

K. **Rhynchelytrum nerviglume**
   'Pink Crystals'. Natal ruby grass (2)

L. **Rudbeckia fulgida.** Coneflower (3)

M. **Phlomis russeliana** (2)

N. **Hemereocallis 'Stella de Oro'.** Daylily (4)

O. **Tithonia rotundifolia.**
   Mexican sunflower (1)

P. **Ricinus communis 'Dwarf Red Spire'.**
   Castor bean (1)

Q. **Celosia, Castle series.**
   Plume cockscomb (7)

FEATURING
ORNAMENTAL GRASSES

If you think of grass as nothing more than a flat green surface demanding hours of tedious watering and mowing, this planting will be a revelation. The decorative grasses used here come in all forms: foliage in fountains, shafts, and tussocks, blossoms and seed heads in spikes and plumes. And not all are green. You'll see steely blue-gray, near-red, and variegated leaves—and many change color in autumn, adding still more variety to the landscape. To highlight the grasses, the planting also includes a number of bright flowers and a shrubby annual with big, tropical-looking burgundy leaves.

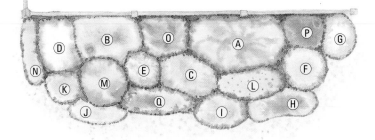

Planting area: About 25' × 8'

A GARDEN IN CONTAINERS

Deck the deck with lots of pots! You can achieve a bountiful display of annuals and perennials without a real plot of ground—great news for flower lovers limited to deck or patio gardening. And even if you do have a garden, you can create a colorful transition zone from house to yard with plants growing in pots carefully chosen to enhance the living bouquets they hold. Many of the plants shown here are described in the encyclopedia beginning on page 84; for still more good container choices, see pages 42–43. Try other annuals and perennials as well, such as the sweet-scented heliotrope and dainty twinspur shown in container G.

PLANT LIST

A. Acer palmatum 'Bloodgood'. Japanese maple (1)
AS UNDERPLANTING: **Viola odorata.** Sweet violet (4)

B. Polygonatum odoratum 'Variegatum'. Solomon's seal (1)
AS UNDERPLANTING: **Campanula poscharskyana.** Serbian bellflower (2)

C. Coleus × hybridus (mixed colors) (4)

D. Hosta 'Gold Standard' (1)

E. Impatiens, New Guinea Hybrid 'Tango' (1)

F. Limonium perezii. Statice (1)
Chrysanthemum paludosum (3)
Verbena, Tapien hybrid, purple selection (1)

G. Heliotropium arborescens. Common heliotrope (1)
AS UNDERPLANTING: **Diascia rigens.** Twinspur (3)

H. Catharanthus roseus, Mediterranean series, apricot selection. Madagascar periwinkle (2)

I. Begonia, Semperflorens Group, Cocktail series (3)

J. Phormium 'Apricot Queen' or **'Duet'.** New Zealand flax (1)
AS UNDERPLANTING: **Helichrysum petiolare 'Limelight'.** Licorice plant (2)

K. Tagetes patula, Aurora strain. French marigold (5)

L. Coreopsis grandiflora 'Early Sunrise' (2)
AS UNDERPLANTING: **Lobelia erinus 'Crystal Palace'** (4)

PLANTING AND CARE

Flourishing garden beds, brimming with dazzling flowers and healthy foliage—that's what most gardeners envision when they plant annuals and perennials. In this chapter, you will discover how to make that picture a reality. As a first step, learn about your soil: its type, how to work it, and how to improve it with organic amendments. It's just as important to prepare the beds well and set out the plants properly.

Once your annuals and perennials are safely in the ground, they'll require attention to basic care such as watering, mulching, fertilizing, staking, and/or pruning. We also discuss common-sense pest and disease control (including photographs of a number of troublemakers) and offer suggestions for dealing with pesky weeds.

At the end of the chapter, we cover ways to start your own annuals and perennials (and biennials, too). These plants can all be grown from seed—sown directly in garden beds, in a wildflower meadow, or in containers (to transplant later to the garden). Perennials can also be propagated by division and by taking stem and root cuttings.

In spring, set out annuals around blooming tulips (or other springtime bulbs). As the tulips fade, the annuals will take over, carrying the flower show into summer.

PREPARING THE SOIL

It's no secret that the healthiest and most attractive annuals and perennials grow in "good" soil. On these pages, we discuss the composition of garden soil, then move on to instructions for making compost to improve your soil; preparing planting beds; and using raised beds to deal with soil problems.

LEARNING ABOUT YOUR GARDEN'S SOIL

All soils are based on mineral particles formed by the natural breakdown of rock. They also contain varying amounts of organic matter, air, and water, as well as numerous living creatures—earthworms, nematodes, bacteria, fungi, and many others. The size and shape of a soil's mineral particles determine its basic characteristics.

Clay soils, also called heavy soils, are made up of very small particles that pack together tightly, producing a compact mass with microscopic pore spaces (the area between soil particles). Drainage is usually slow, since water and nutrients percolate slowly through the tiny pores. Clay soil is not easy for roots to penetrate, and during prolonged rainy spells (or if overwatered), it remains saturated, even to the point of causing root rot. Working clay soil is a miserable job: it's sticky when wet and rock-hard when dry. On the plus side, its slower drainage does allow you to water and fertilize less often.

While some annuals and perennials thrive in perpetually moist areas (see the list on page 17), most require well-drained soil. To check drainage, dig a 1½- to 2-foot-deep hole and fill it with water. After it drains, fill it again. If this second amount of water drains away in an hour or less, the drainage is good. If it remains for several hours or more, the soil drains poorly. To help improve drainage, you can add organic matter—but if drainage is extremely slow, you may need to plant in another (better-drained) part of the garden or in raised beds (see page 65).

At the other end of the spectrum are sandy (light) soils, with large, irregularly rounded particles and large pore spaces that allow water and nutrients to drain away freely. Plants growing in sand are unlikely to suffer root rot, but you will need to water them more often to keep their roots moist. You'll be fertilizing more often, too, to replace nutrients leached away by the necessary frequent watering.

Fortunately, most garden soils fall somewhere between the extremes of clay and sand. The best ones for plant growth, referred to as loam, have mineral particles in a mixture of sizes. They also contain a generous proportion of organic matter—and in fact, adding organic amendments (see "Making a Planting Bed," page 64) is one basic way to bring both clay and sand closer to loam in structure. These materials gradually loosen clay soils, improving drainage; in sandy soils, on the other hand, they enhance moisture retention by wedging into the large pore spaces between soil particles.

MAKING COMPOST

Composting is a natural process that converts raw organic materials into an invaluable soil amendment. You can make compost in several ways. The simplest method, called *slow* or *cold* composting, is to pile garden debris such as leaves, branches, and other trimmings in an out-of-the-way corner; eventually, the pile will decompose.

If you'd like to speed up the process, you can employ *hot* composting. This takes a bit more effort than cold composting: you provide optimum conditions for the organisms responsible for decay (by giving them the mixture of oxygen, water, and carbon- and nitrogen-rich nutrients they need), causing the pile to heat up quickly and decompose in a few months. Hot composting has the additional advantage of destroying many (though not all) weeds and disease pathogens.

You can make hot compost in a freestanding pile or use an enclosure, such as a wire cylinder or wooden bins. In both cases, the fundamentals of the process are the same.

GATHER MATERIALS. You will need more or less equal amounts by volume of brown matter and green matter. Brown matter is high in carbon and includes dry leaves, hay, and woody prunings. Green matter is high in nitrogen; it includes grass clippings, green leaves, fruit and vegetable trimmings, and manure. *Do not* compost bones, cat or dog waste, badly diseased plants or plant parts, or pernicious weeds such as bindweed and quackgrass.

CHOP MATERIALS. Shredding or chopping your raw materials into smaller pieces (ideally no more than an inch or two long) allows decay-producing organisms to reach more surfaces, speeding up the composting process. Use a lawn mower or shredder-chipper; or chop the materials with a machete on a large wooden block.

When you build a freestanding compost pile, make it at least 3 feet high and wide. This provides a mass of material great enough to generate the microbial activity needed for heating the pile thoroughly. When siting the pile, be sure to allow space alongside for turning.

BUILD THE PILE. Building the pile like a layer cake makes it easier to judge the ratio of brown to green materials. Start by spreading a 4- to 8-inch layer of brown matter over an area at least 3 feet square; then add 2 to 8 inches of green matter. Make layers of grass clippings only 2 inches deep; less-dense green materials can be layered more thickly. Add another layer of brown matter and sprinkle with water. Mix these first three layers with a spading fork. Continue adding layers (about two at a time), watering, and mixing until the pile is about 3 feet tall.

TURN THE PILE. In just a few days, the pile will heat up. In time, it will decompose on its own, but you can hurry things along considerably by turning the contents to add more oxygen—which is needed by the organisms responsible for decomposition. Using a spading fork or pitchfork, restack the pile, placing materials originally on the outside in its center; also add water to keep the pile moist. Continue turning the pile weekly, if possible, until most of the materials have turned into dark, crumbly compost, ready to add to planting beds or to spread as mulch.

THREE-BIN COMPOSTING SYSTEM

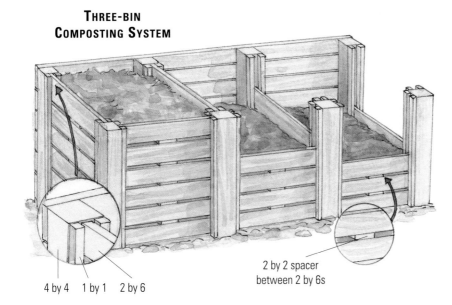

4 by 4   1 by 1   2 by 6

2 by 2 spacer
between 2 by 6s

ACID OR ALKALINE SOIL: THE PH SCALE

Soil may be acid, neutral, or alkaline. A pH of 7 indicates a neutral soil; soils with a pH below 7 are acid, while those with a pH above 7 are alkaline. In general, alkaline soils are found in dry-summer regions with low rainfall, while acid types are associated with high rainfall and humid summers.

Most annuals and perennials grow well in soils ranging from moderately acid to somewhat alkaline; a few, as noted in the plant encyclopedia beginning on page 84, *require* somewhat acid or alkaline soils. Extreme acidity or alkalinity, however, causes problems, since it makes some nutrients chemically unavailable to plant roots. If poor plant growth makes you suspect that your soil is strongly acid or alkaline, have it tested. The kits sold in nurseries and garden centers will give you a ballpark reading. For more precise information, send a soil sample to a laboratory (look under "Laboratories—Analytical" in the Yellow Pages or check with your Cooperative Extension Office). Such tests can also uncover any nutrient deficiencies. The lab will tell you how and when to collect the sample and will give advice on correcting any problems the analysis reveals.

In a three-bin composting system, the left bin holds new green and brown material; the center bin contains partially decomposed material, while the right one holds finished or nearly finished compost. Turn the material in each bin weekly, moving decomposed material to the right. The right bin will be empty for a few weeks at the start.

MAKING A PLANTING BED

You may already have well-prepared garden beds and borders, ready to receive annual and perennial plants or seeds. However, if you're planting in a new area (such as a former lawn) or in a new garden, you'll need to put some time and effort into soil preparation to encourage your new plants to grow quickly and robustly. Begin by removing sod and controlling weeds; then loosen the soil and work in amendments.

1 Use a sharp spade to cut sod into sections, then push the spade under each section to sever the roots. Lift the sections away with your hands. (For more information on eliminating weeds and sod, see page 77.)

2 In small areas, you can use a spading fork to loosen the soil; for larger beds, you may wish to use a rotary tiller. The soil should be slightly damp when you work it; don't try to dig soil that's too wet or completely dry. Dig to a depth of 10 to 12 inches, breaking up clods of earth and removing stones as you go.

3 The next step is to amend the soil with organic matter, fertilizer, and any materials needed to correct pH. As mentioned on page 62, organic matter improves both clay and sand—and it helps plants grow even better in loam, too. Organic materials include compost (homemade or purchased), nitrogen-fortified wood by-products (such as ground bark and sawdust), aged manure, and peat moss; other choices may be available locally.

Use generous quantities of organic matter, spreading at least a 3- to 4-inch-thick layer over the loosened soil. (Aged manure can be an exception; too much can burn roots and leach excess nutrients into the groundwater. To be on the safe side, spread it in a layer just 1 inch thick.) As a rule of thumb, a cubic yard of organic material should cover 100 square feet of planting bed to a depth of 3 inches.

Phosphorus and potassium (two of the major plant nutrients) should be placed near plant roots to have the greatest benefit (see "Fertilizing," page 70), so it's best to work a fertilizer high in these nutrients, such as a 5-10-10 product, into the soil before planting. Spread the fertilizer over the soil, using the amount indicated on the label. Also add any amendments needed to alter soil pH at this time (see page 63).

4 With a spading fork or tiller, incorporate all the amendments evenly into the soil. Then level the bed with a rake and water well. If possible, let the soil settle for a few weeks before setting out plants or sowing seed. When you do plant, the soil will be easy to work, and planting will be a pleasure.

LEFT: Interlocking concrete blocks form the sides of this raised bed.

BELOW: A raised bed bursting with flowers is enclosed with boards held in place by sturdy posts.

BUILDING RAISED BEDS

Many gardeners choose to plant annuals and perennials in some sort of raised bed. This arrangement has a number of advantages. Such beds offer a good way to cope with problem soils. If the native soil is heavy clay, for example, the increased height will allow for better drainage. If your soil is too acidic or alkaline to grow favorite annuals or perennials, you can fill the bed with imported topsoil with a more neutral pH. In addition, raised beds made of decorative materials add interest to a garden's overall design. They bring plants closer to eye level, define boundaries, and, when filled with tall-growing plants, can help provide privacy by enclosing a deck, patio, or seating area.

The simplest raised beds are made by piling amended soil on the area you want to plant. For a slightly more formal look, though, you can enclose the bed with some sort of border; this helps contain the soil, as well. Good choices for borders include wooden boards (1½ to 2 inches thick), bricks, or stone. Whatever method you choose, loosen the existing soil first to ease penetration by roots and water. Then create the planting mound or fill the enclosure with good topsoil (either purchased or dug from pathways or other parts of your garden) amended with plenty of organic matter.

A low, brick-edged raised bed filled with perennials and other favorite plants adds color and structural variety to a courtyard garden.

SELECTING AND PLANTING

Choose your annual and perennial plants wisely, set them out carefully in well-prepared soil, and you'll soon have a flourishing garden. For information on starting plants from seed, see page 78.

CHOOSING PLANTS

Nurseries and garden centers sell annuals and perennials in various containers. Annuals are most often available in cell-packs or 4-inch pots, though you'll sometimes find them sold in gallon-size containers. Perennials are also sold in smaller containers as well as in gallon-size (or occasionally larger) pots.

Small plants are generally the best buy, and once in the ground, they usually become established more quickly and put out new growth sooner than larger ones. When you shop, look for compact plants with good foliage color and a root ball that holds together well but is not tangled or matted. Try to avoid plants in full bloom; they have already put so much energy into producing flowers that they will have little left to establish new roots in your garden. Once you bring the plants home from the nursery, put them in a shaded location and keep the soil moist until planting time.

WHEN TO PLANT

As noted at right, the ideal planting time depends upon the particular plant. Whatever the season, though, try to set out your plants during cool, cloudy, calm weather; they will get established more quickly if not subjected to stress from heat, bright sun, and wind. It's best to avoid planting in the heat of summer—but if you must do so, be sure to shade the new plants temporarily and pay special attention to watering once they are in the ground.

1-gallon pot

4-inch pot

Cell-pack with 1-inch cells

In addition to the containers shown above, you may find annuals and perennials sold in jumbo packs with six 2½-inch cells.

ANNUALS. These plants fall into two groups, cool-season and warm-season, differing in their bloom season and preferred planting time.

Cool-season annuals include calendula, pansy *(Viola)*, sweet pea *(Lathyrus)*, and many others (see the plant encyclopedia beginning on page 84). Also called hardy annuals, these plants perform best in the cool soil and mild temperatures of fall and early spring. They can withstand fairly heavy frosts; indeed, if they are to bloom vigorously, they must develop roots and foliage during cool weather. Gardeners in cold-winter areas should plant them in very early spring, as soon as the soil can be worked. Where winters are mild, they can be planted in fall for bloom in winter and early spring. To ensure winter flowers in these regions, timing is important: plant while the days are still warm enough to encourage growth but when day length is decreasing. If you plant too early in fall, the plants will rush into bloom before they become established; if planted too late, they may not flower until spring. Where winters are mild, cool-season annuals can also be planted in late winter or very early spring for spring blooms.

Warm-season annuals include cosmos, sunflower *(Helianthus)*, zinnia, and numerous other favorites. They grow and flower best in the warm months of late spring, summer, and early fall. They are tender to cold and may perish in a late frost if planted too early in spring. In cold-winter climates, set them out after all danger of frost is past; in mild-winter climates, plant in midspring. (In desert regions of the Southwest with very hot summers, however, certain warm-season annuals, such as petunias, are typically planted in early fall for bloom in later fall and winter.)

BIENNIALS. Most biennials are set out as small plants in fall to bloom the following spring or summer. However, larger plants may be available at nurseries in spring; set these out in the garden immediately for bloom within a few months.

PERENNIALS. If you're planting an entire new bed of perennials, do so in early spring or early autumn. If you are adding just a few new plants, try to set out summer- or autumn-flowering sorts in early spring, so that they will be well established by bloom time. For the same reason, plant spring bloomers in early fall.

SETTING OUT PLANTS FROM CONTAINERS

Before planting, prepare a bed as described on page 64—or, if you are setting out plants in an existing bed, work a shovelful of organic matter into the soil before planting each one. Then set out plants as illustrated below, spacing them far enough apart to prevent crowding. Once you've finished planting, spread a thin layer of mulch (see page 70) around the plants to keep the soil cool, conserve moisture, and discourage weeds. To lessen the possibility of rot, be sure to keep the mulch an inch or two away from each plant's crown.

1 Soak the plant, still in its pot, in a bucket of water for about 30 minutes or until the soil is completely dampened.

2 Dig a hole for each plant, making it the same depth as the container and an inch or two wider.

3 With your fingers, lightly separate matted roots. If there's a pad of coiled white roots at the pot bottom, cut or pull it off so the new roots will form and grow into the soil.

4 Place each plant in its hole so that the top of the root ball is even with the soil surface. Firm soil around the roots; then water each plant with a gentle flow that won't disturb soil or roots.

PLANTING BARE-ROOT PERENNIALS

Nurseries and mail-order companies sell some perennials as bare-root plants. These have most or all of the soil removed from around the roots, which are then surrounded with organic packing material and enclosed in plastic bags. If you'll be setting out such plants within a day or two after receipt or purchase, open the bags slightly, add a little water, and store in a cool place. If planting must be delayed by more than a few days, pot up the plants in small containers or heel them in—that is, plant them temporarily in a shallow trench in the garden.

Before planting bare-root perennials in their permanent position, prepare a planting bed as shown on page 64. If you are adding plants to an existing bed, work a shovelful of organic material into the soil for each perennial.

Remove the packing material and soak the roots in water for about 30 minutes. Dig a hole about twice as wide as the root system, as shown below. Then make a cone of soil in the center to support the roots. Set the plant on the cone of soil and spread the roots evenly. Fill the hole with soil so that the crown of the plant is level with or slightly above the soil, then water well. Finally, spread a thin layer of mulch around the plant.

INSTALLING A WINDOW BOX

Window boxes overflowing with annuals and perennials dress up your home, painting a colorful picture whether you're working outside or enjoying the view from indoors. And it's easy to change the plants with the seasons.

The boxes may be constructed of fiberglass, metal, or wood. If you opt for a wooden box, choose (or make) one of decay-resistant redwood or cedar. Be sure the box has drainage holes; one ½- to ¾-inch hole per foot of box length is ideal. Since water must drain away from house walls and foundations when the box is mounted, make certain that the holes are near the front of the box. To keep the soil from washing out, put a piece of plastic mesh or a layer of gravel in the box bottom.

Window boxes are heavy when planted, so it's essential to provide adequate support, such as sturdy brackets. If the box is to decorate a wooden wall, you'll need to take steps to discourage dry rot. Rather than attach the box directly to the wall, bolt one or two pressure-treated 2 by 2s or 2 by 4s to the wall, then fasten the back of the box to these horizontal runners.

PLANTING ANNUALS AND PERENNIALS IN CONTAINERS

Containers of all sorts—pots in varying sizes, window boxes, hanging baskets—offer a wonderful way to showcase annuals and perennials. The best choices for this sort of display are plants that bloom over a long period or have good-looking foliage throughout the growing season. On pages 42 and 43, you'll find lists of annuals and perennials well suited to container gardens.

In general, container-grown plants are more effective if spaced more closely than they would be in the ground. Place taller plants near the center; set lower-growing and cascading sorts around the edge. Be sure to think about how much sun or shade the plants need, then position the containers accordingly.

Note: Make sure that any container you use has at least one drainage hole.

SOIL MIXES. Plants in containers need fast-draining yet moisture-retentive soil, with a structure loose enough to allow roots to grow easily. Quick drainage means roots won't run the risk of suffocating in soggy soil; good moisture retention saves you from having to water constantly. Regular garden soil, even if it's good loam, is too dense for container use; it forms a solid mass that roots cannot penetrate easily, and it remains soggy for too long after watering. A better bet is one of the packaged potting mixes sold at nurseries or garden centers.

WATERING. Because they have only a limited amount of soil from which to draw moisture, container-grown plants require more frequent watering than those grown in the ground. During hot or windy spells, this can mean daily attention; in cool weather, it may be sufficient to water weekly or even less often. Check the soil in containers and water when the top inch or two is dry. When you do water, be sure to moisten the entire soil mass. A drip irrigation system can make watering container plants almost effortless; kits designed for this purpose are widely available.

Chosen for their attractive foliage, the plants in this container provide color and interest over a long season.

You can reduce watering frequency somewhat by adding soil polymers to your potting mix or by using a mix that already includes them. These tiny, gel-like granules absorb hundreds of times their weight in rain or irrigation water, holding it (and the dissolved nutrients it contains) for plants to use. Follow package instructions carefully for the amounts to add; if you use too much, some of the particles may ooze to the surface.

FERTILIZING. Because frequent watering leaches nutrients from the potting mix, container plants need regular feeding. Liquid fertilizers are easy to use; start right after planting and repeat at least every 2 weeks. You can also mix a controlled-release fertilizer into the potting mix before planting.

PLANTING A HANGING WIRE BASKET

Hanging baskets bring plants to eye level, decorating entryways, arbors, and patio overheads. Wire baskets are traditionally lined with loose sphagnum moss, but you can also purchase preformed liners made of sphagnum or coco fiber (a by-product of coconut farming).

Choose a wire basket at least 12 inches in diameter, since smaller baskets are more difficult to keep moist. Use a high-quality potting mix and add a controlled-release fertilizer and soil polymers (see facing page) to it. Small plants from cell-packs are easiest to insert in the basket.

1 Push soaking-wet sphagnum moss through the mesh from the inside to make an inch-thick lining that extends 1 inch above the basket rim.

2 Place enough potting mix in the basket to fill it by about one-third. Poke holes through the moss every

few inches all around the circumference of the pot, just above the potting mix. Gently push one plant, root ball first, through each hole, so that the roots sit atop the soil. Add more mix, covering the roots; gently tamp down.

3 Continue planting and adding potting mix in tiers. Finish by filling the basket almost to the top with mix; then plant the top surface. Water the basket well, then keep it moist but not soggy. In warm weather, you may need to water daily.

CASCADING PLANTS FOR HANGING BASKETS AND WINDOW BOXES

A few favorite trailing plants are listed here; check the encyclopedia beginning on page 84 for other choices.

Calibrachoa
Coleus
Convolvulus tricolor
Helichrysum petiolare
Impatiens walleriana
Ipomoea tricolor

Lobelia erinus
Lobularia maritima
Pelargonium peltatum
Petunia × hybrida
Tropaeolum majus
Verbena × hybrida

Ivy geranium *(Pelargonium peltatum)* cascades from a hanging planter.

CARING FOR ANNUALS AND PERENNIALS

Like other garden plants, annuals and perennials need basic care such as watering, mulching, fertilizing, pruning, and staking. Some perennials may need winter protection, as well; and most will need periodic dividing and rejuvenating (see page 81).

WATERING

All plants, even drought-tolerant sorts, must have water to grow and bloom. General moisture requirements for specific plants are noted in the encyclopedia beginning on page 84; in addition, you'll find a list of good choices for dry soil on page 16 and for perpetually moist conditions on page 17.

Also be sure to take climate, soil type, and the age of the plant into account when you're deciding how much and how often to water. If you garden where summers are long, hot, and dry, you will of course need to water more often than you would in a cool, moist climate. Likewise, if your soil is light and sandy, it will require more frequent irrigation than clay or highly organic soil. Young plants (including those that can withstand dry conditions when mature) need more frequent watering than do those with deeper and more extensive root systems.

APPLYING WATER. How you choose to water your plants depends on how often they need watering and how much water you have at your disposal. If watering is only necessary during the occasional dry spell, hand watering or a hose-end sprinkler will usually suffice. (However,

ABOVE: A minisprayer (also called a micro-sprayer) gently showers plants with water.

BELOW: A soaker hose lets water ooze slowly and steadily into the soil.

sprinklers that give off a strong spray may topple taller plants.) Where regular irrigation is needed all summer, use soaker hoses laid among the plants; or install a drip system outfitted with emitters (spaced to water each plant) or minisprayers. Drip irrigation is an especially good choice where water is scarce or expensive: it allows you to apply water only where it is needed, with no loss to runoff or wind.

If you're growing long, regular rows of plants, as in a cutting garden, you may opt to water in furrows. Dig a 6- to 8-inch-deep furrow along one or both sides of the row. Then let a hose run at one end of the furrow until the furrow is full.

Regardless of the watering system you choose, test the soil for moisture before you turn on the faucet by digging down a few inches with your fingers or a trowel. For small, newly transplanted annuals and perennials and those that require regular to ample moisture, water when the top inch or so of soil is dry. For established plants that require only moderate water, you can wait until the top 3 to 4 inches are dry.

Aim to soak the root zone when you water. Most annuals and perennials send their roots down to a foot or so, and large-growing sorts have even deeper roots. By watering the entire root zone rather than just the top few inches, you'll encourage the roots to grow deeply. Deeper roots have access to more moisture, letting the plants go longer between waterings; they are also less subject than shallow roots to the drying effects of heat and wind.

MULCHING

A layer of mulch around and between annuals and perennials serves several purposes. It helps conserve water, aids in suppressing weed growth, and, as it decomposes, improves the soil. Good mulches include compost (homemade or commercial), bark (ground, shredded, or chips), wood chips, pine needles, and various agricultural by-products such as ground corncobs and apple or grape pomace. Apply the mulch in a layer 1 to 2 inches thick, keeping it away from the plants' crowns (where the stems and roots join) to avoid the possibility of rot.

FERTILIZING

When plants are actively growing, they need a steady supply of nutrients. Most of the necessary nutrients are already present in soil, water, and air, but gardeners may sometimes need to supplement them—particularly the major nutrients nitrogen (N), phosphorus (P), and potassium (K). The label on a package of fertilizer notes the percentage (by weight) of each major nutrient the product contains, always presenting them in N-P-K order. For example, a 5-10-10 product contains 5 percent nitrogen, 10 percent phosphorus, and 10 percent potassium, while a 12-0-0 fertilizer contains 12 percent nitrogen but no phosphorus or potassium.

Products containing all three major nutrients are known as *complete* fertilizers. Those lacking in one or two of them are called *incomplete* and can be useful when a soil test indicates a deficiency in a certain nutrient. Of the three major nutrients, nitrogen is most likely to be in short supply: not only is it water-soluble and easily leached from soil by rainfall and watering, but it's also the nutrient used most extensively by plants. Phosphorus and potassium, in contrast, cannot move through the soil in solution and must be placed near the root zone to do the most good. The best way to get them there is to dig fertilizer thoroughly into the soil when you prepare it for planting. These two nutrients won't need to be supplemented as often as nitrogen.

NATURAL AND CHEMICAL FERTILIZERS. You can buy fertilizers in either natural (organic) or chemical (synthetic) form. *Natural* fertilizers are derived from the remains of living organisms and include blood meal, bone meal, cottonseed meal, and some animal manures, such as bat guano. Most contain lower levels of nutrients than chemical products. They release their nutrients more slowly, as well: rather than dissolving in water, they are broken down by microorganisms in the soil, providing nutrients as they decay. Most are sold and applied in dry

For best results, plant annuals and perennials in a well-prepared bed enriched with organic matter and fertilizer.

form; you scatter the fertilizer over the soil, then dig or scratch it in. A few (fish emulsion, for example) are available as concentrated liquids to be diluted before application.

Many natural fertilizers are high in just one of the three major nutrients. For example, blood meal and cottonseed meal are good sources of nitrogen; bone meal is high in phosphorus, while greensand is a natural source of potassium. Some manufacturers combine a variety of organic products in one package to make a complete fertilizer.

Chemical fertilizers are manufactured from the chemical sources listed on the label. They may be sold as dry granules or as soluble crystals or concentrated liquids to be diluted in water before use. Because their nutrients are for the most part water soluble, they act faster than organic sorts (though only nitrogen moves through the soil to any extent); types used in liquid form provide nutrients especially quickly, making them a good choice for giving plants a quick boost. You apply the dry kinds as you would natural fertilizers, scratching or digging them into the soil. If you want gradual nutrient delivery rather than quick action, choose controlled-release sorts: they act over a relatively long period (3 to 9 months, depending on the brand) if the soil receives regular moisture.

A FERTILIZING SCHEDULE

As mentioned above, phosphorus and potassium are most effective when placed near plant roots. Thus, it's important to work a fertilizer containing these nutrients (as well as some nitrogen) into the soil before setting out annuals and perennials; a 5-10-10 product is a good choice. This job is easy to do when you're preparing a new planting bed (see page 64). If you're setting out just a few plants in an existing bed, sprinkle a little fertilizer into each planting hole and work it in well, taking care that it does not come in contact with plant roots. In either case, dig in organic matter along with the fertilizer.

For most perennials, this initial fertilizing will be adequate for the first year's growth. After that, you may need to replenish the soil's nutrients. Many gardeners find that a yearly application of compost, spread over the soil as an inch-thick mulch in spring or fall, takes care of all or most nutrient needs, though other gardeners add fertilizer anyway. If you decide to fertilize, do so in spring, as your perennials begin

growing. Use a nitrogen-only (or predominantly nitrogen) product for this pick-me-up, since nitrogen is the nutrient most needed when growth begins and the only one that will leach into the root zone.

Annuals make more demands on soil nutrients than perennials do: they grow much faster, proceeding from seedling to flower in a matter of weeks. An application of fertilizer at planting time should carry the plants through the first half of the growing season. In cool-winter areas, give a second feeding after bloom begins, using a nitrogen fertilizer. Where winters are warmer and the growing season is longer, give supplemental feedings of nitrogen after flowering starts and again in late summer.

Take care not to overfertilize. Too much feeding can result in rank, lanky growth and sparse bloom. In addition, any excess fertilizer can simply wash away, often contaminating the groundwater.

PRUNING

Annuals and perennials aren't woody plants, but some still need pruning, in the form of pinching, deadheading, thinning, and/ or cutting back. Besides controlling growth, this sort of pruning often encourages more profuse bloom. To do most of these jobs, you can use small hand pruners (or even just your thumb and forefinger), but you may prefer hedge or grass shears for large-scale cutting back.

PINCHING. Nipping off growing tips increases branching from buds lower on the stem, making for a compact, bushy plant with more branches and therefore more flowers. Since pinching reduces a plant's height, it can make staking unnecessary in

some cases. The branches of petunias and some geraniums *(Pelargonium)* should be pinched back by about one-third two or three times during the growing season to prevent legginess, give denser growth, and encourage repeat flowering. Florists' chrysanthemum *(Chrysanthemum × morifolium)*, too, should be pinched several times from spring until late summer to produce dense, leafy growth.

Perennials with a tendency toward ranginess benefit from a single pinching in late spring to early summer; these include the taller asters and artemisias, eupatorium, sneezeweed *(Helenium)*, phlox, and false dragonhead *(Physostegia)*. This type of pinching can also delay bloom; if you pinch back half a clump of asters in early summer, for instance, that section will come into blossom a bit later than the unpinched section, prolonging the flowering season by a few weeks.

DEADHEADING. This rather grim-sounding term simply refers to removing spent flowers. It's done partly for aesthetic reasons: the plant looks fresh and full of vigor without a drab load of dead flowers. Beyond this, however, deadheading prevents plants from setting seed. It thus keeps prolific self-sowers from swamping you with volunteer seedlings; and in many cases, it induces longer bloom, since a deadheaded plant often continues to produce flowers in an attempt to form seed and complete its life cycle. Of course, if you want to save seed for future planting, you'll avoid deadheading. In addition, some annuals and perennials and most ornamental grasses have attractive seedheads that many gardeners leave in place until winter or early spring, both to decorate the garden and to provide food for seed-eating birds.

THINNING. When you thin a plant, you cut out stems at or near the base. Thinning is sometimes done to reduce the size of a plant that is impinging on its neighbors. It's also a useful way to improve air circulation around and within a plant, thus discouraging powdery mildew in susceptible annuals and perennials such as bee balm *(Monarda)*, border phlox *(Phlox paniculata)*, and zinnia.

CUTTING BACK. This involves shearing or clipping off rangy growth and spent flowering stems, all at once. It improves the plant's appearance and often promotes new bushy growth and flowering stems. Cut back spreading, low-growing annuals such as lobelia and sweet alyssum *(Lobularia)* by about half when flowering diminishes; then water and apply fertilizer to stimulate another round of bloom.

Most perennials should be cut back at some point after flowering ends but before growth gets underway the following spring. This yearly removal of old growth makes the garden look neater, provides space for fresh new stems and leaves to grow, and deprives certain pests (especially snails and slugs) of potential hiding places.

PRUNING TECHNIQUES

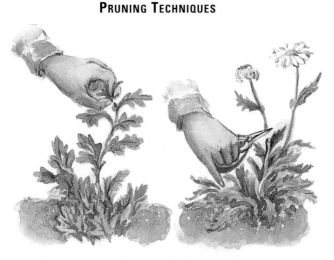

Pinching growing tips makes plants more compact and bushy.

Deadhead spent flowers to encourage more bloom and prevent seeding.

Thinning helps control the size of plants and improves air circulation.

Cutting back improves appearance and may promote more bloom. Hold the stems together in a bunch and cut them all at once.

PROVIDING WINTER PROTECTION FOR PERENNIALS

In colder climates, perennials sometimes need winter protection—not so much to shield them from cold (as is often thought) as to protect them from abrupt fluctuations in temperature. Assuming you have chosen plants hardy to the low temperatures typical for your region, winter damage generally occurs when the plants are subjected to alternate spells of freezing and thawing, a process that ruptures their cells, which then decay. Newly planted perennials without firmly established roots may be heaved from the ground by freeze-thaw cycles; the exposed roots are then likely to be killed by cold and desiccation.

Snow provides excellent protection for garden plants, but if you can't count on a good snow cover for most of the winter, it's best to lay down an insulating blanket of an organic material. Evergreen boughs, salt hay, marsh hay, and pine needles are all good choices; avoid materials such as leaves, which can pack down into an airtight mass. Wait until the soil freezes; then put the protection in place. Use two layers of evergreen boughs (setting the top layer at right angles to the bottom one) or about 6 inches of hay or pine needles. When spring arrives, remove the material gradually, taking it off before the plants put on much growth but not so soon that emerging leaves and shoots can be killed by a late freeze.

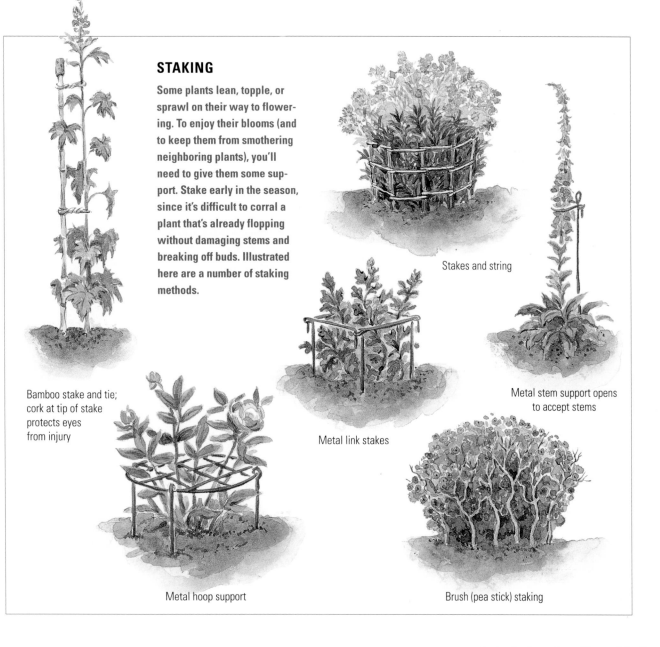

STAKING

Some plants lean, topple, or sprawl on their way to flowering. To enjoy their blooms (and to keep them from smothering neighboring plants), you'll need to give them some support. Stake early in the season, since it's difficult to corral a plant that's already flopping without damaging stems and breaking off buds. Illustrated here are a number of staking methods.

Stakes and string

Bamboo stake and tie; cork at tip of stake protects eyes from injury

Metal link stakes

Metal stem support opens to accept stems

Metal hoop support

Brush (pea stick) staking

DISEASES, PESTS, AND WEEDS

Most garden problems caused by diseases, pests, and weeds can be prevented through careful culture—and the problems that do occur can usually be managed without resort to chemicals, as noted on these pages.

DISEASES AND PESTS

Prevention is the most important step in managing diseases and pests: you won't have to solve problems that don't get a chance to crop up in the first place. Do your best to keep plants healthy and stress free. Set them out at the recommended planting time in well-prepared soil, and give them the care they need throughout the growing season. Be sure to choose plants adapted to your growing conditions; a plant that requires a cool, moist climate, for example, is quite likely to fall prey to diseases and pests if grown in a hot, dry region. Whenever possible, select varieties resistant to pests or diseases; some of these are described in the encyclopedia beginning on page 84. When you buy plants, look them over carefully to be sure you won't be importing problems to your garden. Finally, keep the garden free of debris that can harbor pests and disease-causing organisms. A thorough fall or winter cleanup is especially effective.

Check the plants growing in your garden frequently; regular tours give you a good opportunity to notice problems before they get out of hand. If you do spot trouble, take action only if the infestation is severe. A few aphids or chewed leaves are not cause for alarm, and problems often disappear quite quickly on

BENEFICIAL INSECTS

Hundreds of species of beneficial insects help gardeners keep pests at bay. The half-dozen we describe here are likely to be naturally present in your garden; some (as noted) can be purchased from nurseries or mail-order firms. To encourage beneficials, set out flowering plants that provide food for them. Good choices include yarrow *(Achillea)*, feverfew *(Chrysanthemum parthenium)*, coreopsis, cosmos, and sweet alyssum *(Lobularia)*, as well as herbs such as cilantro, dill, and fennel.

ASSASSIN BUGS. Slim, ½- to ¾-inch-long insects; may be red, black, brown, or gray. They feed on a wide variety of pests.

DAMSEL BUGS. Dull gray or brown, ½-inch-long, very slender insects with a long, narrow head. Nymphs resemble the adults but are smaller and have no wings. Both nymphs and adults feed on aphids, leafhoppers, and small worms.

GROUND BEETLES. Shiny black insects from ½ to 1 inch long. Smaller species eat other insects, caterpillars, cutworms, and grubs; some larger species eat slugs and snails and their eggs.

LACEWINGS. Adults are inch-long flying insects that feed only on nectar, pollen, and honeydew, but larvae devour aphids, leafhoppers, thrips, and many other insects, as well as mites. They resemble ½-inch-long alligators and are commercially available.

LADY BEETLES. Also known as ladybugs, these beetles and their larvae (which look like ¼-inch-long, six-legged alligators) feed on aphids, mealybugs, and the eggs of many insects. You can buy lady beetles, but they often fly away as soon as you release them. Freeing them at night or keeping them in cages for a few days after purchase may encourage them to remain in your garden.

SYRPHID FLIES. Adults, also known as flower or hover flies, look a bit like bees but have just one set of wings; they feed only on nectar. Larvae (tapered green or gray maggots with small fangs) consume dozens of aphids each day.

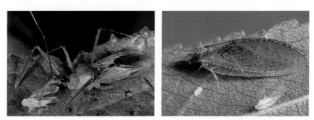

Assassin bug   Lacewing

Damsel bug   Lady beetle

Ground beetle   Syrphid fly

their own as pests die out naturally or move on. In many cases, natural predators will take care of infestations for you; some of the most important beneficial insects are shown on the facing page. Because damaging pests and beneficial or harmless creatures are often quite similar in appearance, it's crucial to identify the organisms you find accurately. For help with identification, check the photos and descriptions on these pages or consult your Cooperative Extension Office or a local nursery.

MANAGING DISEASES AND PESTS. You have a range of options for managing problems. Start with physical and/or biological solutions; turn to chemical controls only when all other methods fail.

Among the simplest of *physical* controls is handpicking: you just remove and destroy pests, infected leaves, or even whole plants, if necessary. Other physical approaches include strong water jets, which can knock pests from plants and often kill them, and various barriers and traps (see the descriptions of individual pests). *Biological* controls are effective in some cases, and they do not harm nontarget creatures. A familiar biological control is *Bacillus thuringiensis (Bt)*, a bacterium which, once ingested by susceptible pest larvae, causes them to stop feeding and eventually die.

As a last resort, turn to *chemical* controls, focusing on less toxic pesticides such as insecticidal soap, neem-based products, and products containing pyrethrins (the active ingredient is derived from a dried flower). Be aware that, despite their relatively low toxicity, these products will still kill beneficial and harmless insects. Use them only on plants that are being attacked and only when pests are present, and follow the label directions exactly. The management suggestions given below and on page 76 do not include recommendations for more toxic chemicals, since their registration and availability change frequently. If you feel you need stronger controls, consult your Cooperative Extension Office for advice.

DISEASES

DISEASE	DESCRIPTION	MANAGEMENT
Botrytis (gray mold)	Fungal disease. Soft, tan to brown spots or blotches appear on flowers and leaves; these later become covered with coarse gray mold.	Remove and discard dead or infected plant parts. Clean planting area thoroughly in autumn, disposing of all dead and fallen leaves and stems.
Powdery mildew	Fungal disease. Shows up as a powdery white to gray coating on leaves, stems, and flower buds. Heavy infestations debilitate and disfigure plants. Favored by moist air, poor air circulation, and shade—but needs dry leaves to become established.	Improve air circulation by thinning crowded plants. Spray with water to wash off fungus. Discard infected plant parts. Spray with copper soap fungicide, neem oil, or potassium bicarbonate.
Root rot	Fungal disease; sometimes called water mold. Active in warm, wet, or poorly drained soils. Young leaves turn yellow and wilt; plants may be stunted or may wilt and die, even in moist soil.	Keep soil moist, but do not overwater plants. Improve drainage or plant in raised beds. Remove and discard diseased plants.
Rust	A great many rust fungi exist, each specific to a certain plant. Yellow, orange, red, or brown pustules appear on leaf undersides; the powdery spores are spread by wind and water.	Plant resistant varieties. Improve air circulation. Remove infected leaves immediately; in winter, clean up all fallen leaves and debris. If watering from overhead, be sure plants will dry before dusk.

Botrytis

Powdery mildew

Root rot

Rust

PESTS

PEST	DESCRIPTION	MANAGEMENT
Aphids	Soft-bodied, rounded insects that range from pinhead to matchhead size. May be black, white, pink, or pale green. They cluster on new growth, sucking plant juices; heavy infestations distort growth. Some kinds transmit viral diseases.	Hose off with strong jets of water. Spray with insecticidal soap or a natural pesticide containing pyrethrins.
Cutworms	A variety of soil-dwelling caterpillars of various colors. They feed at night and on overcast days; during daylight hours, they hide underground, curled up in a C shape. Most cut the stems of young plants.	Protect young transplants from cutworms by encircling each with a can (with both ends removed) or a paper cup with the bottom cut out. Handpick at night.
Geranium budworms (tobacco budworms)	Striped caterpillars up to ¾ inch long; may be greenish, tan, or reddish. Besides geraniums, they attack petunias and other flowers, burrowing into buds and feeding from the inside. They also eat leaves and stems.	Remove dried-up buds and flowers that may harbor the pests. In fall, clear away dead annuals and infested parts of other plants to remove eggs. *Bt* kills budworms if applied before the caterpillars enter buds.
Japanese beetles	Half-inch-long beetles with a distinctive metallic green sheen; attack foliage of many plants. Major pests in the eastern U.S., they have been gradually moving westward.	Don't bring infested plants or soil (containing larvae) into unaffected areas. Handpick, use traps, or spray with a natural pesticide containing pyrethrins.
Leaf miners	A catchall term for certain moth, beetle, and fly larvae that tunnel within plant leaves, leaving a nearly transparent, twisting trail on the surface.	Pick off and destroy infected leaves. Neem extract may discourage adults from laying eggs on leaf surfaces, but once the insect is inside the leaf, sprays are not effective.
Mites	Tiny spider relatives found on leaf undersides (webbing is often present); leaf surface is pale and stippled. Foliage eventually dries out, turns brown. To spot them, hold a piece of white paper under affected foliage and tap plant. Disturbed mites drop onto the paper; they look like specks of pepper. Infestations increase rapidly in hot weather.	Hose off plants with strong jets of water. You can purchase predatory mites that feed on harmful mite species; lacewing larvae are also effective. Spray with insecticidal soap, sulfur, or neem oil.
Slugs and snails	Both are night-feeding mollusks; snails have shells, slugs do not. They feast on leaves, stems, and flowers, leaving tell-tale trails of silvery slime.	Handpick and destroy. Containers filled with beer and set at ground level attract the pests, which then fall in and drown. Use barriers: surround plants or beds with rings of diatomaceous earth, or enclose containers and raised beds with copper strips. Use bait containing nontoxic iron phosphate (Sluggo), which is not hazardous to other creatures.
Thrips	Near-microscopic pests that feed by rasping soft flower and leaf tissue. Leaf surfaces take on a shiny, silvery or tan cast.	Hose off plants with strong jets of water. Spray with insecticidal soap.
Whiteflies	Tiny white pests that fly up in a cloud when disturbed; they suck plant juices from leaf undersides. Damaged foliage is sometimes stippled with yellow and may eventually curl and turn brown.	Handpicking heavily infested leaves helps reduce populations. Yellow sticky traps (available commercially) can trap significant numbers. Hose off plants frequently with jets of water. Spray with insecticidal soap, neem extract.

Aphids

Geranium budworms

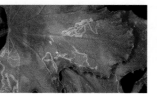
Leaf miners

Whiteflies

WEEDS

Weeds are plants growing where gardeners don't want them to grow. Besides being unsightly in the garden, they rob desirable plants of water, nutrients, and sunlight; some may also harbor diseases or harmful insects. Management does take effort, but working at it consistently for several years can significantly reduce the weed population in your garden.

MANAGING WEEDS. Winning the battle against weeds starts with prevention. Weed seeds often hitchhike into the garden in mulches, animal manure, or purchased topsoil, so ask about possible weed problems before you buy these products. After applying any of them, check frequently for new weeds and dispatch them immediately. Also check the soil of container-grown nursery plants and reject any with visible weeds.

Besides working to prevent weeds from showing up in the first place, you'll need to control those already present in your garden. For best success at this job, learn to distinguish between annual, biennial, and perennial weeds. *Annual* weeds—like annuals grown for ornament—grow shoots and leaves, come into flower, set seed, and die within a period of less than a year. Familiar examples include crabgrass, purslane, and spotted spurge. *Biennial* weeds, such as mullein, produce a cluster of leaves in their first year, then flower, set seed, and die the following year. *Perennial* weeds live for several years; they reproduce by setting seed and, in most cases, by producing spreading roots, bulbs, or tubers, making control more difficult. Common perennial weeds include bindweed, quackgrass, and dandelions.

You can control weeds by physical means or, if absolutely necessary, by chemical methods. Once you have destroyed them, take steps to prevent them from returning. Mulching bare soil around plants is an effective deterrent; see page 70 for more on organic mulches.

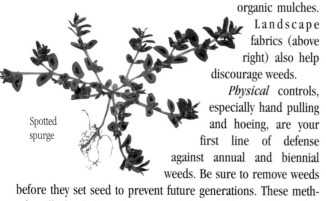

Spotted spurge

Landscape fabrics (above right) also help discourage weeds.

Physical controls, especially hand pulling and hoeing, are your first line of defense against annual and biennial weeds. Be sure to remove weeds before they set seed to prevent future generations. These methods will also help control perennial weeds, but you'll need to catch the plants while they're young. Once they have passed the seedling stage, it is usually necessary to dig out their roots—just pulling them up by hand (or cutting off the tops with a hoe) leaves behind root fragments, which will resprout. Even with assiduous digging, you'll probably have to repeat the process several times.

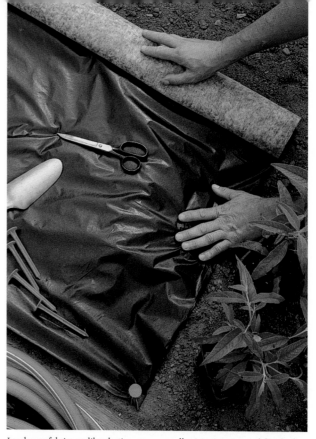

Landscape fabrics, unlike plastic, are porous, allowing air, water, and dissolved nutrients to reach the soil. Sold in nurseries and garden supply centers, these fabrics are best used to prevent weed growth around fairly permanent plantings of perennials; they aren't suited for beds of annuals where you change plants often. To install, unroll the fabric and use a knife or scissors to cut slits where you want to set out plants. After planting, cover the fabric with a 2-inch layer of mulch.

Smothering is another physical control. This technique effectively kills sod and weeds in areas earmarked for future planting. After mowing or cutting off the top growth, put down a layer of heavy cardboard, newspapers (make the layer at least three dozen sheets thick), or black plastic. Overlap these materials so weeds can't grow through the cracks. Anchor the covering with a layer of bark chips or other organic mulch. Leave the smothering materials in place for at least a full growing season; allow a year or more for tough perennial weeds.

Presprouting is a physical control useful for preparing planting beds for annuals or perennials in weedy areas. Dig out existing weeds and spread amendments over the soil. Till or dig the soil, water, and then wait a week or two for weed seeds to germinate. When they're only a few inches high, scrape them away. Then sow or transplant, disturbing the soil as little as possible to avoid bringing more weed seeds to the surface.

Chemical control of weeds with herbicides poses serious risks and, in most cases, should be used only when other methods have failed. Many herbicides can damage desirable plants if they drift through the air or run off in irrigation or rainwater. Some persist in the soil, hindering the growth of later plantings. If you do use herbicides, read the label carefully and follow directions exactly.

PROPAGATION

In gardening usage, "propagation" is a general term for the many ways of starting new plants. Annuals, biennials, and perennials can all be started from seed. For perennials, other options include division and taking root, stem, or basal cuttings; either of these methods will give you an increased supply of plants to expand your own beds and borders and to share with friends and neighbors. A greenhouse or cold frame (see page 82) is the ideal place to raise young plants resulting from division or cuttings—and to harden off those grown from seed.

SOWING SEEDS

Starting from seed is an economical way to get lots of plants. It also allows you to experiment with new and unusual varieties, since most seed catalogs (see page 189) and nursery seed racks offer more choices than you are likely to find among ready-to-plant young plants in pots and cell-packs. You can sow seeds directly outdoors—in a planting bed or cutting garden, for example—or in containers for later transplanting to the garden. Or, if you're planting wildflower seeds, you may want to create a natural meadow; this is a distinct garden style that involves a particular planting method (see page 80).

SOWING SEEDS IN THE GARDEN. Many fast-growing annuals and a few perennials can be sown right where they are to grow, either to cover an entire bed or to fill in empty patches among other plants. This is also a good way to grow a garden of flowers for cutting. Direct sowing saves the trouble of starting seeds indoors and transplanting the young plants. And some annuals grow better when sown directly in the garden, since they have delicate root systems or taproots that make successful transplanting difficult (though not impossible). Such plants include clarkia, California poppy *(Eschscholzia)*, sweet pea *(Lathyrus)*, love-in-a-mist *(Nigella)*, some poppies *(Papaver)*, and nasturtium *(Tropaeolum)*.

Plan to sow cool-season annuals and hardy perennials as soon as the soil can be worked in spring (some may also be sown in fall); wait until after the last frost to sow warm-season annuals and tender perennials. (For more on cool- and warm-season annuals, see page 66.)

Start by preparing a planting bed as described on page 64—even if you're planting only a small area. You can broadcast seeds, creating a natural-looking planting, or plant them in orderly rows. To broadcast, scatter seeds evenly over the prepared soil; then rake lightly, barely covering the seeds. To sow in rows, make furrows with a hoe or rake, following the seed packet instructions for depth and spacing. Sow seeds evenly, then cover them with soil to the recommended depth, patting them into the soil with your hands. Water the bed or rows of seeds with a fine spray, keeping the soil surface moist but not dripping wet. After the seedlings are up and growing, gradually cut back on watering, being sure to keep the root zone moist. When the seedlings have developed two sets of true leaves, thin them to the spacing recommended on the seed packet.

GROWING BIENNIALS

As noted on page 7, biennials typically complete their life cycle in 2 years. During their first year, they grow from seed into leafy but nonblooming plants. They live through the winter (experiencing the cold temperatures that most require if they are to bloom), then flower, set seed, and die in the following year.

To grow biennials, sow seeds in containers or directly in the garden at the time indicated on the seed packet—typically in mid- to late spring or in summer. Transplant seedlings started in containers into the garden in early fall, setting them in well-prepared soil; water as needed. In areas where the ground freezes, place a protective mulch of straw or chopped leaves around the plants, taking care not to smother the foliage rosettes. In spring, pull back the mulch and feed with a high-nitrogen fertilizer as soon as new growth begins.

The first-year foliage clump of biennial foxglove *(Digitalis purpurea)*.

In the second year, flowering spikes appear.

SOWING SEEDS IN CONTAINERS. Many annuals and perennials turn in the best performance when started in containers indoors, then transplanted outside later in the season. It's easier to provide young plants in containers with the warm temperatures and bright light they need for quick growth, and it's also easier to protect them from insects and birds. The information on the packet will help you decide when to plant. Timing does vary, but most annuals should be sown at some point from late winter to midspring—somewhere between 4 and 10 weeks before it's time to set them outdoors. Sow seeds of most perennials within this same winter-to-spring time period. Many kinds will be ready to transplant by early summer or fall (avoid planting in the heat of midsummer). Others, though, may not be mature enough until the following spring.

You can select from a variety of containers, including flats or trays (with or without dividers), small individual pots, and cell-packs. If you're reusing old containers, scrub them out and soak them for half an hour in a solution of 1 part household bleach to 9 parts hot water to destroy any disease organisms. Then proceed as directed below.

SEEDS TO SEEDLINGS

1 Fill each container to within ½ inch of the rim with damp seed-starting or potting mix, firming it gently. Scatter seeds thinly over the surface. Check the seed packet for recommended planting depth and cover with the proper amount of mix. (As a rule of thumb, cover seeds to a depth equal to twice their diameter.) Label each container with the plant's name and the date. Moisten lightly. Covering containers loosely with damp newspaper helps keep soil moist—but don't cover if the seed packet informs you that the seeds need light to germinate.

Place the containers in a warm spot. When the seeds sprout, uncover the containers, if necessary; then move them to a location where they'll be in bright light, such as a greenhouse or sunny window. (Or give them 12 to 14 hours of fluorescent light each day, setting the light 6 to 8 inches above the tops of plants.) Water with a fine mist when the soil surface feels dry.

2 When the seedlings develop their second set of true leaves, it's time to transplant them to larger containers, such as 3-inch plastic pots. Fill the new containers with moist potting mix. Remove the seedlings from their original pots by squeezing each pot's sides and turning it upside down, keeping one hand around the soil ball. Once the soil ball is out of the pot, carefully pull it apart with both hands and set it down on a flat surface.

3 To separate the seedlings, separate the fragile roots with a toothpick or skewer or tease them apart with your fingers.

4 Poke a hole in the new container's potting mix. Handle each seedling by the leaves to avoid damaging the tender stem; support the soil ball with your finger. Place each seedling in its new container and firm the mix around it. Water immediately, then set the pots in bright light (but keep them out of direct sunlight for a few days). Fertilize weekly with a fertilizer sold for starting seeds or with a liquid type diluted to half-strength.

About 10 days before the seedlings are ready to plant outdoors, harden them off so they can withstand bright outdoor sun and cooler temperatures. Stop fertilizing and set the seedlings outside for a few hours each day in a wind-sheltered spot in filtered light. Over the next week, gradually increase exposure until plants are in full sun all day. (Plants that prefer shade are an exception; they should not be exposed to day-long sun.) Alternatively, you can harden off seedlings by placing them in a cold frame (see page 82), opening its cover a bit more each day (as well as at night). Set out seedlings in the garden as shown on page 67.

PLANTING A WILDFLOWER MEADOW

For a carefree, natural look, gardeners turn to mixes of wildflowers and other easy-to-grow annuals and perennials. Though the word "meadow" conjures up the image of a sweeping, grassy expanse, a meadow-type garden can also be established in more confined spaces—in a small planting bed, around a mailbox, even in a container. Planted in a carefully prepared site, a wildflower meadow can give you months of pleasure, and provide food and nectar for butterflies and beneficial insects at the same time.

If you garden in a mild-winter climate, sow wildflowers in fall or early winter. In cold-winter areas, spring planting is more successful. Many sorts of wildflower mixes are available; most contain both native and non-native annuals and perennials, though you can find native-only mixtures. It's a good idea to choose a mix geared to your region—a so-called Midwestern wildflower mix, for example. Most wildflowers grow best in a sunny spot, but mixes for partially shaded sites are available. Local nurseries and mail-order firms (see page 189) sell wildflower seed mixes.

Follow these steps to sow and care for your meadow.

1 Cultivate the soil, removing all weeds. Most garden soils need no additional organic matter to support wildflowers successfully, but if your soil is very heavy clay or very sandy, spread on an inch or two of compost and work it in. Soak the soil thoroughly, then wait for weed seeds to germinate. When they do (allow about 3 weeks), hoe or pull them.

2 Rake the soil lightly to form shallow grooves. Broadcast the wildflower seeds over the soil according to package directions (you'll need about 1 ounce per 100 square feet). Rake lightly again to cover the seeds; water well. Continue watering just enough to keep the surface of the soil moist until seedlings appear.

3 Pull out any weeds as soon as they germinate. To help you tell the difference between weeds and wildflowers, sow some of the wildflower seeds in a nursery flat at planting time. When the seedlings in the flat come up, compare them with seedlings in the meadow planting; any seedlings that show up in the meadow but not in the flat are probably weeds.

4 Water and weed regularly during growing season. As the flowers fade, cut the plants back, shaking seeds from the faded blooms over the ground to provide a new flowering meadow next year.

Brilliant poppies *(Papaver),* clarkias, and bachelor's buttons *(Centaurea cyanus)* glow in this wildflower meadow.

DIVIDING PERENNIALS

To divide a perennial, you dig it up, separate it into sections, and replant the pieces. Besides giving you new plants, division rejuvenates overgrown plants, improving bloom and overall appearance. Most perennials can be divided either in fall or in early spring. If you plan to divide in fall and you live in a cold-winter climate, do the job early enough in the season to let roots get established before freezing weather arrives (generally 6 to 8 weeks before the first hard frost).

Step-by-step instructions for dividing perennials are given below. A day or two before dividing, thoroughly moisten the soil around the clump. To make the plants easier to handle, many gardeners cut back the stems of larger perennials, leaving about 6 inches of foliage. If you'll be planting in a new bed, prepare the area (see page 64) in advance, so you can replant the divisions promptly. If you're replanting in the same location, place the divisions in a shady spot and cover them with damp newspapers while you replenish the soil.

To divide large, tough, or overgrown perennials such as these daylilies *(Hemerocallis),* pry the roots apart with two spading forks inserted back to back in the center of the clump.

1 Loosen the soil in a circle around the clump, cutting 6 to 12 inches beyond the plant's perimeter with a shovel or spading fork. Then dig under the roots to free them from the soil. Lift the whole clump out of the ground; or, if it's too heavy to lift, cut it into sections. Set the clump (or pieces) in a convenient working spot, such as a path.

2 Gently tease some soil from the root ball so you can see what you are doing. For larger, fibrous-rooted perennials such as daylilies *(Hemerocallis),* hose off as much of the soil as possible.

3 Now make the divisions. Look at the plant, noting natural dividing points between stems or sections. You can easily divide some perennials by pulling the clumps apart by hand. Those with mats of small, fibrous roots can be cut with a knife, small pruning saw, or trowel; types with thick, tough roots may require a sharp-bladed shovel or an ax. Try to divide the clumps into good-sized sections, which will grow and bloom more quickly than small divisions. Trim any damaged roots, stems, or leaves from the divisions.

4 Replant the divisions as soon as possible, then keep them well watered while they get established. You can also plant divisions in containers (a good idea if they're very small) to set out later or share with other gardeners.

TAKING ROOT CUTTINGS

Some fleshy-rooted perennials—acanthus, sea holly *(Eryngium)*, and phlox, for example—can be increased from root cuttings. For most perennials, root cuttings are best made in late winter to early spring, when the plant is still dormant but close to beginning growth. (Exceptions are bleeding heart, *Dicentra*, and Oriental poppy, *Papaver orientale*; these are dormant in late summer or fall, and you should take root cuttings then.)

To obtain roots for cuttings, you can dig up an entire plant or just a section of its roots. Using a sharp knife, remove vigorous, healthy pieces of root. Those growing closest to the plant's crown will form new plants most quickly. Being sure to note which end was closest to the crown, cut the pieces into 2- to 4-inch-long sections. If you have only a few cuttings, you can insert them upright in a container filled with damp potting mix, with the top cut ends just at soil level. For larger numbers of cuttings (or for very thin pieces of root), fill a flat to within an inch of the top with potting mix. Lay the cuttings flat on top of the mix, then cover them with ½ inch more mix.

Water the planted containers well, then place them in a growing area such as a greenhouse or cold frame and provide

protection from direct sun. Once stems and green leaves have formed, move the containers into full light and water them as needed. When the young shoots are several inches tall and new roots have formed (check by gently digging up a cutting), transplant them to individual pots and feed with liquid fertilizer.

COLD FRAMES

Used to protect tender plants or rooted cuttings during the colder months, as well as to harden off seedlings, a cold frame is simply a box with a transparent lid or cover. It acts as a passive solar energy collector and reservoir. During the day, the sun's rays heat the air and soil in the frame; at night, the heat absorbed by the soil radiates out, keeping the plants warm.

You can buy a ready-made cold frame or build your own, using rot-resistant lumber. For the cover, use a recycled window or staple polyethylene film to a wooden frame. Make the cold frame about 3 feet wide (so you can reach all the plants) and as long as you like; a longer frame will need several covers. The frame should slope from back to front to allow water to run off and to capture more heat. Place the frame in a site protected from harsh winds; if possible, orient it to face south. Sinking the frame 8 to 10 inches into the ground increases heat retention.

Ventilation is vital to prevent overheating. Open the cover when the temperature inside reaches 70 to 75°F/21 to 24°C; keep a minimum-maximum thermometer inside the frame to help keep track of temperature fluctuations. Close the cover in late afternoon to trap heat. On very cold nights, drape the frame with an old blanket to provide extra insulation.

TAKING STEM OR BASAL CUTTINGS

Most perennials, including tender ones often grown as annuals (such as begonia, coleus, and *Pelargonium*), can be propagated from stem or basal cuttings.

Stem cuttings, also called softwood cuttings, are taken from pieces of the stem or shoot. Basal cuttings, recommended for a few perennials, are quite similar; they consist of entire young shoots, cut from the parent plant so that each retains a piece of firm tissue at its base. They are rooted in the same way as stem cuttings, shown below. Take stem and basal cuttings during the active growing season from spring until late summer; the plant encyclopedia beginning on page 84 notes the best time to take them for each perennial.

1 Prepare containers first. Use clean pots or flats with drainage holes. Fill them with a half-and-half mixture of perlite and peat moss, or with perlite or peat moss alone. Dampen the mixture.

2 Gather material for cuttings early in the day, when plants are full of moisture. The parent plant should be healthy and growing vigorously. With a sharp knife or bypass pruners, snip 5- to 6-inch-long pieces from the plant, choosing vigorous young tip or side shoots.

   Remove and discard any flower buds, flowers, and small shoots growing laterally from the main stem. Then trim the stems into 3- to 4-inch lengths, each with at least two nodes (growing points). Make the lower cut just below a node, since new roots will form at this point. Remove leaves from the lower half of the cutting.

3 Dip the lower cut ends of the cuttings in liquid or powdered rooting hormone; shake off any excess. (Many gardeners omit this step and still get good results.)

   Using the end of a pencil, make 1- to 1½-inch-deep holes in the rooting medium, spacing them 1 to 2 inches apart; then insert the cuttings. Firm the medium around the cuttings and water with a fine spray. Label each container (or group of plants within a container) with the name of the plant and the date.

   Enclose each container in a plastic bag. Close the bag to maintain humidity, but open it for a few minutes every day to provide ventilation. Set the containers in a warm, shaded (but not dark) location.

4 The cuttings will usually take hold and begin growing roots in 1 to 5 weeks. To check, gently pull on a cutting; if you feel resistance, roots are forming. At this point, expose the cuttings to drier air by opening the bags; if the cuttings wilt, close the bags again for a few days (opening them briefly each day for ventilation).

   When the plants seem acclimated to open air, transplant each to its own 3- to 4-inch pot of lightweight potting mix. When they're well rooted and growing new leaves, they're ready to go into the ground.

ENCYCLOPEDIA OF ANNUALS AND PERENNIALS

The realm of annuals and perennials is a vast one, including enough plants to keep gardeners busy and happy for years—and each spring, nurseries introduce even more enticing choices. The following pages present a diverse selection that includes long-time favorites as well as promising newer varieties. You'll also find special features on ornamental grasses (pages 126–129), varieties of vegetables attractive enough to decorate beds and borders (page 151), and flowering annual vines (pages 180–181).

Each entry in this encyclopedia begins with the plant's botanical name; any alternate botanical names (former names that are still widely used or new ones that haven't yet taken hold) appear in parentheses. Entries that describe a number of species and hybrids are headed simply by the plant's genus—*Achillea*, for example. Other entries cover only a single species and are headed by both genus and species, as in the case of *Ageratum houstonianum*.

Next, we give the plant's common name or names (if there are any) and its botanical family. The plant is then identified as a perennial, biennial, or annual; annuals are further identified as cool-season or warm-season (see page 66). The following line notes the *Sunset* climate zones (see pages 184–188) in which the plant will succeed.

Recommended exposure is indicated next. *Full sun* means the plant grows best with day-long bright, unshaded sun. *Partial shade* and *light shade* refer to spots that are sunny in the morning but shaded in the afternoon, or to those that receive no direct sun but still get plenty of light. *Full shade* indicates that the plant prefers little or no direct sunlight.

Moisture needs are identified as well. *Moderate water* and *little water* apply to plants that need some moisture but prefer to have the soil go somewhat to quite dry between waterings. *Regular water* means the plant requires steady moisture, but the soil shouldn't remain saturated. A few plants need *ample water;* these grow happily in soggy soil.

Finally, we note the range of flower colors and the main bloom season for each plant.

ACANTHUS

ACANTHUS, BEAR'S BREECH
Acanthaceae
PERENNIALS
ZONES 4–24, 28–32, 34, 39, EXCEPT
    AS NOTED
FULL SUN OR PARTIAL SHADE
MODERATE TO REGULAR WATER
✿ ❀ ✿ FLOWERS IN LATE SPRING, SUMMER

Acanthus spinosus

A good choice for a garden accent, a thriving clump of acanthus has a bold, sculptural look—and when bloom time comes, it provides a strong vertical effect as well. Borne on arching stems, the dark green, 2-foot-long leaves are attractively lobed; in some species, the leaf margins are spiny. Rigid flower spikes rise to a height of 3 to 4 feet, set with tubular blossoms surrounded by spiny bracts (modified leaves). *A. balcanicus (A. hungaricus)* has deeply lobed leaves with wide gaps between the lobes; it blooms profusely in summer, bearing white or pale pink blossoms with purple bracts.

The most commonly grown species, *A. mollis* (Zones 5–24, 28–32), has shiny deep green leaves that are not as deeply lobed as those of the other two species described here. White flowers with purple-flushed bracts bloom from late spring to early summer. '**Latifolius**' has larger leaves than the species, flowers less freely, and reputedly tolerates more cold. *A. spinosus,* another species that blooms from late spring to early summer, has finely cut, spiny-margined leaves and white blossoms with purple bracts.

CULTURE. Where hardy, acanthus are almost too easy to grow. The roots spread rapidly underground, especially in loose, moist, well-enriched soil. To save yourself the task of constantly fighting the plants back, either allow them plenty of space or confine the roots with an 8-inch-deep barrier. Where summers are hot, locate acanthus in partial shade; hot sun causes the leaves to wilt. In dry-summer regions, plants go dormant if not regularly watered.

Propagate acanthus by dividing the clumps. In mild-winter regions, do the job at some time from fall through late winter; in cold-winter regions, wait until spring. Note that any roots left in the soil will sprout, forming new clumps.

Ranging from foot-tall front-of-the-border plants in soft pastels to 5-footers with brilliant yellow flowers, yarrows are carefree, generously blooming perennials. Most species have aromatic gray or green leaves that are narrow, fernlike, and finely dissected. The flowers, appearing in summer and early fall, are tiny daisies packed tightly into flattened or somewhat rounded heads. They make good fresh cut flowers and also dry nicely for winter arrangements.

A. filipendulina 'Gold Plate' is one of the tallest yarrows, producing 6-inch-wide, deep yellow flower clusters on 5-foot stems that may require staking. A related hybrid, 'Coronation Gold', tolerates a wide range of soils and climates; its shiny golden flower heads are 3 to 4 inches across, carried on strong, 2- to 3-foot stems.

Common yarrow, *A. millefolium*, forms a spreading mat of green to gray-green leaves. The species is a roadside weed with off-white flowers on 1- to 2-foot stems. Gardeners grow various selected forms and hybrids, including 'Cerise Queen', a 1½-footer with magenta flowers; 2- to 3-foot-tall 'The Beacon' ('Fanal'), with rich red blossoms centered in yellow; 3-foot-tall 'Fireland', with flowers that open red, then fade to pink and gold; and 3- to 4-foot 'Credo', bearing light yellow blooms that fade to creamy white. The **Summer Pastels** strain features 2-foot plants that flower the first year from seed in a range of colors, including white, purple, apricot, and yellow.

A. 'Moonshine', a popular hybrid with gray-green, filigreelike foliage, has deep lemon yellow flowers on 1- to 2-foot stems. The related hybrid 'Anthea' bears light yellow blooms on plants that tend to be more erect in habit.

A. ptarmica goes by the common name "sneezeweed" (note that it isn't the same plant as another sneezeweed, *Helenium*). The species can be quite invasive, but selected forms such as 'Angel's Breath' and double-flowered 'The Pearl' are less aggressive. They grow about 2 feet tall and produce white blossoms that are often used in bouquets as a substitute for baby's breath (*Gypsophila*).

CULTURE. Yarrows grow best in reasonably good, well-drained soil. They are drought tolerant once established but look more attractive with moderate watering. Cut out the spent stems after flowering. Divide crowded clumps in spring.

The curious helmet- or hood-shaped flowers of monkshood are set closely along tall, leafy spikes that rise above attractive clumps of dark green, deeply lobed foliage. These plants can substitute for delphiniums in shady locations; they are effective in borders or near a bog garden. Keep in mind, however, that all parts of monkshood are poisonous, and be especially careful not to locate it where the tuberous roots could be mistaken for edible roots.

Summer-blooming *A.* × *cammarum* 'Bicolor' grows to 4 feet and produces two-tone blossoms of white and violet blue. Flowering later (in late summer and early autumn) is *A. carmichaelii (A. fischeri)*, bearing dense, branching clusters of deep purple-blue flowers on 2- to

ACHILLEA
YARROW
Asteraceae (Compositae)
PERENNIALS
ZONES A1–A3; 1–24, 26, 28–45
FULL SUN
LITTLE TO MODERATE WATER
✿❀✿✿✿✿ FLOWERS IN SUMMER,
  EARLY FALL

Achillea 'Moonshine'

ACONITUM
MONKSHOOD, ACONITE
Ranunculaceae
PERENNIALS
ZONES A1–A3; 1–9, 14–21, 34–45
FULL SUN OR PARTIAL SHADE
REGULAR WATER
✿✿✿❀✿ FLOWERS IN SUMMER, FALL

Aconitum

Aconitum napellus

4-foot stems. An early-summer bloomer is *A.* **'Ivorine'**, a compact, 1½-foot-tall form topped with many clusters of creamy white flowers. Common monkshood, *A. napellus,* flowers in late summer; it grows 2 to 5 feet tall and is available in blue, violet, pink, and white forms.

CULTURE. Plant monkshood in moist, fertile soil enriched with compost. Plants grow best in cool-summer regions with some winter chill; they are difficult to establish in warm, dry climates. Clumps can remain undisturbed for years with no loss of vigor and bloom quality—and in fact, it's best not to disturb established plants. If you want to increase your plantings, however, you can carefully separate and replant the tuberous roots in very early spring. Mulch new plants and transplanted roots the first winter.

ADENOPHORA

LADY BELLS
Campanulaceae (Lobeliaceae)
PERENNIALS
ZONES A2, A3; 1–10, 14–24, 30–43
FULL SUN OR LIGHT SHADE
MODERATE TO REGULAR WATER
✿ ❀ FLOWERS IN SUMMER

These are slim, erect plants with narrow, leafy stems that bear rows of charming, fragrant, bell-like, typically blue flowers along their upper portions. They look much like campanulas (to which they are related) and may substitute for them in the hot, humid climates where campanulas often fail. Group several plants together for the showiest display.

Common lady bells, *A. confusa,* grows 2 to 3 feet tall and 2 feet wide. The nodding flowers are deep blue. Lilyleaf lady bells, *A. liliifolia,* is similar but smaller, just 1½ feet high and a foot wide; its blooms are pale lavender blue or, in some forms, white.

CULTURE. Plant lady bells in rich, well-drained soil. When buying container-grown plants, look for young ones, since older plants have deep, fleshy roots that do not transplant readily. For the same reason, it's best not to divide clumps— division harms the roots and is rarely successful. Instead, propagate lady bells by sowing the fine seeds outdoors in containers in fall (as soon as seed ripens) or indoors in late winter. Plants may self-seed abundantly; pull out seedlings you don't want.

Adenophora confusa

AGAPANTHUS

AGAPANTHUS, LILY-OF-THE-NILE
Amaryllidaceae
PERENNIALS
ZONES VARY
FULL SUN OR LIGHT SHADE
LITTLE TO REGULAR WATER
✿ ❀ FLOWERS IN SUMMER

These elegant, stately, summer-blooming plants feature fountainlike clumps of handsome, strap-shaped foliage that send up sturdy, 1- to 5-foot stems topped with rounded clusters containing dozens of tubular flowers. Colors include almost every shade of blue, from the palest tints to deep midnight, as well as sparkling white.

A number of species and hybrids are available. Two typically evergreen choices are *A. africanus (A. umbellatus)* and *A. praecox orientalis (A. orientalis);* both are successful in Zones 6–9, 12–24, 28–31, H1, H2. *A. africanus* has leaves that reach about a foot long and 1½- to 2-foot flower stalks carrying 6-inch-wide clusters of 20 to 50 blue flowers. **'Albus'** is a white-flowered cultivar that looks especially showy in the night garden.

A. praecox orientalis grows altogether larger than *A. africanus,* with 1- to 2-foot-long leaves and 4- to 5-foot stems carrying 8- to 12-inch-wide heads of up to 100 blue or white flowers. Hybrid selections include 3- to 4-foot-tall **'Midknight Blue'**, with exceptionally deep blue flowers, and the outstanding dwarf **'Peter Pan'**, with foliage clumps just 1 foot tall and profuse blue flowers atop 1- to 1½-foot-high stems.

Agapanthus 'Peter Pan'

The more cold-hardy **Headbourne Hybrids** and *A. inapertus* (both suitable for Zones 4–9, 12–21, 28–31, warmer parts of 32) are deciduous in winter. The Headbourne Hybrids have fairly narrow, upright leaves and 2- to 3-foot-tall stems bearing 6-inch-wide flower heads; colors include many shades of blue as well as white. *A. inapertus* is taller, reaching 4 to 5 feet in bloom, and features deep blue blossoms in drooping, 4- to 6-inch-wide clusters.

CULTURE. Tough and durable, agapanthus thrive in loamy soil with regular water, but they tolerate poor soils, and, once established, can get along with little or no irrigation. They flower most freely in sun but also grow and bloom fairly well in light shade. Clumps can remain in place for many years before they need dividing; when it's time to divide, do the job in early spring.

In zones too cold for in-ground planting, grow agapanthus in containers placed in the garden, around a pool, or on a deck or patio. When winter weather comes, move the containers to a frost-free place and allow the crowns to dry out; as spring approaches, move them into bright light and begin to water again.

Agapanthus praecox orientalis

These showy mint-family members have aromatic foliage, often delightfully reminiscent of licorice; in summer and fall, they send up blossom spikes set with whorls of small, tubular flowers. Though frequently planted in herb gardens, they are equally at home in borders and large containers.

A. barberi (Zones 2–24, 29–32, 34, 39), reaching 2 feet tall, has 6- to 12-inch spikes of reddish purple flowers. Its ovate green leaves are about 2 inches long. Anise hyssop, *A. foeniculum* (Zones A3; 1–24, 28–41), forms an erect, bushy plant to 5 feet tall, clothed in lance-shaped, gray-green, 2- to 3-inch leaves with downy undersides. Its dense clusters of lilac-blue flowers are borne in 4-inch spikes. It blooms the first year from seed and reseeds freely. Korean hummingbird mint, *A. rugosa* (Zones 4–24, 28–33), bearing purplish blue blossoms, grows about 5 feet tall. Its ovate, tooth-edged, 2½- to 3-inch-long leaves are glossy green with a purplish tinge.

Among hybrid agastaches are **'Blue Fortune'**, to 3 feet tall, with blue blossom spikes; and the shorter **'Firebird'**, which grows just 1½ to 2 feet tall and bears coppery orange-red blooms. Both grow in Zones 4–24, 28–33. **'Apricot Sunrise'** (Zones 2–24, 29–32, 34, 39) is a 2½-footer with pale orange flowers.

CULTURE. Plant agastaches in well-drained soil. They tolerate some drought but grow and bloom best with regular water. A full-sun location will yield the most prolific flower show, but you'll get a good performance in light shade as well. Propagate by seed sown indoors in late winter, division in spring, or stem cuttings.

AGASTACHE
AGASTACHE, HYSSOP
Lamiaceae (Labiatae)
PERENNIALS
ZONES VARY
FULL SUN OR PARTIAL SHADE
MODERATE TO REGULAR WATER
✿ ✿ ✿ ✿ ✿ FLOWERS IN SUMMER, FALL

Agastache 'Blue Fortune'

Floss flower is a reliable favorite for color from summer until frost, a good choice for edging borders and for use in beds and containers. In mild-winter areas, it can be grown as a fall- and winter-flowering annual. The plants have a mounded form, with soft, hairy green leaves that are usually heart shaped at the base. Individual flowers are tiny but are borne in dense clusters resembling powder puffs. Among the many blue-blossomed varieties are some of the truest blues available to gardeners. These include dwarf sorts (about 6 inches in height) such as **'Blue Danube'** (**'Blue Puffs'**), **'Dwarf Blue Bedder'**, and **'Royal Delft'**; 8- to 10-inch-high **'Blue Lagoon'**, with masses of navy blue flowers; and foot-tall **'Capri'** and **'Southern Cross'**, bearing blue blossoms with brightly contrasting white centers. **'Blue Horizon'**, to 2½ feet tall, is an excellent

AGERATUM
houstonianum
FLOSS FLOWER
Asteraceae (Compositae)
WARM-SEASON ANNUAL
ZONES 1–45
FULL SUN, EXCEPT AS NOTED
REGULAR WATER
✿ ✿ ✿ FLOWERS IN SUMMER AND FALL, EXCEPT AS NOTED

Ageratum houstonianum 'Blue Horizon'

choice for the middle of a border; it's also a popular cut flower. Floss flowers with blossoms in other colors include **'Pink Powder-puffs'** and white **'Summer Snow'**, both 9 inches high.

CULTURE. Plant floss flower in rich, moist soil. Choose a full-sun location except in hot-summer climates, where filtered shade is best.

Sow seeds indoors 8 to 10 weeks before warm weather is expected. (In mild-winter regions, you can sow or set out young plants in late summer or early fall.) The seeds need light to germinate, so barely press them into the potting mix. Be sure soil has warmed thoroughly in spring before setting out transplants. Pinch back after planting to promote bushiness. To help keep the plants looking neat and encourage continuous bloom, deadhead regularly.

ALCEA rosea
(Althaea rosea)
HOLLYHOCK
Malvaceae
PERENNIAL, BIENNIAL, OR WARM-SEASON
    ANNUAL
ZONES 1–45
FULL SUN, EXCEPT AS NOTED
REGULAR WATER
✿✿✿✿✿ FLOWERS IN SUMMER

An old-fashioned favorite now enjoying a revival, hollyhock forms a clump of big, rough, more or less lobed leaves with a rounded heart shape. At bloom time, it sends up spikes of 3- to 6-inch-wide, funnel-shaped flowers that may be single, semidouble, or double. The blossom spikes of some older single-flowered varieties can reach 9 feet tall, but newer selections tend to be quite a bit shorter. A fine background plant, hollyhock is especially attractive planted against a fence or near a gate. It's generally grown as a biennial but often lives over for several years, making it a short-lived perennial. Some strains are grown as annuals; they bloom the first year from seed, provided seed is started indoors early in spring.

Chater's Double strain grows 6 to 8 feet tall and has ruffled double flowers in a wide range of colors. **'Nigra'**, a classic single-flowered type, bears deep chocolate maroon blossoms on 6- to 8-foot spikes; the 5-foot-tall **Country Romance** strain, also single flowered, offers a mix of colors. Mixed-color strains that bloom the first year from seed include double-flowered **Summer Carnival,** which grows 5 to 6 feet tall, and 2½-foot-tall **Majorette,** with semidouble flowers.

Alcea rosea

CULTURE. Hollyhock grows best in moderately rich, well-drained soil. Give it full sun except in the hottest climates, where partial shade is better. The tall flowering spikes may need staking in windy sites. Rust (see page 75) can damage leaves and shorten the life of the plants. Pick off infected leaves as soon as you notice them.

For blossoms in the current year, sow seed indoors in early spring; transplant seedlings into the garden as soon as warm weather arrives. To grow hollyhock as a biennial, sow seed in the garden (in the spot where plants are to grow) from spring into summer, up to 8 weeks before the first frost. Or sow in pots and transplant into the garden in late summer or in spring. Plants often self-sow, providing plenty of volunteers.

Alcea rosea

Alchemilla mollis

A soft-looking plant for the front of the border, lady's-mantle forms a mound of rounded, velvety gray-green, about 6-inch-wide leaves that glisten when beaded with droplets of dew or rain. In late spring or summer, frothy sprays of yellow-green blossoms offer a soothing contrast to brighter flowers. The plant reaches 1½ to 2 feet high and spreads 2 to 2½ feet across. **'Thriller'** is a floriferous selection with larger, pleated-looking leaves.

CULTURE. Lady's-mantle requires good soil that is moist but well drained. In regions with mild summers, plant in sun or light shade. In warm-summer areas, a location in partial shade is important—but even if given a shady spot, plants tend to be short lived where summers are long, hot, and dry. Lady's-mantle doesn't require division to stay healthy, but you can divide in early spring (before flowering) to increase your supply of plants. Self-sown seedlings often appear.

ALCHEMILLA mollis
LADY'S-MANTLE
Rosaceae
PERENNIAL
ZONES A2, A3; 1–9, 14–24, 31–43
FULL SUN OR LIGHT SHADE
REGULAR WATER
✿ FLOWERS IN LATE SPRING, SUMMER

Growing from tuberous roots, alstroemerias form spreading clumps of wiry, upright, 1- to 4-foot stems topped in late spring and summer by clusters of long-lasting, lilylike blossoms. Bright colors, bicolor combinations, and beautiful markings give the flowers an exotic appearance; they are excellent for cutting. Evergreen varieties bloom for a longer season if spent flower stems are removed. Gently pull the stems away from the root; this encourages new growth. (Don't simply cut them off at the base, since this slows new growth and bloom.)

Cordu and **Meyer** are hybrid strains that are evergreen where temperatures remain above freezing. They form compact, 1- to 3-foot-tall clumps and bloom over a long season, in colors including white, pink, red, lilac, and purple, usually bicolored and spotted. Another evergreen alstroemeria is 3- to 4-foot-high ***A. aurea (A. aurantiaca)***, bearing blossoms in yellow, orange, or orange red, liberally marked with dark stripes and flecks; **'Lutea'** is a named selection with yellow flowers marked in carmine. Both the species and 'Lutea' do best in mild-winter areas of the West Coast, and both tend to spread widely, sometimes becoming invasive.

Parrot lily, ***A. psittacina (A. pulchella)***, also evergreen, grows to 2½ feet tall and sports dark red flowers tipped with green and spotted with deep purple.

Deciduous alstroemerias are represented by the **Ligtu** hybrids, which produce leafy shoots 2 to 5 feet tall in late winter and into spring. As the leaves begin to brown, the flowering shoots appear, with blooms following in early to midsummer. Flowers come in colors including orange and orange shades (peach, salmon, shrimp) as well as red and near-white; all are flecked and striped with deeper colors. Plants go dormant after flowering.

CULTURE. Alstroemerias require well-drained soil enriched with organic matter. Plants do well everywhere in light shade (and must have afternoon shade where summers are hot); in cool-summer areas, they'll also take full sun. Handle the brittle roots carefully, setting them 6 to 8 inches deep and 1 foot apart. In warm regions, it's a good idea to mulch with ground bark, shredded leaves, or other organic material to help keep the soil cool. The plants tolerate some drought but grow best if given regular moisture (the Ligtu hybrids are exceptions: after they become dormant, they need no water unless winter rains fail). Mulch to protect the roots over winter.

Listing continues>

ALSTROEMERIA
ALSTROEMERIA, PERUVIAN LILY
Liliaceae
PERENNIALS
ZONES 5–9, 14–24, 26, 28, 31, 32
  (WARMER PARTS), 34; H1
LIGHT SHADE, EXCEPT AS NOTED
REGULAR WATER, EXCEPT AS NOTED
✿❀✿✿✿ FLOWERS IN LATE SPRING,
  SUMMER

Alstroemeria aurea

Established clumps can be divided, but because plants reestablish slowly after transplanting, it's usually best to start new plants from seed. Sow in fall, winter, or earliest spring, either directly in the garden or in individual pots for later transplanting

Note that contact with alstroemeria foliage may cause an allergic skin reaction in some people.

AMSONIA
BLUE STAR FLOWER
Apocynaceae
PERENNIALS
ZONES VARY
FULL SUN OR LIGHT SHADE
MODERATE TO REGULAR WATER
✿ FLOWERS IN LATE SPRING, SUMMER

Amsonia ciliata

These elegant perennials form handsome, bushy clumps of 2- to 3-foot stems. The small (½- to ¾-inch), star-shaped blue blossoms are borne in clusters during late spring and summer. The foliage turns a lovely golden yellow in autumn; it hangs on until frost, then drops. *A. ciliata* (Zones 2–24, 28–41), with pale blue blooms, grows 2½ to 3 feet tall, its stems crowded with 2-inch leaves that look needlelike but are soft and silky to the touch. *A. tabernaemontana* (Zones 2–24, 28–45) reaches 2 to 2½ feet; it has shiny, willowlike leaves and bears nodding clusters of slate blue flowers.

Amsonia ciliata

CULTURE. Easy to grow and undemanding, these plants thrive in average, well-drained soil in full sun or light shade. In very shady sites, they may become leggy and require staking. They are tolerant of occasional lapses in watering. Clumps increase steadily in size but seldom require division to maintain top appearance; however, you can dig and divide in early spring to increase your plantings. You can also propagate blue star flowers by taking stem cuttings in summer.

ANCHUSA
Boraginaceae
PERENNIALS, BIENNIALS, AND
    WARM-SEASON ANNUALS
ZONES VARY
FULL SUN
MODERATE TO REGULAR WATER
✿ FLOWERS IN SUMMER

Anchusa capensis

Clusters of blue summer blossoms, larger and showier than those of the related forget-me-not (*Myosotis*), characterize these plants. Cape forget-me-not, *A. capensis,* is grown as an annual in all zones; in Zones 6–24, it can also be treated as a biennial (see "Culture," below). Rich blue blossoms with white centers are clustered on hairy, branching stems to 1½ feet tall; the narrow, 5-inch-long leaves are rough in texture. **'Blue Angel'** is a free-flowering, compact selection (to 9 inches high).

Bearing bright blue flowers, Italian bugloss, *A. azurea* (*A. italica;* Zones 1–24, 29–45), is a short-lived perennial with flower stems that grow as tall as 4 feet in some selections; they rise from clumps of hairy, lance-shaped, 4- to 16-inch-long leaves. **'Dropmore'** is a widely available cultivar with deep blue flowers; it grows 4 feet high. **'Loddon Royalist'**, to 3 feet tall, is a bushier, sturdier plant with lovely gentian blue blooms. Dark blue–flowered **'Little John'** is a compact selection reaching just 1½ feet.

CULTURE. These plants need well-drained soil. Provide enough water to keep the roots moist but not saturated; they tend to rot in overly wet soil. Deadhead spent flowers to encourage a second bloom flush. Taller varieties may need staking. *A. azurea* declines after its second year; to rejuvenate the clump, divide and replant it. You can also propagate it by root cuttings taken in early spring.

To grow *A. capensis* as an annual, sow seed indoors 8 to 10 weeks before the last frost; keep temperatures at about 85°F/29°C during the day, 70°F/21°C at night. When the soil is warm, transplant seedlings into the garden. In warmer regions, where this plant can be grown as a biennial, sow seed in the garden in summer or early fall; keep soil moist until germination occurs. Plants will bloom the following summer.

Anemone tomentosa 'Robustissima'

Prized for late-season bloom, these graceful perennials are especially effective in front of a dark hedge or near the back of a border. They can be slow to establish, but once settled in, they spread widely. Japanese anemone, **A. × hybrida** (Zones 2b–24, 30–43), produces clumps of dark green, deeply veined, divided leaves at the ends of long leafstalks. The wiry, somewhat leafy flower stems typically reach 3 to 5 feet tall and bear loose sprays of cupped, gold-centered flowers resembling wild roses. Classic varieties include 3- to 4-foot **'Honorine Jobert'**, with single white flowers, and 3-foot **'Königin Charlotte'** (**'Reine Charlotte'**, **'Queen Charlotte'**), with semidouble pink blooms. **'Alice'** is a shorter selection (to about 2 feet tall) with semidouble light pink blossoms.

A. tomentosa 'Robustissima' (**A. vitifolia** 'Robustissima'; Zones 2b–9, 14–21, 30–43) forms a spreading clump of three-leafleted leaves. At bloom time, branching stems to about 3½ feet tall rise from the foliage clump, bearing single pale pink flowers.

CULTURE. Both *A. × hybrida* and *A. tomentosa* 'Robustissima' grow best in well-drained soil enriched with organic matter. Plant in light or partial shade or in filtered sun; where summers are cool, plants will also do well in full sun. Clumps don't need dividing for rejuvenation, but you can dig and transplant rooted shoots in spring to increase your supply of plants. Or propagate by root cuttings taken in late winter.

ANEMONE
Ranunculaceae
PERENNIALS
ZONES VARY
LIGHT SHADE, EXCEPT AS NOTED
REGULAR WATER
❀ ✿ FLOWERS IN LATE SUMMER, FALL

Delightful for sunny gardens and for cutting, snapdragons bloom abundantly, bearing solid-colored as well as bicolored blossoms that come in every shade but blue. In most climates, they are at their best in spring and early summer, but in mild-winter regions, they'll bloom in winter and early spring and may even live for several years. In addition to the familiar "snapping" snapdragon with upper and lower "jaws," you'll find types with double, bell-shaped, and azalea-shaped flowers. The flowers are borne in spikes above medium green, lance-shaped leaves. Dwarf forms are suitable for edging, small beds, and containers, while taller sorts provide vertical accents and are among the choicest annuals to include in perennial beds and borders. Snapdragons are most often sold in mixed colors (as both transplants and seeds), but some strains and varieties are also offered in separate colors.

Dwarf "snapping" snapdragons (6 to 12 inches tall) include **Floral Showers, Palette,** and rust-resistant **Royal Carpet** strains. Among intermediate types (1 to 2 feet tall) you will find strains such as **Rainbow, Sonnet, Ribbon,** and rust-resistant **Monarch;** others include **'Night and Day'**, with scarlet-and-white blooms, and heirloom **'Black Prince'**, with bronze foliage and deep crimson flowers. Tall-growing sorts (to 3 feet) include **Rocket** and double-flowered **Double Supreme** strains.

Bell-flowered snapdragons include **Bells Mixed** (8 to 12 inches tall), **La Bella** (to 1½ feet), and **Bright Butterflies** (2½ feet high). Among azalea-flowered types are

ANTIRRHINUM majus
SNAPDRAGON
Scrophulariaceae
PERENNIAL GROWN AS COOL-SEASON
    ANNUAL
ZONES A3; 1–45
FULL SUN
REGULAR WATER
✿ ❀ ✿ ✿ ✿ FLOWERS IN SPRING AND
    SUMMER, EXCEPT AS NOTED

Antirrhinum majus

Antirrhinum majus

foot-tall **Sweetheart** (which is resistant to rust) and 2½-foot **Madame Butterfly**. In a class of their own are the cascading snapdragons, grown for a trailing growth habit that makes them ideal for hanging baskets; these include **Cascadia** and **Lampion** strains.

CULTURE. Grow snapdragons in well-drained soil enriched with organic matter. Sow seed from late summer to early spring, about 10 weeks before you plan to set plants out in the garden. Press seeds into the surface of the potting mix rather than covering them. Keep pots or flats at fairly low temperatures—around 50°F/10°C at night, about 65°F/18°C during the day. Pinch young plants to encourage bushy growth and more flowers. In colder climates, set out plants in spring; in mild-winter regions, set out in early fall. If snapdragon seedlings are set out early enough in fall to reach bud stage before night temperatures drop below 50°F/10°C, they'll start blooming in winter and continue until weather gets hot. If set out later, they usually won't bloom until late winter or early spring.

Snapdragons are susceptible to rust, a disease which disfigures the leaves (see page 75). To help prevent this problem, plant rust-resistant varieties (note that these are resistant, not immune) and fertilize regularly. Also keep plants well watered—but avoid overhead watering (or water only in the morning or on sunny days, so foliage will dry before nightfall). If rust persists, change planting locations from one year to the next.

AQUILEGIA
COLUMBINE
Ranunculaceae
PERENNIALS
ZONES VARY
LIGHT SHADE, EXCEPT AS NOTED
REGULAR WATER
✿ ✿ ✿ ✿ ✿ ✿ FLOWERS IN SPRING, EARLY SUMMER

Graceful and full of charm, columbines have lacy foliage and intricate, delicate flowers. Heights vary from only a few inches to 4 feet; leaves are typically lobed and gray green, with a shape reminiscent of maidenhair fern foliage. The erect or nodding blossoms, carried on slender, branching stems, appear in spring and early summer. Many sorts have sepals and petals in contrasting colors, and most have backward-projecting spurs. There are also short-spurred sorts, spurless types, and kinds with double flowers.

Three North American species are especially noted for their stately form. Rocky Mountain columbine, *A. caerulea* (Zones A1–A3; 1–11, 14–24, 32–45), has classic long-spurred, blue-and-white flowers on 1½- to 3-foot stems; the blooms are held erect and reach about 2 inches wide. Canadian columbine, *A. canadensis* (Zones A1–A3; 1–10, 14–24, 30–45), is a 1- to 2-footer with nodding red-and-yellow flowers about 1½ inches wide. A selected form, *A. canadensis* 'Corbett', bears creamy yellow blooms. Golden columbine, *A. chrysantha* (Zones 1–11, 14–24, 31–45), forms a many-branched plant 3 to 4 feet high; its pure yellow flowers are 1½ to 3 inches across.

The Japanese native *A. flabellata* (Zones A2, A3; 1–9, 14–24, 31–45) forms a compact mound growing 8 inches to 1½ feet high; it is well suited to the front of the border. It bears nodding, 1½-inch-wide, lilac-blue or creamy white flowers and has thicker, darker leaves than other columbines. European columbine, *A. vulgaris* (Zones A2, A3; 1–10, 14–24, 32–45), grows 1 to 2½ feet tall and has nodding, 2-inch blossoms in blue, violet, or white; the species has blooms with very short spurs, but some selected forms are spurless.

Aquilegia,
McKana Giants strain

Many hybrid columbine strains are available. Among these are double-blossomed **Spring Song,** with flowers in a range of colors, and the graceful, long-spurred **McKana Giants,** in bicolors and solid colors that include white, blue, purple, pink, peach, red, and yellow. Both Spring Song and the McKana Giants reach 3 feet tall and grow in Zones A2, A3, 1–10, 14–24, 32–45.

CULTURE. Columbines are not fussy about soil type, but they must have good drainage. Plant them in light shade or filtered sun; where summers are cool, plants also grow well in sun. Cut back old stems for a second crop of flowers. Most columbines are not long lived; plan on replacing them every 3 to 4 years. If you let the spent flowers form seed capsules, you'll get a crop of volunteer seedlings—but if you're growing hybrids, the seedlings may differ from the parents. Seedlings from species (if grown isolated from other columbines) should closely resemble the parents, however.

Leaf miners (see page 76) are a potential pest, especially on hybrids. Cut off affected foliage; new leaves will soon appear.

Aquilegia chrysantha

ARTEMISIA

ARTEMISIA, WORMWOOD
Asteraceae (Compositae)
PERENNIALS
ZONES VARY
FULL SUN
LITTLE TO MODERATE WATER,
   EXCEPT AS NOTED
❀ FLOWERS IN LATE SUMMER; MOST
   ARE GROWN PRIMARILY FOR GRAY
   OR WHITE FOLIAGE

Artemisias are valued for their interesting leaf texture and for the aromatic, silvery gray or white foliage that always enhances its surroundings—providing an admirable foil for vivid flower colors and blending subtly with soft blues, lavenders, and pinks. In height, the plants vary from about 1 foot to over 4 feet tall; some are shrubby (woody based), while others die back in winter.

Among the taller shrubby species is southernwood, *A. abrotanum* (Zones 2b–24, 27–41), with finely cut gray-green foliage on a spreading, bushy plant 3 to 5 feet high. Common wormwood, *A. absinthium* (Zones 2–24, 29–41), grows 2 to 4 feet tall and has silvery gray, finely divided leaves. 'Lambrook Silver' is a 2-foot form with especially finely cut foliage. A related hybrid is *A.* 'Powis Castle' (Zones 2–24, 29–34), with soft, silvery gray-green foliage that forms a splendid lacy mound to 3 feet tall and 6 feet wide.

Two other shrubby species are shorter, useful when you want a foreground accent in soft, shimmering silvery gray. *A. stellerana* 'Silver Brocade' (Zones A1–A3; 1–10, 14–24, 29–45), with beautiful felted, lobed leaves, is one of several plants called dusty miller. It forms a dense, low-growing mound to 1 foot tall and 2 feet wide. *A. schmidtiana* 'Silver Mound' (Zones A1–A3; 1–10, 14–24, 29–41), is another dense, low grower, reaching just 1 foot high and wide. In hot, humid climates, its foliage tends to rot in summer.

Unlike the plants described above, *A. ludoviciana* 'Silver King' (Zones 1–24, 29–41) is deciduous, with stems that die down at the onset of frost. During the growing season, it reaches 2 to 3½ feet, with many slender, spreading branches covered in silvery white, 2-inch leaves. 'Silver Queen' is a shorter selection with slightly larger leaves. Both spread widely and can be seriously invasive in a small garden. Plant them where they can colonize freely; or confine them with an 8-inch-deep barrier around the roots.

White mugwort, *A. lactiflora* (Zones 1–9, 14–21, 29–41), also dies down in winter. This is the only artemisia grown primarily not for foliage, but for its attractive flowers: elegantly plumed spikes of small, creamy white blossoms that appear in late summer atop upright, 4- to 6-foot stems clad in dark green, lobed leaves. Plants in the **Guizhou Group** (often sold as *A. lactiflora* 'Guizho') feature handsome purple-red stems.

CULTURE. All artemisias require well-drained soil, and all tolerate drought except for *A. lactiflora*, which needs regular moisture during the growing season. Cut back stems of shrubby kinds fairly heavily in late winter or early spring to keep growth compact. For the two deciduous species, cut spent stems down to the basal rosette of leaves in autumn or early spring.

Propagate clump-forming artemisias by division in early spring. The tall, shrubby kinds may propagate themselves by layering (that is, stems that come in contact with the soil may form rooted sections); these layers can then be separated from the parent plant in spring. All artemisias can be propagated by stem cuttings in spring or summer.

TOP: *Artemisia schmidtiana* 'Silver Mound'
BOTTOM: *Artemisia* 'Powis Castle'

ARUNCUS
GOATSBEARD
Rosaceae
PERENNIALS
ZONES VARY
SUN OR SHADE, EXCEPT AS NOTED
REGULAR TO AMPLE WATER
❀ FLOWERS IN SUMMER

Well suited to woodland gardens, the goatsbeards resemble airy astilbes, with elegant, feathery plumes of tiny white summer flowers rising above slowly spreading clumps of finely divided leaves.

At just 1 foot tall and wide, *A. aethusifolius* (Zones 1–9, 14–17, 31–43) is an excellent choice for the front of the border. The deep green, finely divided foliage gives the plant a delicate look; the flower plumes add a graceful note at bloom time.

A much larger species is *A. dioicus* (Zones A2, A3; 1–9, 14–17, 31–43). It forms a 4-foot-tall, shrublike mound of broad, fernlike leaves topped with a foam of blossoms in many-branched clusters to 20 inches long. **'Kneiffii'** is only half as tall as the species, with leaves finely divided into threadlike segments. **'Child of Two Worlds' ('Zweiweltenkind')** reaches about 5 feet tall; its branched flower clusters droop gracefully.

Aruncus dioicus

CULTURE. Plant goatsbeards in moist soil. You can grow them in sun or shade except in hot-summer regions, where they require shade throughout the day. They do not thrive where summers are both hot and dry.

A. dioicus has large, deep roots that make the plant difficult to move or divide once established. The smaller *A. aethusifolius* is easier to divide (do the job in spring). Both species can be propagated by seed sown indoors in late winter.

ASCLEPIAS tuberosa
BUTTERFLY WEED
Asclepiadaceae
PERENNIALS
ZONES 1–45
FULL SUN
LITTLE TO MODERATE WATER
✿ ✿ ✿ ✿ FLOWERS IN SUMMER

Asclepias tuberosa, Gay Butterflies strain

The common name may label it a weed—but gardeners (and butterflies too!) count this rugged, easy-to-grow plant a desirable one. Each spring, the dormant root sends up many stems clothed in lance-shaped leaves to 4 inches long. Stems reach 2 to 3 feet tall by bloom time in summer, when many small, starlike flowers are carried in broad, flattened clusters at the stem tips. Vivid orange is the usual color, but other bright hues also occur naturally. The aptly named **Gay Butterflies** strain is a mix containing red, orange, pink, yellow, and bicolored flowers; **'Hello Yellow'** bears vibrant yellow blossoms.

In some regions, butterfly weed is a favorite food of monarch butterfly caterpillars, which can quickly eat plants almost to the ground. In these parts of the country, some gardeners like to set out other perennials nearby, providing a temporary screen for the demolished butterfly weed (the plants grow back rapidly).

CULTURE. Plant butterfly weed where you want it to grow permanently; the plants establish slowly but are long lived. Plant in well-drained soil, since too much moisture around the roots, especially in winter, can lead to rot. Butterfly weed is drought tolerant but performs best with moderate watering. Because the stems emerge later in spring than those of many other plants, mark the location of your plantings (or leave the old stems in place as markers).

The easiest way to increase a planting is to raise new plants from seed sown indoors in late winter, but you can also take root cuttings or divide clumps in spring. When dividing, dig deeply, removing as much of the root system as possible.

Typically blooming in late summer and autumn, asters bear cheerful daisy flowers (usually just ½ to 1 inch wide) in a wide variety of colors, on plants that range from low front-of-the-border mounds to imposing 6-footers. White wood aster, *A. divaricatus* (Zones 1–10, 14–24, 31–43), is a spreading plant up to 2 feet high with dark stems and a generous show of flowers in pure white aging to pink. Unlike most asters, it grows well in shade. Heath aster, *A. ericoides* (Zones 1–10, 31–43), reaches 3 feet high; it has narrow leaves and a strong horizontal branching pattern. It's a profuse bloomer with blossoms in white, pink, or blue. Often sold as a form of *A. ericoides* is *A. pringlei* **'Monte Cassino'**, successful in Zones 1–24, 31–43. An especially good cut flower, it produces tall stems—up to 5 feet—set with short branches bearing clouds of starry white blossoms.

The hybrid *A. × frikartii* (Zones 2b–24, 31–43) has produced excellent selections with exceptionally long flowering seasons. **'Mönch'** and **'Wonder of Staffa'** are bushy plants in the 3-foot range; both bear clear lavender-blue, 2- to 3-inch-wide blossoms from early summer to fall in most areas, almost all year in mild-winter areas (with regular deadheading). These plants may be short lived.

Smooth aster, *A. laevis* (Zones 1–10, 14–24, 31–45), grows 3½ feet tall and has blue or purple blossoms. The selection **'Bluebird'** bears charming clusters of violet-blue flowers on arching stems. Cultivars of calico aster, *A. lateriflorus* (Zones 1–10, 14–21, 31–45), are attractive and easy to grow. **'Horizontalis'** is a bushy, mounding 2½-footer with spreading branches bearing white flowers with reddish centers; in fall, the tiny dark green leaves take on a reddish tint that echoes the bloom colors. **'Prince'** has even darker foliage and bears flowers centered in deeper red.

An old-fashioned classic fall bloomer is New England aster, *A. novae-angliae* (Zones 1–24, 31–43). It rises to 6 feet or more in its basic form, bearing great, airy sprays of violet-blue flowers; the stems are clothed in grayish green, hairy leaves. Several pink and nearly red selections are available, including 3- to 4-foot-tall, bright rose **'Andenken an Alma Pötschke'** (**'Alma Pötschke'**) and 3-foot **'Honeysong Pink'**. **'Purple Dome'** is a compact selection that forms a 1½- to 2-foot mound covered in violet-blue flowers.

Another old favorite is New York aster, also known as Michaelmas daisy (*A. novi-belgii*; Zones 1–24, 31–42). Like *A. novae-angliae*, it blooms primarily in violet blue, but it grows only 3 to 4 feet high and has smooth foliage. Its hundreds of cultivars range in height from about 1 foot to well over 5 feet. A few choice selections are foot-tall **'Professor Anton Kippenburg'**, with semidouble lavender-blue blossoms; 2- to 3-foot **'Winston Churchill'**, sporting handsome red flowers; and **'Climax'**, a 5- to 6-foot giant bearing outstanding medium blue blooms that measure 2 to 3 inches across.

CULTURE. Asters are undemanding plants, needing only a sunny location (except for *A. divaricatus*, which prefers shade), and reasonably good, well-drained soil. *A. novi-belgii* is particularly susceptible to powdery mildew; keeping it well watered helps minimize this problem. Most of the taller asters flop over by flowering time. To deal with this problem, either stake them early in the season or cut back the stems by about one-third in early summer (early to mid-June) to make them more compact (plants cut back this way may bloom a bit later than unpruned plants). While most asters don't need winter protection, the cultivars of *A. × frikartii* may benefit from a blanket of evergreen boughs in the colder zones.

Especially vigorous asters, notably *A. novae-angliae* and *A. novi-belgii*, spread rapidly and can become invasive. Dig and divide the roots at least every other year in spring, replanting only the strong divisions from the clump's perimeter. Other kinds of asters need dividing only when vigor diminishes and the center of the clump becomes bare and woody. Asters can also be propagated by stem cuttings taken in summer.

ASTER

Asteraceae (Compositae)

PERENNIALS

ZONES VARY

FULL SUN, EXCEPT AS NOTED

REGULAR WATER

✿ ✿ ✿ ✿ ✿ FLOWERS IN LATE SUMMER
AND FALL, EXCEPT AS NOTED

TOP: *Aster × frikartii* 'Wonder of Staffa'
BOTTOM: *Aster novae-angliae* 'Purple Dome'

ASTILBE

ASTILBE, FALSE SPIRAEA,
MEADOWSWEET
Saxifragaceae
PERENNIALS
ZONES 1–7, 14–17, 32–43
   (BUT SEE "CULTURE," BELOW)
PARTIAL SHADE, EXCEPT AS NOTED
REGULAR WATER
✿ ❀ ✿ ✿ FLOWERS IN LATE SPRING,
   SUMMER

Airy and plumelike, astilbe's flower clusters are an invaluable addition to summer borders and woodland gardens—and they're good for cutting, as well. Either upright or gracefully arching, the floral plumes rise above clumps of handsome, fernlike leaves; they are held on wiry stems that range from 6 inches to 5 feet high. By selecting varieties carefully, making sure that bloom times overlap, you can enjoy flowers from late spring or early summer right through to summer's end.

Most astilbes sold in nurseries are listed as *A. × arendsii,* though some have been reclassified into other species. **'Deutschland'** flowers in late spring—early in the season for an astilbe—bearing dense plumes of white flowers on 1½-foot stems. **'Fanal'** also blooms quite early, carrying its blood red flowers on 1½- to 2½-foot stems. Blooming in mid- to late summer, **'Ostrich Plume'** (**'Straussenfeder'**, often listed as a hybrid of *A. thunbergii*) features drooping pink clusters on 3- to 3½-foot stems. Among *A. × arendsii* selections, those with deeper flower colors tend to have bronzy new leaves.

A. chinensis is a late-summer bloomer that tolerates somewhat drier soils than other astilbes. One of its well-known cultivars is **'Pumila',** with rosy lilac flower spikes on foot-tall stems held stiffly upright over spreading mats of foliage. Pink-flowered **'Finale',** to 20 inches tall, is one of the latest to bloom. Another late-blooming selection is *A. c. taquetii* **'Superba'** (*A. taquetii* **'Superba'**), which grows 4 to 5 feet tall and has bright pinkish purple flowers.

Summer-blooming *A. simplicifolia* **'Sprite',** an excellent front-of-the-border plant, has bronze-tinted foliage and abundant shell pink, drooping spires on 1-foot stems. The blossoms are followed by attractive, long-lasting rust-colored seed heads.

CULTURE. Grow astilbes in moist but not saturated soil enriched with plenty of organic matter. They thrive in light shade, though they can take full sun in cool-summer climates if given plenty of moisture. Tall kinds are self-supporting and require no staking. When bloom production declines noticeably (after 3 to 5 years), divide the clumps in early spring. Survival in the coldest zones (1, 2a, 43) depends on good snow cover.

Astilbe × arendsii
'Fanal'

Astilbe × arendsii 'Ostrich Plume'

AURINIA saxatilis
(Alyssum saxatile)
BASKET-OF-GOLD
Brassicaceae (Cruciferae)
PERENNIAL
ZONES 1–24, 32–43
FULL SUN
MODERATE WATER
✿ ✿ FLOWERS IN SPRING

Providing a welcome splash of bright color in spring, basket-of-gold forms a spreading mound (9 to 12 inches high and 1½ feet wide) of narrow, gray-green, lance-shaped leaves 2 to 5 inches long. Individual flowers are small, but they come in many rounded, 1-inch clusters that virtually cover the plant. Basket-of-gold is a traditional component of large-scale rock gardens, and it also looks good at the front of a sunny border or spilling over a wall.

In addition to the basic bright yellow form, you can choose **'Citrina',** with pale yellow blossoms; **'Compacta',** which forms a smaller, tighter-growing clump; **'Silver Queen',** a compact grower with pale yellow blooms; and **'Dudley Nevill Variegated'** (**'Dudley Neville Variegated'**), an apricot-flowered form with leaves handsomely edged in creamy white.

Aurinia saxatilis 'Dudley Nevill Variegated'

CULTURE. Plant basket-of-gold in a sunny location in average, well-drained soil (if soil is too rich, the plant tends to become sprawling and untidy). After the flowers finish, shear the plant back by about a third to keep it compact and to divert energy from seed production (thus preventing excess volunteer seedlings). Basket-of-gold is short lived in hot, humid areas; gardeners in such regions often treat it as a biennial, setting out new plants in fall for spring bloom, then removing them once the show is over. Propagate basket-of-gold by division in fall or by stem cuttings taken in spring or summer.

Baptisia australis

Reliable, long-lived, large-scale perennials native to the eastern and midwestern U.S., the false indigos bloom in late spring and early summer, carrying spires of sweet pea–shaped flowers above clumps of bluish green, cloverlike foliage. Dark brown to black, inflated-looking seedpods add interest later in summer and on into fall. Plants emerge early in spring and grow quickly to their full size.

White false indigo, **B. alba,** grows 2 to 3 feet tall and spreads to about 3 feet wide. Foot-long spikes of white blossoms (sometimes blotched with purple) contrast well with the charcoal gray stems. The more widely grown blue false indigo, **B. australis,** is a larger plant, reaching 3 to 6 feet tall and 4 feet wide. Its flowers are deep indigo blue. **'Purple Smoke'**, a hybrid between *B. alba* and *B. australis,* grows 4½ feet tall and has violet blooms with dark purple centers.

CULTURE. False indigos are easy to grow, needing only moderately fertile, nonalkaline soil. Their deep taproots make them drought tolerant once established. Clumps gradually increase in size but do not require division—and in fact, established plants resent transplanting. To start more plants, sow seed in early spring, after danger of frost is past; or transplant volunteer seedlings.

BAPTISIA
FALSE INDIGO
Fabaceae (Leguminosae)
PERENNIALS
ZONES 1–24, 28–45
FULL SUN
MODERATE WATER
✿ ✿ ❀ FLOWERS IN LATE SPRING, EARLY SUMMER

Bearing abundant clusters of single or double blossoms, fibrous begonias form mounding, 8- to 12-inch tall plants with succulent stems and glossy green or bronze leaves. In most regions, they bloom from spring straight through until frost; in the hottest climates, though, gardeners grow them as winter-blooming annuals. Use them in beds and borders, as an edging, or as superb container plants; they can also be grown as houseplants. Many varieties are offered. The foot-tall **Cocktail** series has rounded dark bronze leaves and single flowers in scarlet, rose, pink, white, and bicolors; the **Lotto** series features extra-large (2-inch-wide) flowers in red or pink on compact, 8-inch-high plants with green leaves. Plants in the early-blooming **Super Olympia** series also grow 8 inches high and have green foliage; they bear flowers in pink, red, white, coral, and bicolors.

Begonia, Semperflorens group

Listing continues>

BEGONIA,
Semperflorens group
FIBROUS, BEDDING, OR WAX BEGONIAS
Begoniaceae
PERENNIALS OFTEN GROWN AS WARM-SEASON ANNUALS
ZONES 14–28, H1, H2 AS PERENNIALS; ANNUALS ANYWHERE
PARTIAL SHADE, EXCEPT AS NOTED
REGULAR WATER
❀ ✿ ✿ FLOWERS IN SPRING, SUMMER, AND FALL, EXCEPT AS NOTED

Begonia, Semperflorens group

CULTURE. Grow fibrous begonias in rich, moisture-retentive soil. Give them partial shade except in cool-summer areas, where they'll thrive in full sun (dark-foliaged kinds, however, will take full sun even in warm climates if well watered).

Fibrous begonias take 3 to 4 months to grow from seed to transplanting size. Sow the dustlike seeds thinly on the potting mix; do not cover them with mix. Lay plastic wrap loosely over the container so the mix stays moist, then keep at 70°F/21°C. After the seedlings sprout (in 2 to 3 weeks), make sure night temperatures don't drop below 60°F/18°C. You can also propagate these plants from stem cuttings. Take them in late summer and grow over winter indoors; or take in spring from indoor plants.

BERGENIA
Saxifragaceae
PERENNIALS
ZONES A1–A3, 1–9, 12–24, 30–45, EXCEPT AS NOTED
LIGHT TO FULL SHADE, EXCEPT AS NOTED
MODERATE TO REGULAR WATER
✿ ❀ ✿ ✿ FLOWERS IN WINTER, EARLY SPRING

Even if bergenias never flowered, they'd be worth planting for their handsome foliage alone. Growing in informal rosettes 1 to 1½ feet high, the substantial, oval to nearly round leaves are leathery and deeply veined; they grow up to a foot long and are borne on equally long leafstalks. They often take on purple tints in cold weather. Graceful clusters of small flowers appear on thick, leafless, 1- to 1½-foot stalks.

B. ciliata is the most elegant-looking species, though it's less hardy than the rest (Zones 5–9, 14–24, 29–34, 39). Its lustrous light green leaves are covered with short, silky hairs; they are damaged by frosts and die down completely in the colder zones of the range. The early-spring flowers are light pink or white, often darkening with age.

Also blooming in early spring is heartleaf bergenia, *B. cordifolia,* with glossy, wavy-edged leaves that partially conceal the rose or lilac flowers. Winter-blooming bergenia, *B. crassifolia,* bears its dense clusters of rose, lilac, or purple flowers any time from midwinter to early spring, depending on climate. The blossoms are held above clumps of glossy, rubbery leaves.

Named hybrid bergenias are increasingly available from specialty nurseries. Choices include **'Abendglut' ('Evening Glow'),** a slightly shorter selection with dark red blooms and leaves that turn dark red in cold weather; **'Baby Doll',** which grows about 1 foot tall and has soft pink flowers; **'Bressingham White'; 'Bressingham Ruby';** and **'Bressingham Salmon'.**

CULTURE. Though bergenias tolerate dry shade and poor soil, their foliage and flowers are much more attractive when the plants are given good soil and regular watering. In mild- and warm-summer areas, they prefer filtered sun to full shade; where summers are cool, they can also take full sun. Divide crowded clumps and replant vigorous divisions in late winter or early spring.

Bergenia 'Bressingham Salmon'

BRUNNERA macrophylla
BRUNNERA, SIBERIAN BUGLOSS, PERENNIAL FORGET-ME-NOT
Boraginaceae
PERENNIAL
ZONES 1–24, 31–45
LIGHT SHADE, EXCEPT AS NOTED
REGULAR WATER
✿ FLOWERS IN EARLY SPRING

In early spring, airy sprays of little (¼-inch) azure blue flowers resembling forget-me-nots *(Myosotis)* rise above lush clumps of heart-shaped dark green leaves to 4 inches wide and 6 inches long. As the season progresses, the leaves become larger and the stems grow taller, reaching 1½ to 2 feet by the time flowering is over. The foliage stays attractive for the rest of the growing season, making brunnera a good choice for a small-scale ground cover under high-branching shrubs or near a shady pool or stream. Several selections offer variegated foliage; among these is **'Dawson's White' ('Variegata'),** with elegant creamy white bands along the leaf margins.

Brunnera macrophylla 'Dawson's White'

CULTURE. Brunnera looks best when grown in well-drained, moisture-retentive soil. It's at home anywhere in light shade; where summers are cool, you can also plant it in sun. Keep in mind, however, that variegated forms always require shade to keep their leaves from scorching. Brunnera self-sows freely once established; it can also be propagated by dividing clumps in fall or taking root cuttings in late winter.

E asy to grow and long blooming, calendula brings glowing color to the garden from spring to midsummer (from fall through spring, where winters are mild). The plant grows 1 to 2½ feet tall, with aromatic, slightly sticky green leaves and single or double, daisylike flowers 2½ to 4 inches across.

Besides making excellent cut flowers, the blossoms have edible petals that add a tangy flavor to salads, egg dishes, and fish. When cooked with rice, they give the grain a saffron color. In times past, both leaves and petals went into vegetable stews—hence the common name "pot marigold."

Dwarf strains (12 to 16 inches high) include early-blooming **Bon Bon,** with 2½-inch-wide flowers in a mix of bright and soft yellows, oranges, and apricots; and **Calypso,** which has larger (3- to 4-inch) blossoms in orange or yellow with black centers. **Touch of Red** grows 16 to 18 inches tall and features 2½-inch-wide flowers in cream, yellow, and orange; the petal tips and backs are mahogany red. The **Kablouna** series (20 inches tall), bearing 3-inch-wide flowers with a crested, pompomlike center, comes in all the calendula colors. The **Prince** series grows 2 to 2½ feet high and bears long-stemmed, 3-inch-wide blooms in golden yellow and orange.

CULTURE. Calendula thrives in full sun and rich soil; it also does well in average soil as long as drainage is good. Deadheading helps prolong bloom. The plants will self-sow, though seedlings' flowers may differ from those of the parents.

Sow seeds in place in the garden as soon as soil can be worked in spring. Or start seeds indoors in late winter, then set out seedlings in early spring. In mild-winter areas, you can sow seed or set out transplants in late summer or early fall.

CALENDULA officinalis
CALENDULA, POT MARIGOLD
Asteraceae (Compositae)
COOL-SEASON ANNUAL
ZONES 1–45; H1
FULL SUN
MODERATE WATER
❀✿✿ FLOWERS IN SPRING AND SUMMER,
   EXCEPT AS NOTED

Calendula officinalis, Touch of Red strain

I ntroduced to gardeners in the 1990s, these petunia relatives are long blooming and easy to grow. They're smaller overall than petunias, with finer foliage, wiry, slender stems, and trumpet-shaped blooms about an inch across. The plants are "self-cleaning"—the spent flowers drop off cleanly, eliminating the need for deadheading. Two basic forms are available: low-growing trailers and more mounding types that reach 10 inches tall. Plant calibrachoas in containers and hanging baskets; or use them as bedding plants. In most regions, gardeners grow them as annuals that bloom from early summer to autumn, but in mild-winter climates they are truly perennial.

The low-growing **Liricashower** series offers blooms in pink-blushed white, blue, pink, and rose, while the mounding **Colorburst** series has flowers in violet, rose, and red. Plants sold under the common name "million bells" include trailing types in white, blue, and pink, as well as mounding ones in pink, terra-cotta, and yellow.

CULTURE. Plant calibrachoas in moist, well-drained soil. To keep them blooming over a long season, fertilize container-grown plants every 2 weeks and those in the ground once a month. Growers propagate the plants through tissue culture; seed is not available.

CALIBRACHOA
CALIBRACHOA, MILLION BELLS
Solanaceae
PERENNIALS USUALLY GROWN AS
   WARM-SEASON ANNUALS
ZONES 2–43
FULL SUN OR PARTIAL SHADE
REGULAR WATER
✿✿❀✿✿✿ FLOWERS IN SUMMER, FALL

Calibrachoa

CALLISTEPHUS chinensis

CHINA ASTER

Asteraceae (Compositae)

WARM-SEASON ANNUAL

ZONES 1–45

FULL SUN

REGULAR WATER

✿ ❀ ✿ ✿ ✿ FLOWERS IN SUMMER

Callistephus chinensis

Treasured by gardeners for its brilliant colors and usefulness as a cut flower, summer-blooming China aster is a fast-growing, bushy annual related to perennial asters. The 1½- to 4-inch flowers come in white, yellow, and shades of pink, purple, and red, and are available in a variety of forms. You'll find blossoms resembling chrysanthemums or daisies (both single and double) and those that look like peonies or pin-studded pincushions; and the flowers may have quilled, spidery, incurved, or ribbonlike petals or crested centers. Plant height varies from 8 inches to about 2½ feet; the medium green leaves are coarsely toothed and reach 3 inches long.

Low-growing varieties include the 8-inch-tall, double-flowered **Pinocchio** series, bearing dense, rounded, 1½-inch-wide flowers with incurved petals; it comes in a wide range of colors. Another low-growing double form is the 10-inch **Asteroid** series, with larger (4-inch) blossoms in mixed as well as many individual colors. Taller sorts especially well suited for cutting include the 20-inch **Massagno** series, bearing 3½-inch double flowers with thin, spidery petals, and **Single California Giant,** which features 3-inch single blooms on 2½-foot plants. Both are sold in mixed colors.

CULTURE. Plant China aster in rich, loamy or sandy soil with a neutral to slightly alkaline pH. Taller varieties may need staking, which should be done while plants are young.

After the danger of frost is past, sow seed in place in the garden. For earlier blooms, you can start seed indoors 6 to 8 weeks before the last-frost date. Transplant seedlings carefully, since they are very sensitive to root disturbance.

China aster (along with many other kinds of plants) is subject to aster yellows, a viral disease transmitted by leafhoppers. Symptoms include yellowed foliage and pale leaf veins; flowers may be small, deformed, or nonexistent. To control the disease, spray to keep the leafhopper population in bounds; also discard infected plants (to prevent further spread) and destroy nearby weeds, which may harbor the disease. China aster is also susceptible to aster wilt or stem rot, caused by a parasitic soil-dwelling fungus that enters plants through their roots; many varieties are at least somewhat resistant to this disease. Overwatering (especially in heavy or poorly drained soil) produces ideal conditions for both aster yellows and aster wilt. To prevent a buildup of disease organisms, don't plant China aster in the same location in successive years.

CAMPANULA

CAMPANULA, BELLFLOWER

Campanulaceae (Lobeliaceae)

PERENNIALS, BIENNIALS, AND BIENNIALS
 GROWN AS ANNUALS

ZONES 1–9, 14–24, 31–45, EXCEPT
 AS NOTED

FULL SUN, EXCEPT AS NOTED

MODERATE TO REGULAR WATER

✿ ✿ ❀ ✿ ✿ FLOWERS IN SPRING, SUMMER

A vast and varied group, campanulas range in form from stately back-of-border plants to low, spreading or compact mounds suitable for use at the front of the border, in rock gardens, and as small-scale ground covers. The five-petaled flowers are typically bell-shaped, but some kinds have upward-facing, cup-shaped blossoms, while others are star-shaped.

Canterbury bells, **C. medium,** is the popular campanula of cottage gardens. Though it is usually grown as a biennial (it flowers the second year from seed, then dies), some varieties can be grown as annuals. The narrow, lance-shaped, 6- to 10-inch-long leaves form a clump that sends up erect, leafy, 2- to 3-foot flowering stems in spring and summer. Borne in loose spikes, the

Campanula medium 'Calycanthema'

upward-facing bells reach 2 inches across; colors include blue shades, purple, pink, and white. The popular cup-and-saucer version, 2½-foot-tall 'Calycanthema', has an unusual flower form: each cuplike flower is seated on a flattened corolla that forms the "saucer." Forms of *C. medium* grown as annuals tend to be shorter in stature and include the 14-inch-tall **Dwarf Bells** strain, which has flowers in mauve, lilac, pink, and white, and 'Russian Pink', to 15 inches high.

The perennial campanulas discussed here are divided into two groups—those with upright flowering stems and those that form spreading mounds. In the descriptions that follow, the second category is represented only by Dalmatian and Serbian bell-flowers, *C. portenschlagiana* and *C. poscharskyana*.

Tussock bellflower, *C. carpatica,* is the shortest of the upright campanulas, topping out at about 1 foot. Wiry, branching stems rise from low clumps of narrow, 1½-inch-long leaves in late spring, bearing cup-shaped, 1- to 2-inch-wide flowers in white and various blue shades; bloom continues into summer if the spent flowers are removed. 'White Clips' and 'Blue Clips' are reliable selections. Somewhat taller (1 to 2 feet or more) is summer-blooming clustered bellflower, *C. glomerata* (Zones A1, A2; 1–10, 14–24, 31–45). Its dense clusters of flaring, typically blue-violet, inch-wide bells are carried on erect stems above clumps of broadly lance-shaped, 2- to 4-inch-long leaves. Named selections vary in flower color and plant height. 'Crown of Snow' is a 1½- to 2-foot plant with white flowers; 'Superba', to 2½ feet, bears blossoms in an intense, glowing violet; purple 'Joan Elliott' grows to 1½ feet.

Tallest of the widely grown campanulas is *C. lactiflora* (Zones 1–9, 14–24, 31–34, 39). Its upright stems, clothed with 3-inch, pointed leaves, top out in the 3- to 5-foot range. Large, conical clusters of open, starry-looking, 1-inch-wide bells bloom in summer. Named selections include pale pink, 3- to 4-foot-high 'Loddon Anna'; 3-foot-tall, blue-violet 'Prichard's Variety'; and dwarf 'Pouffe', which forms a mound of pale blue flowers just over 1 foot tall.

Graceful peach-leafed bluebell, *C. persici-folia,* has leafy, 2- to 3-foot stems above low clumps of narrow, 4- to 8-inch-long leaves. In summer, each stem bears loose spires of cupped, outward-facing, inch-wide bells in blue, pink, or white. Named selections include 'Chettle Charm', with white flow-ers edged in pale violet blue, and 'Telham Beauty', with larger (3-inch) blue blossoms. Spotted bellflower, *C. punctata,* forms a rosette of heart-shaped, 3- to 5-inch basal leaves. In summer, arching stems to 2 feet high bear nodding, elongated, 2-inch bells in white, lilac, or pink, typically marked with spots on the inside. 'Cherry Bells' has reddish flowers edged in white.

Campanula persicifolia

Campanula punctata

Forming a low (6-inch-high) mound of roundish, ¾- to 1½-inch-wide leaves, easy-to-grow Dalmatian bellflower, *C. portenschlagiana* (Zones 2–9, 14–24, 31–41), produces purplish blue, bell- to cup-shaped, inch-wide flowers from late spring through summer. The more aggressive Serbian bellflower, *C. poscharskyana,* has clumps of heart-shaped, about 1-inch-long leaves and spreads by rooting runners to form a solid foliage carpet. Starlike, ½- to 1-inch-wide blooms in soft blue or white appear along semi-upright, foot-tall stems in spring to early summer.

Listing continues>

Campanula portenschlagiana

CULTURE. Plant campanulas in well-drained soil that has been enriched with organic matter. Most need regular watering for good performance, though *C. portenschlagiana* and *C. poscharskyana* are somewhat drought tolerant. Campanulas grow well in full sun except in warm-summer areas, where they need partial shade. Tall kinds require staking. To encourage repeat bloom, remove spent flowers. Slugs and snails can be serious pests; for controls, see page 76.

To grow *C. medium* (Canterbury bells) as a biennial, sow seeds outdoors in late spring or early summer, either in place or in a nursery bed for later transplanting; transplant, if necessary, in fall or early spring. In colder regions, protect plants over winter with a mulch of evergreen boughs or salt hay. Start seed of annual varieties indoors in early spring; most kinds require 16 to 20 weeks to reach blooming size. Barely press seeds into the soil surface—they need light to germinate.

To propagate perennial campanulas, dig and divide crowded clumps in early spring. Plants can also be propagated by stem cuttings or, for the species and some named varieties, by seed sown indoors in late winter.

CANNA
CANNA LILY, INDIAN SHOT
Cannaceae
PERENNIALS
ZONES 6–9, 12–31, WARMER PARTS OF 32;
  H1, H2; OR DIG AND STORE
FULL SUN
AMPLE WATER
✿ ✿ ✿ ✿ ✿ FLOWERS IN SUMMER, FALL

Bringing a bold, tropical accent to borders and container gardens from summer into autumn, cannas flaunt spikes of big, showy, irregularly shaped flowers and large leaves that may be rich green, bronzy red, or variegated. In size, the plants range from dwarfs only a few feet high to giants that reach 6 feet or taller. Numerous varieties (most are hybrids between several species) are available. Just a few of the many choices are **'Pretoria'** (**'Bengal Tiger'**), a 6-footer with dramatic green-and-yellow striped leaves and bright orange flowers; 4-foot **'Wyoming'**, with bronzy purple foliage and orange blooms; and the lower-growing **'Pfitzer Chinese Coral'** and **'Pfitzer Crimson Beauty'**, both just 2½ to 3 feet tall.

Canna 'Pretoria'

CULTURE. Cannas require moist soil enriched with organic matter. They thrive in hot, bright locations. Cut stems to the ground as they finish flowering; new stems will continue to appear throughout summer and early fall. Every 3 or 4 years, divide crowded clumps in early spring. Dig the rhizomes and cut them apart; let the cuts heal (this takes about 24 hours), then replant, covering with 2 to 4 inches of soil.

In the colder parts of their range, protect cannas with a 6-inch layer of mulch over winter. Beyond their hardiness limit, cut off the stalks and dig the rhizomes after the first frosts have killed the leaves. Let rhizomes dry in a warm place for a few days; then place in a box, cover with dry peat moss, and store in a frost-free location over winter. In spring, plant the rhizomes indoors in pots about 4 weeks before the usual last-frost date. Transplant to the garden after weather has warmed.

Creating a colorful show throughout the heat of summer and on into late autumn, Madagascar periwinkle flourishes in dry as well as humid conditions. The bushy plant typically reaches 1 to 2 feet high and wide. Single, phloxlike, 1- to 2-inch-wide flowers, often featuring a contrasting eye, are set off perfectly by glossy green, 1- to 3-inch-long leaves. Depending on the variety you choose, you can plant Madagascar periwinkle to edge a border, as a small-scale ground cover, or to trail over the sides of a pot or window box.

The **Pacifica** and **Cooler** series form compact, 15-inch plants with 2-inch-wide flowers; both are available in mixed colors and in a wide range of individual colors. Plants in the trailing **Mediterranean** series spread to 2½ feet wide but grow only 5 to 6 inches high. Colors include white, deep rose, lilac, and apricot (some apricot varieties have a large deep rose eye).

Catharanthus roseus

CULTURE. Madagascar periwinkle thrives in well-drained, average to rich soil. Sow seed indoors 12 weeks before the usual last-frost date. To avoid disease, take care not to overwater seedlings. Transplant to the garden after the weather has warmed in spring. To increase your supply of a favorite color (of either seed-raised or nursery plants), take cuttings in spring or early summer.

CATHARANTHUS roseus (Vinca rosea)
MADAGASCAR PERIWINKLE
Apocynaceae
PERENNIAL USUALLY GROWN AS
    WARM-SEASON ANNUAL
ZONES 1–45; H1, H2
FULL SUN OR PARTIAL SHADE
MODERATE WATER
✿ ✿ ✿ ✿ ✿ FLOWERS IN SUMMER, FALL

Brilliant and long lasting, celosias are stunning in the summer garden and equally striking for indoor arrangements—both as fresh cut flowers and dried for winter bouquets. In the garden, they're effective massed as well as in combination with other annuals in vivid colors; they also make good container subjects.

Three popular kinds of celosias are derived from *C. argentea,* a white-flowered tropical species with narrow leaves to 2 inches or more long. Plume cockscombs (often sold as *C.* 'Plumosa') range in height from 10 inches to 3 feet; as the name indicates, they have feathery flower plumes. Low-growing varieties include the **Kimono** series, only 10 inches tall, and the 14-inch-high **Castle** series; both are available in a wide variety of individual colors and as mixtures. Among the taller sorts, 20-inch-tall **'Apricot Brandy'** has deep orange plumes; the 3-foot-tall **Sparkler Mix** is a popular choice for cut flowers.

Crested cockscombs (often sold as *C.* 'Cristata') grow from 6 inches to over 3 feet high and feature velvety, fan-shaped flower clusters that are often strangely contorted or fluted, resembling enormous rooster combs. The **Amigo** series features 6-inch-wide flower heads in magenta, red, rose, scarlet, and yellow on plants only 6 inches high; most have green leaves. **'Amigo Mahogany Red'**, however, boasts dark purple foliage topped by dark maroon flower heads. **'Prestige Scarlet'** is a dense, branching plant 15 to 20 inches tall and wide.

CELOSIA
CELOSIA, COCKSCOMB
Amaranthaceae
WARM-SEASON ANNUALS
ZONES A3; 1–45; H1, H2
FULL SUN
MODERATE WATER
✿ ✿ ✿ ✿ ✿ FLOWERS IN SUMMER

Celosia 'Apricot Brandy'

Listing continues>

Celosia 'Flamingo Feather'

Wheat celosias (often sold as *C.* **'Spicata'**) include upright, branching plants to 2½ feet tall with slim, cylindrical flower spikes. Varieties include **'Flamingo Feather'**, with blossoms in soft pink and white, and **'Purple Flamingo'**. All may reseed.

CULTURE. Plant celosias in moist but well-drained soil that has been enriched with organic matter. They thrive in hot, humid weather but not in chilly conditions—so don't sow or transplant too early. Tall varieties may need staking. To dry the flowers, cut them just as they open fully and hang them upside down in a warm, dry, airy place.

Sow seed indoors 6 to 8 weeks before the last expected frost. To avoid shocking the seedlings, use lukewarm water when watering; once the plants are up, keep them out of cold drafts. Set out transplants when they are still fairly young (or purchase small plants); older plants do not transplant as successfully and generally produce fewer flowers.

CENTAUREA
Asteraceae (Compositae)
PERENNIALS AND COOL-SEASON ANNUALS
ZONES VARY
FULL SUN
MODERATE WATER
✿ ✿ ✿ ✿ ✿ ✿ FLOWERS IN SPRING AND
    SUMMER, EXCEPT AS NOTED

Centaurea cyanus

Among these easy-to-grow plants for the border or wild garden, the best known is the annual bachelor's button or cornflower (*C. cyanus;* Zones 1–45, H1, H2). In most areas, it blooms in spring and early summer, but in desert areas it is planted for flowers in winter and early spring. The plant grows 1 to 1½ feet high, with gray-green, narrow, 2- to 3-inch-long leaves and 1½-inch, thistlelike flowers in white, blue, purple, pink, rose, or wine red (blue varieties are traditional favorites for boutonnières). **'Jubilee Gem'** is a bushy, compact 1-footer with deep blue flowers; the 16-inch **Polka Dot** strain features all the bachelor's button colors.

C. cineraria, one of a number of plants called dusty miller, is grown for its clumps of lobed, velvety white leaves. Perennial only in Zones 8–30, it is popular as an annual in regions beyond its hardiness range. Though its foliage is the main attraction, it also bears yellow blooms in summer.

Centaurea hypoleuca 'John Coutts'

Showy-flowered perennial centaureas include two species hardy in Zones 1–9, 14–24, 29–43. Summer-blooming Persian cornflower, *C. dealbata* (usually offered in the cultivar **'Steenbergii'**), forms spreading clumps of lobed, 8- to 12-inch-long leaves that are soft green on the upper surfaces, gray green beneath. It bears thistle-like purple flowers with white centers on slender, 2-foot stems. *C. hypoleuca* **'John Coutts'** (sometimes listed as a variety of *C. dealbata*) is more compact, with deep rose pink blooms from late spring to mid-summer. It has the same foliage color as *C. dealbata,* but the lobed, wavy-edged leaves are smaller (6 to 8 inches long) and lance shaped.

CULTURE. Plants grow vigorously in moderately fertile, well-drained soil. For best performance, add lime to acid soils. Taller varieties usually require staking.

While perennial species (including *C. cineraria*) are most easily grown from purchased plants, annual *C. cyanus* is easy to start from seed sown in place in spring, at about the time of the last expected frost. Or sow indoors 6 to 8 weeks before the last frost. (In desert regions, sow seed in fall for flowers in winter and spring.) When you plant, be sure to cover seed with ⅛ to ¼ inch of soil; darkness helps germination. Transplant seedlings grown in pots carefully, since too much root disturbance stunts the plants.

With the exception of *C. cineraria,* clumps of perennial species spread easily and may need to be divided every 3 to 4 years to renew growth and keep plantings in bounds.

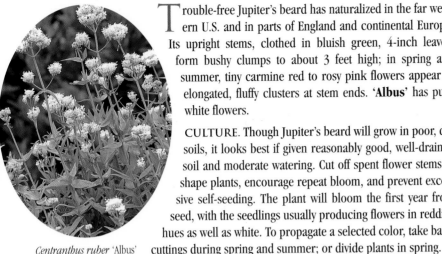

Trouble-free Jupiter's beard has naturalized in the far western U.S. and in parts of England and continental Europe. Its upright stems, clothed in bluish green, 4-inch leaves, form bushy clumps to about 3 feet high; in spring and summer, tiny carmine red to rosy pink flowers appear in elongated, fluffy clusters at stem ends. **'Albus'** has pure white flowers.

CULTURE. Though Jupiter's beard will grow in poor, dry soils, it looks best if given reasonably good, well-drained soil and moderate watering. Cut off spent flower stems to shape plants, encourage repeat bloom, and prevent excessive self-seeding. The plant will bloom the first year from seed, with the seedlings usually producing flowers in reddish hues as well as white. To propagate a selected color, take basal cuttings during spring and summer; or divide plants in spring.

Centranthus ruber 'Albus'

CENTRANTHUS ruber
JUPITER'S BEARD, RED VALERIAN
Valerianaceae
PERENNIAL
ZONES 2–9, 12–24, 28–43; H1
FULL SUN OR LIGHT SHADE
LITTLE TO MODERATE WATER
❀✿✿ FLOWERS IN SPRING, SUMMER

Forming a silvery gray, 6- to 8-inch-high mat of stems clothed in narrow, ¾-inch leaves, snow-in-summer is covered in small, snowy white flowers in early summer—hence the common name. It makes an excellent edging and is especially effective setting off a border of brightly colored flowers. Or use it between stepping-stones or as a ground cover.

CULTURE. As long as drainage is good, snow-in-summer will grow in any soil. Where summers are hot, it looks best with some afternoon shade. Shear off faded flowers after bloom ends. Start with nursery plants; or sow seed outdoors in early spring after danger of frost is past, either in place or in containers for later transplanting. When a planting begins to show bare patches, divide and replant in fall or early spring.

Cerastium tomentosum

CERASTIUM tomentosum
SNOW-IN-SUMMER
Caryophyllaceae
PERENNIAL
ZONES A1, A2; 1–24, 32–45
FULL SUN, EXCEPT AS NOTED
MODERATE TO REGULAR WATER
❀ FLOWERS IN EARLY SUMMER

Honeywort grows 1 to 2 feet tall, with gray-green, 2½-inch leaves that seem to clasp its sturdy stems. Small, nodding clusters of unusual tubular flowers surrounded by showy bracts (modified leaves) appear at the stem tips from spring until early summer in most climates—but in mild-winter areas, bloom often begins in late winter and continues until hot weather arrives. The species has bicolored flowers in yellow and maroon. More widely grown, however, is **'Purpurascens'**; its flowers, bracts, and upper leaves are purplish blue, making the top of each stem look as though it's been dipped in purple dye.

CULTURE. Give honeywort full sun and well-drained, average soil. In mild-winter climates, sow seed outdoors in autumn, in the spot where the plants are to grow. In colder regions, sow seed outdoors in spring, just after the last-frost date; or sow indoors 8 weeks before the last-frost date. The plant may self-sow but does not do so profusely enough to become a pest.

CERINTHE major
HONEYWORT
Boraginaceae
COOL-SEASON ANNUAL
ZONES 1–24, 32, 34–45
FULL SUN OR LIGHT SHADE
REGULAR WATER
✿✿ FLOWERS IN SPRING AND SUMMER, EXCEPT AS NOTED

Cerinthe major 'Purpurascens'

CHELONE

TURTLEHEAD

Scrophulariaceae

PERENNIALS

ZONES 1–9, 14–24, 28–43

FULL SUN OR LIGHT SHADE

AMPLE WATER

✿ ❀ ✿ FLOWERS IN LATE SUMMER, FALL

Chelone obliqua

These natives of the southeastern U. S. bear inch-long, puffy, two-lipped flowers of a vaguely reptilian appearance—hence the common name "turtlehead." From spring into summer, the plants are clumps of good-looking, glossy foliage; then, as bloom time approaches, leafy, branching stems rise 2 to 3½ feet, bearing blossoms in branching spikes. *C. glabra* has white flowers tinged with rose. *C. lyonii*, the most widely available species, produces rose pink flowers. *C. obliqua* has rosy purple blossoms; its cultivars include deep rose '**Bethelli**', more floriferous than the species, and white '**Alba**'.

CULTURE. Grow turtleheads in naturally damp places, such as in bog gardens or along stream banks. They also succeed in borders if grown in soil enriched with organic matter and given plenty of water. In general, turtleheads do well in full sun or light shade, though *C. lyonii* needs partial shade in hot-summer regions. *C. obliqua* is more tolerant of heat and sun.

When clumps become crowded, divide them in spring; or increase your supply of plants by stem cuttings taken in spring or summer.

CHRYSANTHEMUM

Asteraceae (Compositae)

PERENNIALS AND COOL-SEASON ANNUALS

ZONES VARY

FULL SUN, EXCEPT AS NOTED

REGULAR WATER, EXCEPT AS NOTED

✿ ❀ ✿ ✿ ✿ FLOWERS IN SPRING,
      SUMMER, AND FALL, EXCEPT AS NOTED

While the name "chrysanthemum" is often associated with fall-blooming mums, the genus also includes other favorite spring- and summer-flowering daisies, among them annuals such as tricolor chrysanthemum and crown daisy. Perennial sorts include brightly colored painted daisy, feverfew, and the popular Shasta daisy. Taxonomists have split *Chrysanthemum* into a number of new genera—and in certain cases, changed their minds and returned some species to the original genus. In the following descriptions, the former, often more familiar names are given first, followed by the new names in parentheses.

ANNUAL CHRYSANTHEMUMS

Tricolor chrysanthemum, *C. carinatum* (*Glebionis carinatum*; Zones 1–45, H1, H2), is an erect, 1- to 3-foot-tall plant with deeply cut bright green foliage. Appearing in early summer in most climates (winter and spring in mild-winter regions), the 3- to 4-inch-wide flowers feature a dark center ringed with contrasting zones of white, purple, red, orange, or yellow. Crown daisy, *C. coronarium* (*Glebionis coronarium*; Zones 1–45, H1, H2), to 2½ feet tall, has coarsely cut light green leaves and 2-inch-wide yellow daisies in spring and summer. '**Primrose Gem**' is lower growing (1 to 1½ feet tall), with golden-eyed semidouble flowers in a softer yellow. *C. paludosum* (*Leucanthemum paludosum*, *Melampodium paludosum*; Zones A1–A3, 1–24), forms a 2- to 6-inch-tall clump of dark green, toothed leaves. In summer, the foliage mound sends up 8- to 10-inch stems topped by yellow-centered, inch-wide, white or yellow blossoms.

Chrysanthemum coronarium

CULTURE. Grow these annuals in full sun, in average to rich, well-drained soil. All can be sown in place in early spring, as soon as the soil can be worked. Or start seed indoors about 8 weeks before the usual last-frost date. (In mild-winter regions, sow *C. carinatum* in fall for winter and spring flowers.) Pinch young plants to encourage bushiness; deadhead to prolong bloom.

PERENNIAL CHRYSANTHEMUMS

The first species described below, *C. frutescens,* is grown as an annual in many parts of the country. The remaining species are raised as perennials everywhere.

Marguerite, ***C. frutescens (Argyranthemum frutescens),*** is a short-lived shrubby perennial in Zones 14–24, 26, 28, H1, H2; elsewhere, it is grown as an annual. It is an excellent container plant in any region. It grows fast—a young plant can expand to a dense, 4- by 4-foot mound of coarsely cut green leaves in just a few months. Summer brings a generous show of 2½-inch flowers. The typical form has single white blossoms with yellow centers, but named selections offer variations; among these are double-flowered **'Snow White'**, pale yellow **'Jamaica Primrose'**, and **'Vancouver'**, with anemone-centered, semidouble pink blooms.

CULTURE. Plant marguerites in a sunny spot, in loose-textured, well-drained soil. Cut plants back lightly and frequently to maintain bushiness, encourage rebloom, and limit size. Even in climates where marguerites are perennial, individual plants last just a few years; start replacements from cuttings taken in spring or summer. In cold climates, you can take cutings in late summer and overwinter them indoors in a bright, cool spot.

Painted daisy, ***C. coccineum (Tanacetum coccineum, Pyrethrum roseum)*** grows in Zones A1, 1–24, 32–41. It forms a bushy, 2- to 3-foot plant with bright green, very finely divided leaves. The long-stemmed, 3-inch-wide blooms are single or double and come in pink shades, red, and white. Flowering starts in midspring where winters are mild, in late spring in colder regions. If you cut the stems to the ground after flowering, plants will sometimes rebloom in late summer. Cultivars include dark red **'James Kelway'** and the double-flowered **Robinson's Hybrids,** available in white, pink, and red.

CULTURE. Painted daisy grows best where summers are warm to hot, but it does not tolerate high humidity. Divide clumps or sow seeds in spring (seedlings flower in their second year).

Shasta daisy, ***C. maximum (C. × superbum, Leucanthemum maximum, L. × superbum),*** succeeds in Zones A1–A3, 1–24, 26 (northern part), 28–43, H1. A charming and versatile summer-flowering perennial for the border, it forms robust clumps of toothed, linear dark green leaves from which rise leafy flower stalks, each topped with one to several showy white daisies. The original forms featured 2- to 4-foot stems bearing 3- to 4-inch single flowers with big yellow centers; **'Alaska'** and **'Polaris'** are good examples, as is the more recently introduced **'Becky'**, which grows exceptionally well in hot, humid regions. **'Esther Read'** is a widely grown, long-blooming cultivar with double white blossoms on 2-foot stems. **'Aglaya'**, another 2-footer, has fringed double flowers. A popular dwarf is 15- to 18-inch **'Snowcap'**.

CULTURE. Shasta daisies thrive in fairly rich, moist soil. They prefer sun but do well in partial shade in hot-summer climates; the double-flowered kinds hold up better in very light shade in all regions. Deadhead to keep the flowers coming. In the coldest zones, mulch around the plants for winter, taking care not to smother the foliage. Clumps increase quickly and usually need division every other year or so. Divide in early spring (in fall in mild-winter areas). Shasta daisies are easy to grow from seed. Catalogs offer many strains, including some that bloom the first year.

Florists' chrysanthemum, ***C. × morifolium (Dendranthema × grandiflorum),*** is the mainstay of the autumn perennial flower show—both in the garden and in containers. It succeeds in Zones 2–24, 26 (northern part), 28–41, H1. Also known simply as garden mum, it's available in an incredible array of flower forms, flower colors, and growth habits. Popular among gardeners are types with single, semidouble, and double

Chrysanthemum frutescens 'Vancouver'

TOP: *Chrysanthemum coccineum*
BOTTOM: *Chrysanthemum maximum*

Chrysanthemum × morifolium 'Debonair'

flowers, in a basic daisy shape or with a pompom, shaggy, or quilled form in colors including white and many shades of yellow, orange, bronze, red, purple, and pink. For general garden display, opt for the lower-growing kinds (usually under 1½ feet) with smaller flowers and a bushy, compact habit; large-flowered exhibition types are often rangy and require staking, even if you pinch them often to control growth. It's also important to consider your climate when choosing mums. The shorter the growing season, the more important it is to select early-flowering types, since fall frosts will destroy late bloomers before the flowers have a chance to open.

CULTURE. Plant florists' chrysanthemum in good, well-drained soil improved with organic matter; also dig in a complete fertilizer before planting. In hot climates, provide shade from afternoon sun. Set out young plants in early spring. Water deeply as needed to keep the soil moist but not saturated: too little water leads to woody stems and loss of lower leaves, while overwatering causes leaves to yellow, then blacken and drop. Several times during the growing season, pinch back all but the lowest-growing mums (the "cushion" type): as soon as a stem reaches 5 inches long, nip out the tip to force branching and create a dense, leafy plant. In cold-winter regions, stop pinching in early summer; in less severe climates (where lows seldom dip below 0°F/−18°C), continue pinching into August. After flowering has finished, cut stems down to about 8 inches; in cold regions, use the cut stems as a mulch over the plants. When growth begins the next year, cut the remaining portion of the stems to the ground. Clumps will need dividing about every other year. Do the job in early spring, replanting small, single-stem divisions from the outside of the clump and discarding the woody center.

Feverfew, ***C. parthenium*** (***Tanacetum parthenium;*** Zones 2–24, 28–45) is an old-fashioned favorite that makes a useful filler in the perennial border and provides excellent cut flowers. Clumps of bright green, somewhat feathery leaves with a pungent, peppery scent send up 2- to 3-foot stems in summer; these produce clusters of white daisies less than an inch across. **'Aureum'** grows 8 to 12 inches tall and has chartreuse foliage; **'Snowball'** reaches 1 to 2 feet and bears double flowers.

CULTURE. Plant this adaptable perennial in full sun in well-drained, average soil. It isn't long lived, but an ample supply of volunteer seedlings usually allows you to maintain your planting. You can also propagate feverfew by dividing the clumps in spring or by sowing seeds in spring for bloom by midsummer.

Chrysanthemum parthenium 'Snowball'

Listed in catalogs as cultivars of ***C. × rubellum*** or ***Dendranthema zawadskii*** are two other pretty chrysanthemums; both grow about 2 feet tall, have finely cut leaves, and succeed in Zones 1–24, 28–43. They bear 2- to 3-inch-wide daisies over a long season, beginning earlier than garden mums and continuing into fall. **'Clara Curtis'** has bright pink flowers; blossoms of **'Mary Stoker'** are an unusual soft yellow with apricot touches.

CULTURE. Give plants full sun and moderate water. When clumps become crowded (usually every other year), divide them in spring.

Cimicifuga simplex

Tall, slender plants with an airy, delicate texture, the bugbanes are at home in woodland gardens or in borders. Clumps of coarse, fernlike dark green leaves may reach 2½ feet; from these rise slim, branching stems that terminate in spikes of small, bristly white flowers. One of the tallest species is black snakeroot, **C. racemosa,** a North American native which easily reaches 6 feet when in bloom—in midsummer in southern regions, in late summer or early fall further north. It has erect flower spikes. The floral plumes of Kamchatka bugbane, **C. simplex,** in contrast, are arching; they appear in autumn on 4-foot stems. Among this species' selections are **'White Pearl',** with especially large, dense flower spikes; **'Atropurpurea',** with 4- to 6-foot blossom stalks and dark reddish purple foliage; and **'Brunette'** (3 to 4 feet tall) and **'Hillside Black Beauty'** (5 to 6 feet tall), with even more richly colored foliage. (The last three selections are sometimes listed as selections of *C. racemosa.*)

CULTURE. Plant bugbanes in soil enriched with organic matter. Where summers are cool or mild, they can be planted in full sun or partial shade; in hot areas, they require some shade (as at the edge of a woodland, for example). Plants seldom need division, but if you want to divide to increase your planting, do so in early spring.

CIMICIFUGA
(Actaea)
BUGBANE, SNAKEROOT
Ranunculaceae
PERENNIALS
ZONES 1–7, 17, 32–45
FULL SUN OR PARTIAL SHADE, EXCEPT AS NOTED
REGULAR WATER
❀ FLOWERS IN SUMMER, FALL

Named for Captain William Clark of the Lewis and Clark expedition, these slender-stemmed annual wildflowers are grown for their clusters of satiny blossoms. They make good cut flowers; cut the stems when the top bud opens (others open successively). Plants range in height from well under a foot to as tall as 4 feet; they grow and bloom best in cool climates and do not tolerate heat and humidity.

Farewell-to-spring, **C. amoena (Godetia amoena)** has two forms in the wild. One is coarse stemmed and sprawling, only 4 to 5 inches high; the other is a slender-stemmed, 1½- to 2½-foot plant. The tapered leaves are ½ to 2 inches long. On both forms, the buds grow upright along the stems, opening into 2-inch-wide, cup-shaped pink or lavender flowers, often with central blotches of contrasting colors. The **Grace** series has lavender, pink, red, or salmon blossoms on 20-inch plants.

C. pulchella is a slim, upright, 1- to 1½-foot plant with reddish stems and narrow, 1- to 2-inch-long leaves. The bright pink to lavender flowers are single or semidouble; each petal has a distinctive three-lobed tip. **'Snowflake'** is a pure white form that grows 12 to 15 inches high.

Mountain garland, **C. unguiculata (C. elegans),** grows from 1 to 4 feet high and has lance-shaped, 1- to 2-inch-long leaves; the inch-wide flowers have petals that are narrow at the base, rounded or lobed at the tip. Wild forms bloom in rose, purple, and white. Varieties include **'Apple Blossom',** with fully double flowers in soft apricot pink, and the **Royal Bouquet** strain, also with double flowers, in colors including white, purple, pink, rose, salmon, orange, and creamy yellow.

CULTURE. Clarkias grow best in sandy soil without added fertilizer. Sow seed in place in the garden—in fall in mild-winter regions, in early spring in colder areas. Plants often self-sow, producing volunteers for next year's garden.

CLARKIA
Onagraceae
COOL-SEASON ANNUALS
ZONES 1–45
FULL SUN
MODERATE WATER
✿❀✿✿✿ FLOWERS IN SPRING, EARLY SUMMER

Clarkia amoena

CLEOME hassleriana (C. spinosa)
SPIDER FLOWER

Capparidaceae

WARM-SEASON ANNUAL

ZONES 1–45

FULL SUN

MODERATE TO REGULAR WATER

✿ ❁ ✿ ✽ FLOWERS IN SUMMER, FALL

Cleome hassleriana

Growing as tall as 5 feet, this substantial annual produces leafy spikes topped in summer and fall by open clusters of blossoms with extremely long, protruding stamens—a feature that gives the flowers a distinctly spidery look. Long, narrow, pointed seedpods follow the blossoms, adding to the plant's unusual appearance. The lower leaves are divided, with leaflets radiating out from the center like fingers of a hand; the upper ones are undivided. Both leaves and stems have a pungent odor and feel somewhat clammy to the touch. The stems are usually set with short spines, so be careful when cutting the flowers for indoor display.

Spider flower provides a colorful, unusual background for a large border; it is also attractive grown as an annual hedge or in a large container. Seeds are sold in mixed or individual colors; the latter group includes **'Helen Campbell'**, with pure white blooms, and **'Purple Queen'**, **'Pink Queen'**, **'Cherry Queen'**, and **'Rose Queen'**.

CULTURE. Spider plant grows well in warm weather, in light, well-drained soil. It self-sows, sometimes to the point of becoming invasive. For flowers earlier in the season, sow seeds indoors 6 to 8 weeks before the last-frost date. Or sow outdoors after the last frost. In either case, mix the seeds with moist potting mix in a plastic bag and chill in the refrigerator for 5 days before planting.

COLEUS × hybridus (Solenostemon scutellarioides)

Lamiaceae (Labiatae)

PERENNIAL USUALLY GROWN AS
    WARM-SEASON ANNUAL

ALL ZONES

LIGHT SHADE, EXCEPT AS NOTED

REGULAR WATER

FLOWERS ARE INSIGNIFICANT; GROWN
    FOR FOLIAGE IN PURPLE, RED, BUFF,
    BROWN, SALMON, ORANGE, YELLOW,
    CHARTREUSE, BICOLORS

Coleus × hybridus 'Plum Parfait'

Valued for its brilliant foliage, coleus forms a bushy plant 1 to 3 feet high. Leaves vary from 1 to 7 inches long and may be toothed or ruffled; in most selections, each leaf displays two or more colors, with contrasting edges, splotches, or veins. The blue flower spikes are attractive, but they're usually pinched out in bud to make the plant more rounded and compact.

Coleus are classic plants for shaded borders and containers, but varieties more tolerant of sun are becoming available. In general, the more red or purple pigment the foliage has, the greater the sun tolerance; examples include **'Cranberry Sun'**, with reddish purple foliage, and **'Plum Parfait'**, featuring ruffled plum-colored leaves edged in pink. Both of these grow 2 to 3 feet high and have 1½- to 3-inch-long leaves. They are sold as cutting-grown plants—as are **'Black Magic'**, a 1½- to 2-footer with 1½- to 2-inch, dark velvety purple leaves bordered in green, and 2-foot **'Saturn'**, bearing purple, 2½- to 3-inch-long leaves sporting a vivid lime center. Many other cutting-grown coleus are offered; all tend to be more uniform in habit than seed-grown sorts.

Among seed-grown coleus, **The Wizard** is a well-known self-branching dwarf strain. It reaches 10 to 12 inches tall and has heart-shaped, 2- to 2½-inch leaves in a wide range of color combinations. Another seed-grown strain is **Giant Exhibition**, featuring 12- to 15-inch plants with huge (6- to 7-inch-long) leaves in a great variety of colors.

CULTURE. Grow coleus in rich, loose, evenly moist, well-drained soil. As noted above, most (though not all) varieties require some shade. Fertilize regularly.

Sow seeds indoors 10 weeks before the last frost. Barely press seeds into the potting mix; they need light to sprout. Pinch seedlings as well as older plants frequently to encourage bushy growth. Set out plants in the garden after all danger of frost is past. You can easily propagate coleus from cuttings—and this method provides a simple way to overwinter favorite varieties. Take cuttings in late summer and keep the resulting plants indoors through winter; then, in early spring, take more cuttings to produce plants for outdoor use.

Consolida ajacis

Prized for its resemblance to the stately perennial delphinium and for its ease of culture, larkspur is an erect, 1- to 4-foot-tall plant with deeply cut, almost fernlike leaves and showy blossom spikes set thickly with single or double, 1- to 1½-inch-wide blossoms. It blooms best in the cool weather of spring and early summer, dying out when hot temperatures arrive. Tall varieties make excellent back-of-border plants and provide charming cut flowers; shorter ones are a good source of color at the front of beds and borders. Note that all parts of this plant are poisonous (especially the seeds).

The **Dwarf Hyacinth Flowering** series offers neat, foot-tall plants with double flowers in white, blue, lilac, violet, and pink. Growing 20 inches tall, the **Earlibird** series is available in white, blue, lilac, or rose. Taller larkspurs include **'Blue Cloud'**, to 3½ feet tall, and 4-foot **'Earl Grey'**, with double flowers in an unusual shade of silvery mauve. The double-blossomed **Giant Imperial** series produces 4-foot plants in colors including white, blue, lilac, pink, salmon, and rose.

CULTURE. Larkspur grows best if sown in place directly in the garden, in a well-prepared planting bed enriched with organic matter. Sow in autumn except in heavy, slow-draining soils; in these soils, plant in spring, about 2 weeks before the last frost. Thin seedlings to avoid crowding; tall varieties may need staking. Larkspurs often self-sow.

Intensely colored, trumpet-shaped blossoms, their throats highlighted by jagged bands of white and yellow, make dwarf morning glory a striking choice for the summer garden. It's a mounding, somewhat trailing plant to 1 foot or a little taller, 2 feet wide. Its flowers, like those of the related annual morning glory vine (*Ipomoea tricolor*, page 180), last only a day and do not open in cloudy weather. Dwarf morning glory is a reliable summer bloomer; in mild-winter climates, it can also be planted in fall for spring flowers. It's effective in a large rock garden, as an edging, draped over the top of a wall, or in hanging baskets.

The **Ensign** series, growing 12 to 14 inches tall, is available in mixed or individual colors. **'Royal Ensign'** has blooms of the classic deep royal blue; **'Red Ensign'** and **'Rose Ensign'** are also offered. **Choice Mixed,** to 16 inches, blooms in white and shades of pink and blue.

Listing continues>

CONSOLIDA ajacis (Consolida ambigua, Delphinium ambiguum)
LARKSPUR, ANNUAL DELPHINIUM
Ranunculaceae
COOL-SEASON ANNUAL
ZONES 1–45
FULL SUN
REGULAR WATER
✿ ✿ ❀ ✿ FLOWERS IN SPRING, EARLY SUMMER

CONVOLVULUS tricolor
DWARF MORNING GLORY
Convolvulaceae
WARM-SEASON ANNUAL
ZONES 1–45
FULL SUN
MODERATE WATER
✿ ✿ ❀ ✿ ✿ FLOWERS IN SUMMER, EXCEPT AS NOTED

CULTURE. Grow dwarf morning glory in a sunny area, in average to moderately rich soil. The seed coat (outer covering) is very hard, preventing the seed from absorbing moisture; nicking each seed with a sharp knife or soaking seeds overnight in warm water before planting will improve germination. Sow seeds in place in the garden after the last-frost date (in mild-winter areas, sow in fall).

Convolvulus tricolor 'Royal Ensign'

COREOPSIS

COREOPSIS, TICKSEED

Asteraceae (Compositae)

PERENNIALS AND WARM-SEASON ANNUALS

ZONES VARY BY SPECIES

FULL SUN

LITTLE TO MODERATE WATER, EXCEPT
    AS NOTED

✿ ✿ ✿ FLOWERS IN SPRING, SUMMER, FALL

Coreopsis tinctoria

Brightening the garden with sunny daisies over a long season, species and varieties of coreopsis range from a few inches to several feet in height. One annual species, summer-blooming ***C. tinctoria*** (Zones 1–45; H1, H2), is widely grown. Known as annual coreopsis and native to much of North America, it's a slender, upright, 1½- to 3-foot-tall plant with wiry stems and lacy-looking leaves to 4 inches long. The species bears the solid yellow blooms common to most other coreopsis, but its cultivars offer variations with maroon centers and petals strikingly striped or marked in dark red, maroon, or purplish-brown. The flowers are 1 to 2 inches wide.

The following perennial choices are native to the southern and eastern U. S. At only 6 inches tall, ***C. auriculata*** 'Nana' (Zones 1–24, 26–45) is the shortest of the group, useful as an edging at the front of a border. It blooms from spring to early fall, sending up stems bearing vivid orange-yellow, 1- to 2½-inch blossoms above a mat of 2- to 5-inch-long leaves. ***C. grandiflora*** (Zones 2–24, 26, 28–43; H1, H2), with narrow, 2- to 4-inch-long leaves, includes several excellent selections that bloom from late spring through summer. '**Early Sunrise**' is a 1½- to 2-footer with semidouble bright yellow, 2-inch-wide flowers; '**Sunray**' is similar but has double blooms in a deeper yellow. ***C. lanceolata*** (Zones 1–24, 26, 28–45; H1, H2) grows 1 to 2 feet high; it has narrow basal leaves to about 6 inches long. Bright yellow, 1½- to 2-inch-wide blossoms bloom in late spring and summer; they are excellent for cutting.

C. rosea (Zones 2b–24, 31–41), reaching 1½ to 2 feet tall, is a fine-textured plant with linear bright green leaves to about 2 inches long. Yellow-centered pink blossoms appear from summer to fall.

As the common name indicates, threadleaf coreopsis, ***C. verticillata*** (Zones 1–24, 26, 28–45), has finely divided, very narrow leaves. Ranging from 1 to 2½ feet tall, the bushy, mounding plant bears bright yellow, 2-inch daisies over a long summer-to-autumn season. '**Moonbeam**' features blossoms of a soft pale yellow on a 1½- to 2-foot plant; foot-tall '**Zagreb**' has golden yellow flowers.

CULTURE. Coreopsis are trouble-free plants, thriving even in relatively poor soil (as long as it is well drained). Once established, they grow well with relatively little water—with the exception of *C. rosea*, which prefers moist soil. Remove spent blossoms to prolong flowering. Most of the perennials spread rapidly and may need frequent division (as often as every 2 to 3 years) to stay in bounds. Both annual and perennial coreopsis can be propagated from seed. Sow seed of annual coreopsis, *C. tinctoria*, in place in the garden after the last frost. Start seed of perennial sorts indoors in late winter.

Coreopsis lanceolata

These shade-loving perennials carry their charming little spurred flowers above handsome clumps of dainty, divided, fernlike leaves much like those of bleeding heart (*Dicentra,* to which they are closely related) or maidenhair fern (to which they are not).

C. cheilanthifolia, growing 8 to 10 inches high, has green foliage and clusters of deep yellow, ½-inch-long flowers in spring. *C. flexuosa* (sometimes called blue corydalis), an introduction from western China, forms a 9- to 12-inch mound of blue-green foliage. Narrow, erect clusters of beautiful sky blue, long-spurred, 1-inch flowers bloom in early spring, often continuing into summer. The plant may go dormant in summer, especially in hot climates, but it will reappear the following spring. Selected forms include '**Blue Panda**', with brilliant gentian blue flowers, and '**Père David**', with lavender to light blue blooms.

A many-stemmed plant with masses of gray-green foliage, *C. lutea* reaches 15 inches tall and bears golden yellow, ¾-inch-long, short-spurred flowers throughout the summer. It often self-sows, popping up in shady places throughout the garden.

CULTURE. Give corydalis rich soil that is moist but well drained. Plants grow well and look good in shady areas among rocks, in open woodland, or near a pool or stream. Divide clumps or sow seed in spring or fall (seed germinates best if freshly collected).

Long-time cottage-garden favorites, cosmos are airy, graceful plants with daisylike, satiny-petalled blossoms. The plants range from 1½ to 4 feet high (or even taller) and have bright green, finely divided leaves. Cosmos are useful for mass color in beds and borders, as background plants, and mixed with other annuals in big containers; they're also first-rate cut flowers (gather them as soon as the blossoms open and immediately place them in cool water).

C. bipinnatus produces 3- to 4-inch-wide flowers in white and shades of lavender, purple, pink, rose, and red; all have tufted yellow centers. The species has single flowers with flat petals, but there are also double-flowered sorts and kinds with quilled petals. The dwarf **Sonata** series produces bushy plants just 2 feet tall; it's available in mixed colors and in single shades including pure white, pink, pink-blushed white, and carmine. The **Seashells** strain has rolled or quilled petals, giving the flowers greater depth and substance; plants grow 3 to 4 feet tall and are usually offered in mixed colors that range from white through pink to red. Also reaching 3 to 4 feet, **Psyche** offers frilly semidouble flowers in pink as well as soft or deep rose. Bred for cut flowers, the **Versailles** strain features 3½-foot-tall, vigorous, strong-stemmed plants with blossoms in a variety of colors.

Yellow cosmos, *C. sulphureus,* produces 2- to 3-inch-wide blossoms in bold shades of yellow, golden orange, and scarlet orange. The dwarf **Ladybird** series packs a lot of color into plants only 12 to 14 inches tall; its semidouble flowers come in vivid shades of scarlet, orange, and yellow. '**Lemon Twist**' offers softer yellow blossoms on plants growing about 2½ feet high; the 3-foot-tall **Polidor** mix flaunts flowers in glowing red, orange, and yellow.

CULTURE. Grow cosmos in well-drained, average soil; if planted in rich soil, they produce foliage at the expense of flowers. Stake taller varieties to keep them upright. Removing spent flowers will encourage more blossoms.

Sow seed in place after danger of frost is past; or, for earlier blossoms, sow indoors 6 weeks before the usual last-frost date. Seed germinates quickly—in only 5 to 10 days. Cosmos often self-sow.

CORYDALIS

Fumariaceae
PERENNIALS
ZONES 2–9, 14–24, 32–35, 37, 39–43
PARTIAL SHADE
REGULAR WATER
✿ ✿ ✿ FLOWERS IN SPRING, SUMMER

Corydalis lutea

COSMOS

Asteraceae (Compositae)
WARM-SEASON ANNUALS
ZONES A3; 1–45
FULL SUN
MODERATE WATER
✿ ✿ ✿ ✿ ✿ FLOWERS IN SUMMER, FALL

Cosmos bipinnatus

DELPHINIUM

Ranunculaceae

PERENNIALS

ZONES VARY

FULL SUN, EXCEPT AS NOTED

REGULAR WATER

✿ ✿ ❀ ✿ FLOWERS IN SUMMER

Delphinium elatum,
Magic Fountains strain

Stately and aristocratic, delphiniums epitomize both the classic English border and the cottage garden. Though these old-fashioned favorites are most often associated with blue flowers, they're available in a range of colors, including white, pink, lilac, and purple. Some of the hybrids have bi- or even tricolored blooms, with the center petals (the "bee") offering a white, black, or gold contrast to the outer petals. Ranging in height from 15-inch dwarfs to 8-foot giants, the plants bear their rounded blossoms on spikes; the lobed or fanlike leaves are variously cut and divided. All delphiniums require considerable effort from the gardener if they are to grow to perfection.

D. × belladonna (Zones 1–9, 14–24, 32, 34, 36–43) is a hybrid group of plants that reach 3 to 4 feet when in bloom. Unlike the well-known *D. elatum* hybrids (see below), which have a central flower stem followed later in the season by smaller branches, these delphiniums produce many flower stems at the same time; they also have airier, more loosely arranged flower clusters than *D. elatum* hybrids and are somewhat longer lived. Selections include light blue **'Belladonna'**, dark blue **'Volkerfrieden' ('People of Peace')**, white **'Casa Blanca'**, and deep turquoise **'Cliveden Beauty'**.

D. elatum is a Siberian native reaching 3 to 6 feet tall; it has small purple flowers and is among the parents of the familiar tall modern delphiniums—complex *D. elatum* hybrids that grow in Zones A1–A3, 1–10, 14–24, 32, 34, 36–41. **Pacific** strain delphiniums (also known as **Pacific Hybrids, Pacific Giants,** and **Pacific Coast Hybrids**) reach 5 to 8 feet under optimal conditions. They're available as seed-raised mixed-color plants and in named series that produce specific colors, including light blue **'Summer Skies'**, medium blue **'Blue Bird'**, dark violet **'Black Knight'**, white **'Galahad'**, and **'Percival'**, which has white flowers with a black center. Many other named varieties in purple, lavender, and pink are sold. Shorter choices include the 2- to 2½-foot-tall **Blue Fountains, Blue Springs,** and **Magic Fountains** strains. Even shorter is the 15- to 20-inch **Stand Up** strain.

CULTURE. Delphiniums grow best in the classic English climate—that is, in regions with cool to warm (not hot), humid summers. They are much less successful where summers are hot, dry, or both. In marginal locations, shelter plants by placing them in dappled sunlight, and take care to provide sufficient moisture. These plants require soil that is cool, moist yet well drained, and slightly acid to slightly alkaline. Add lime to strongly acid soils. Dig plenty of organic matter and a complete fertilizer into the soil a few weeks before planting time. To prevent rot, take care not to cover the crown of the plant. Taller varieties require staking. Slugs and snails can ruin young plants; see page 76 for controls.

During the bloom season, cut off spent blossom spikes just below the lowest flower, leaving part of the stalk and its foliage. Then, when new basal shoots reach about 6 inches tall, cut the old spikes to the ground and apply a complete fertilizer around the plant. The new stems should flower in late summer or early autumn.

Even with the best care, hybrid delphiniums tend to be short lived. You can take basal cuttings in spring or divide clumps and set out individual plants in well-prepared soil—but most gardeners find it easier to start fresh with young seedlings or cutting-grown plants from a nursery. You can also treat delphiniums as annuals by planting them in autumn (in mild-winter regions) or early spring (in all regions) to flower in summer. This is the best tactic in areas that have hot summers and/or mild winters.

Delphinium elatum, Pacific strain,
'Summer Skies'

For centuries, gardeners have enjoyed the many sorts of dianthus for their cheerful flowers and, in most species, delightful clove fragrance. Borne singly or in clusters, the circular, ½- to 1-inch-wide flowers may be single, semidouble, or double; they are often fringed at the edges and may have eyes and petal margins in contrasting colors. All are delightful in low borders, in rock gardens, and as edgings. Annual and biennial sorts are also good choices for containers.

The China pink, **D. chinensis,** may live for more than a year as a biennial or short-lived perennial in warm-winter climates, but it's generally grown as an annual everywhere. Ranging from 6 inches to 2½ feet tall, the dome-shaped plants have stems that branch near the top. The basal leaves are medium green, up to 3 inches long (they often wither before flowering time); the narrow stem leaves are 1 to 3 inches long. Fringed-looking flowers in white and shades of pink and red are produced in loose clusters in late spring or early summer; unlike most other dianthus, they have little or no scent. The **Ideal** series produces foot-tall plants that flower better than most others in summer heat; the blossoms often feature a charming contrasting eye. **Telstar** is a bushy, 6- to 8-inch-tall strain; its blossoms, often with intricately marked eyes, may have smooth-edged or fringed petals.

Sweet William, **D. barbatus,** is generally grown as a vigorous biennial—but some newer fast-maturing varieties are treated as annuals, blooming the first year from seed. These cottage-garden classics reach 20 inches tall and have light to dark green, 1½- to 3-inch-long leaves. In late spring and early summer, dense clusters of small, fragrant flowers bloom in white, pink, rose, red, and bicolors. 'Harlequin', to 1½ feet tall, produces large flower heads that contain blossoms in a mix of colors, ranging from white to deep pink. The **Rondo** series (6 inches tall) and **New Era Mixed** (1½ feet tall) are two sweet Williams that have been bred to bloom the first year if sown in early spring. Both have flowers in white and shades of pink and red, quite often with contrasting central rings or outer edges.

The Allwood pinks, **D. × allwoodii,** are perennial hybrids developed early in the 20th century; they vary somewhat, but most have gray-green foliage and two blossoms per stem. Among the many varieties are '**Aqua**', with double blooms in pure white, and '**Doris**', with salmon pink flowers accented by a deep pink eye; both grow 10 to 12 inches high. '**Horatio**', to just 6 inches tall, has double pink flowers with a dark eye.

Maiden pink, **D. deltoides,** also a perennial, grows well in light shade. The green-foliaged plants spread to form broad, loose mats about 6 inches high, making a good small-scale ground cover. Branched stems bear flowers at their tips in summer. The species has purple to rose-colored flowers. Available varieties include pure white '**Albus**'; deep red '**Vampire**'; and '**Zing Rose**', bearing rosy red blossoms with a darker ring around the eye.

Perennial Cheddar pink, **D. gratianopolitanus (D. caesius),** forms a ground-hugging mat of blue-green leaves; pink flowers appear in summer on 6- to 10-inch stems. Selected forms vary in size and flower color. '**Bath's Pink**' sends up 12- to 15-inch stems bearing fringed soft pink blossoms; smaller-growing cultivars include 6-inch-tall, red-and-white '**Spotty**' and 4-inch '**Tiny Rubies**', with small double blooms in ruby red. The species as well as its varieties grow well in hot, humid areas.

Perennial cottage or grass pink, **D. plumarius** (Zones A1; 1–24, 30–45), forms a loose mat of gray-green foliage. It blooms in early summer, carrying its blossoms on stems 10 to 18 inches tall. Some of the oldest dianthus are classified here, including the legendary 17th-century '**Dad's Favorite**', with ruby-edged double white flowers centered in maroon, and '**Musgrave's Pink**', a classic at least two centuries old that bears intensely fragrant single white flowers with a green eye. Listing continues>

DIANTHUS
Caryophyllaceae

PERENNIALS, BIENNIALS OFTEN GROWN
   AS COOL-SEASON ANNUALS
ZONES A2, A3, 1–24, 30–45,
   EXCEPT AS NOTED
FULL SUN, EXCEPT AS NOTED
MODERATE TO REGULAR WATER
✿ ❀ ✿ ✿ FLOWERS IN SPRING, SUMMER

Dianthus chinensis 'Telstar Scarlet'

Dianthus chinensis 'Telstar Picotee'

Dianthus × allwoodii 'Horatio'

CULTURE. All kinds of dianthus thrive in fast-draining soil. *D. barbatus* and *D. plumarius* need fairly rich soil; the others described here require a light, even gritty, soil. All prefer neutral to slightly alkaline soil; add lime to acidic soils. In hot-summer regions, place plants where they will receive a little afternoon shade. To encourage more flowers throughout summer, remove faded blossoms, breaking or cutting the stems at the nodes where new growth is starting. In colder regions (where winter lows dip to −10°F/−23°C), protect perennial varieties with a loose cover of evergreen boughs.

Most dianthus are easy to grow from seed, and many self-sow. Sow seed of perennials in containers in a cold frame in spring or fall. You can sow seed of annual dianthus (*D. chinensis,* annual forms of *D. barbatus*) outdoors a few weeks before the last frost; or, for earlier flowering, sow indoors 8 weeks before the last frost. To grow *D. barbatus* as a biennial, sow seed in late spring or early summer in a nursery bed; in fall, transplant the young plants to the desired garden location for bloom the following year.

After several years, most perennial dianthus begin to decline. Replace them with plants grown from seed or cuttings. Take stem cuttings in spring from new growth that has not flowered; the cuttings should be about six nodes in length. Stems that spread along the ground may take root where nodes touch the soil; cut these rooted plants from the parent and transplant them.

DICENTRA
BLEEDING HEART
Fumariaceae
PERENNIALS
ZONES 1–9, 14–24, 31–45, EXCEPT
　　AS NOTED
LIGHT SHADE, EXCEPT AS NOTED
REGULAR WATER
❀✿✿ FLOWERS IN SPRING, SUMMER

Dicentra spectabilis

Delicate wands of heart-shaped flowers and finely dissected, almost feathery foliage make bleeding heart a favorite. Eastern and western North America are home to two similar low-growing species. The eastern species is fringed bleeding heart, **D. eximia;** it forms a tidy, non-spreading, 1- to 1½-foot clump of blue-gray foliage. The bare stems rise just above the leaves, carrying dangling deep pink flowers from mid-spring into summer. **'Alba'** is a white-flowered selection. Foot-tall Western bleeding heart,

Dicentra spectabilis 'Alba'

D. formosa, has blue-green foliage; in spring, pale to deep rose flowers are clustered on slim stems that rise 6 to 8 inches above the leaves. Under favorable conditions, this species spreads widely, but it is not invasive. **'Zestful'** is a long-blooming variety with deep rose flowers. **D. f. oregana** is shorter than the species and bears cream blossoms tipped in pink.

Nurseries offer a number of superior 12- to 15-inch selections of uncertain ancestry; they may be hybrids of the above two species or selected forms of one of them. **'Bacchanal',** bearing deep red blooms, is nearly everblooming during the growing season, as is pink-flowered **'Bountiful'.** The hardy selection **'Luxuriant'** (Zones A1–A3; 1–9, 14–24; 31–45) can endure drier soil and stronger light than most; its deep pink flowers appear in spring and early summer.

Common bleeding heart, **D. spectabilis** (Zones A1–A3; 1–9, 14–24, 31–45), native to Japan, is the showiest and largest leafed of the bleeding hearts. Clothed in soft green foliage, the plants grow 2 to 3 feet high; in late spring, branched stems carry nearly horizontal sprays of pendulous, heart-shaped rose pink flowers with protruding white inner petals. **'Alba'** is pure white. Plants begin to die down after flowering and are generally dormant by midsummer, though they tend to last longer in cool-summer climates if given adequate moisture. To fill the gap they leave, plant summer-maturing perennials (such as hostas or ferns) or annuals such as impatiens nearby.

CULTURE. Plant bleeding hearts in light, well-drained soil enriched with organic matter. The roots should be kept cool and moist, but not soggy. Most of these plants prefer filtered sunlight to partial shade, but in cool regions, *D. spectabilis* and the hybrid 'Luxuriant' will tolerate full sun. All but *D. spectabilis* may need dividing after several years. Do this in earliest spring, before growth is really underway. (*D. spectabilis* has brittle roots and is best left undisturbed, though you can divide it during dormancy to increase your plantings.) All can be propagated by root cuttings taken in summer or fall.

Dictamnus albus

Sturdy and long lived, this handsome perennial forms bushy, 2½- to 4-foot-tall clumps of glossy, citrus-scented foliage on sturdy stems; the leaves are composed of 3-inch-long, pointed leaflets. At bloom time in late spring and summer, loose spires of narrow-petaled blossoms with prominent, greenish stamens appear at the stem tips; they are reminiscent of wild azaleas. Pink is the basic color, but nurseries also offer lilac **'Purpureus'** and white **'Albiflorus'**. The seedpods that follow are also attractive. In warm, humid weather, volatile oils from the immature seed capsules may briefly ignite if you hold a lighted match immediately beneath a flower cluster—hence the common names "gas plant" and "burning bush." (This "ignition test" does not harm the plant.)

Gas plant contains phototoxins, chemical substances that make the skin of susceptible people hypersensitive to sunlight following direct exposure to plant parts.

CULTURE. Give gas plant well-drained, moderately fertile soil. It grows best in regions with cool nights. Plants may take 2 to 3 years to settle in and start blooming well, but they can remain in place indefinitely (and should, in fact, be left in one place; they reestablish slowly if divided). Start new plants from seed or from root cuttings taken in late winter.

DICTAMNUS albus
GAS PLANT, BURNING BUSH, FRAXINELLA
Rutaceae
PERENNIAL
ZONES 1–9, 31–45
FULL SUN OR LIGHT SHADE
MODERATE TO REGULAR WATER
✿ ❀ ✿ FLOWERS IN LATE SPRING, SUMMER

These old-fashioned favorites feature tubular flowers shaped like the fingertips of a glove, carried in erect spikes that rise above a rosette of lance-shaped leaves. The classic garden sort, **D. purpurea** (Zones A2, A3; 1–24, 31–41), is a biennial: it develops a clump of large, furry light green leaves during its first year, sends up stately, 4- to 6-foot spires of pendulous blossoms in spring and early summer of the second year, and then usually dies. The 2- to 3-inch-long flowers come in creamy yellow, white, rose purple, or pink, all spotted with purple inside. Garden strains include 5-foot-tall **Excelsior,** with outward-facing flowers in creamy yellow, white, purple, and pink; 3½-foot , apricot pink **'Sutton's Apricot';** and **'Alba',** a pure white form lacking the typical interior spots. As is the case with many other biennials, breeders have developed a fast-growing strain that can be grown as an annual: 3-foot-tall **Foxy,** which flowers in just 5 months from seed and offers a range of colors.

Digitalis purpurea, Foxy strain

DIGITALIS
FOXGLOVE
Scrophulariaceae
PERENNIALS AND BIENNIALS
ZONES VARY
LIGHT SHADE, EXCEPT AS NOTED
REGULAR WATER, EXCEPT AS NOTED
✿ ❀ ✿ FLOWERS IN LATE SPRING, SUMMER

Listing continues>

Digitalis grandiflora

Other species are perennial (though sometimes short lived); they produce the typical clumps of bold leaves but feature somewhat shorter flower spikes. Yellow foxglove, ***D. grandiflora (D. ambigua),*** succeeds in Zones 1–10, 14–24, 31–43. It grows 2 to 3 feet tall and has 2-inch-long pale yellow flowers lightly spotted brown on the inside. Its cultivar '**Carillon**' grows only 12 to 15 inches high. Grecian foxglove, ***D. lanata*** (Zones 2b–10, 14–24, 31–41), has dark green leaves and narrow, 3-foot-tall spikes of 1¼-inch, cream-colored flowers with purplish veining and a small near-white lip. ***D. × mertonensis*** (Zones 1–10, 14–24, 31–41) bears 2- to 3-foot spikes of 2½-inch flowers in a deep pink shade often described as strawberry. Though it is a hybrid, it comes true from seed.

Narrow-leaf foxglove, ***D. obscura*** (Zones 2–10, 14–24, 31–41), grows 1½ feet high; it has lance-shaped leaves and unusual brown-and-yellow flowers just ¾ to 1¼ inches long. ***D. thapsi*** (Zones 2–10, 14–24, 31–41) reaches only a foot high and features drooping, inch-long pink flowers over furry foliage.

Note that all parts of all foxglove species are poisonous if ingested.

CULTURE. Most foxgloves are at their best in filtered sun to light or partial shade; where summers are cool, however, you can plant them in sun. Most kinds also need good soil enriched with organic matter and do best with regular watering. *D. obscura* and *D. thapsi,* however, are exceptions: they prefer full sun to light shade, well-drained soil that is not too rich, and occasional deep watering.

For all species, remove spent flower spikes to encourage repeat bloom in late summer or autumn. If you want seeds to start new plants, leave a few spikes.

Sow seed of biennial foxgloves in late spring or summer—in place in the garden, in an outdoor nursery bed, or in containers. Transplant seedlings from beds or containers to their final location in early fall or in spring. To grow foxgloves as annuals, start seed indoors in midwinter. Set out plants of perennial foxgloves (and biennials bought from a nursery) in early spring. You can divide clumps of perennial kinds in spring.

ECHINACEA purpurea
PURPLE CONEFLOWER
Asteraceae (Compositae)
PERENNIAL
ZONES A2, A3; 1–24, 26-45
FULL SUN, EXCEPT AS NOTED
MODERATE WATER
✿ ✿ ✿ ✿ FLOWERS IN SUMMER

Purple coneflower bears showy, 4-inch-wide daisies with dark, beehivelike centers and rosy purple petals that are typically slightly drooping. Bristly, oblong, 3- to 4-inch-long leaves form dense clumps; from these, sparsely leafed flowering stems rise 2 to 4 feet and bear flowers over a long summer season. '**Bright Star**' is a free-flowering, 2½-foot-tall cultivar with rose-colored blossoms; '**Crimson Star**' reaches 2 feet high, as does '**Bravado**', bearing the typical rosy purple blooms. '**Magnus**', to 3 feet tall, has rose pink flowers with petals that do not droop, but are held horizontally. '**White Swan**' and '**White Lustre**' feature white blooms with an orange-yellow cone.

Echinacea purpurea

CULTURE. Purple coneflower is a trouble-free plant that needs only a sunny spot in average, well-drained soil. In hot-summer regions, it also does well in light shade. It is drought tolerant but performs better with moderate watering. Deadheading encourages repeat flowering and keeps plants looking neat, but many gardeners leave some of the seedheads for birds to enjoy. The clumps spread slowly and may become crowded after 4 years or so. The fleshy rootstocks can be difficult to separate; divide them carefully, making sure that each division has a shoot and roots. You can also increase your supply of plants by taking root cuttings in fall, sowing seed, or transplanting self-sown seedlings (note that these may not bloom true to the parent plants).

Though related to common thistles, these plants have none of their roadside relatives' weediness. Reaching up to 1 foot long, the prickly, deeply cut leaves are usually green on the upper surface, gray and woolly beneath. Upright, well-foliaged stems rise to about 4 feet by bloom time, bearing distinctive spherical flower heads that look like golf ball–size pincushions stuck full of tubular, metallic blue pins.

You'll find globe thistles sold under various species names—*E. exaltatus, E. humilis, E. ritro, E. sphaerocephalus*—but by any name, plants are likely to fit the description above, particularly if you buy '**Taplow Blue**' (which may be sold as a selection of any of those spe-

Echinops

ECHINOPS
GLOBE THISTLE
Asteraceae (Compositae)
PERENNIALS
ZONES A2, A3; 1–24, 31–45
FULL SUN
MODERATE WATER
✿ FLOWERS IN SUMMER, FALL

cies). '**Veitch's Blue**' offers darker blue flowers on stems just 2½ to 3 feet tall. Globe thistles bloom from summer to late fall and are excellent in everlasting arrangements; cut the stems just before flowers open, then hang them upside down to dry.

CULTURE. Given a warm, sunny site, globe thistles thrive with moderate water in well-drained soil of just average fertility. (With rich soil and regular moisture, they can grow too lushly, producing taller stems that require support.) Clumps can flourish undisturbed for years, but to increase your plantings, you can dig and separate them in spring or take root cuttings in early spring.

At first glance, you could mistake these leafy, fine-textured, mounding or spreading plants for perennial asters—but the fleabanes have threadlike petals rather than the flattened ones of asters. Mexican or Santa Barbara daisy, *E. karvinskianus* (Zones 8, 9, 12–28; H1, H2), is a semitrailing, wiry-stemmed plant that can reach 1½ feet high and spread to 3 feet wide, rooting as it spreads. Its pink-tinted white flowers are small (no more than ½ inch wide) but profuse, thickly dappling the foliage over a long, midspring-into-summer period—or virtually all year, in frost-free climates. Tough and adaptable, it grows with little to regular water and self-sows readily. For larger, pale lavender flowers on a more compact plant, look for '**Moerheimii**'.

The other popular fleabanes are selections and hybrids of *E. speciosus* (Zones 1–9, 14–24, 31–43). All are bushy growers to about 2 feet high and wide, with clusters of 1½- to 2-inch, single to double blossoms in summer. Violet-blue '**Darkest of All**' has double flowers; '**Azure Fairy**' ('**Azurfee**') is slightly taller (to 2½ feet), with semidouble lavender-blue blooms. '**Förster's Liebling**' ('**Förster's Darling**'), only 1½ feet tall, has semidouble carmine pink blossoms; fully double '**Quakeress**' is light mauve pink; '**White Quakeress**' is a double-flowered choice with off-white flowers.

CULTURE. All fleabanes grow best in well-drained, fairly light soil (*E. karvinskianus* will even grow in crevices in rock walls). *E. karvinskianus* thrives with any amount of moisture, from little to regular; *E. speciosus* prefers moderate watering. Where summers are cool to moderately warm, all thrive in full sun; in hotter-summer regions, *E. speciosus* and its selections prefer some light shade (and even then will have a shorter bloom season than in cooler climates). All types benefit from cutting back. With the *E. speciosus* group, cut plants back halfway after the first flush of bloom to encourage a repeat performance; for *E. karvinskianus*, cut back plants hard (nearly to the ground) at the start of the growing season. Divide crowded clumps in spring.

ERIGERON
FLEABANE
Asteraceae (Compositae)
PERENNIALS
ZONES VARY
FULL SUN, EXCEPT AS NOTED
WATER NEEDS VARY
✿ ✿ ❁ ✿ FLOWERS IN SPRING AND
   SUMMER, EXCEPT AS NOTED

Erigeron karvinskianus

ERYNGIUM

SEA HOLLY

Apiaceae (Umbelliferae)

PERENNIALS AND BIENNIALS

ZONES 2–24, 29–43, EXCEPT AS NOTED

FULL SUN

MODERATE WATER, EXCEPT AS NOTED

✿ ✿ ❀ ✿ FLOWERS IN SUMMER

Eryngium alpinum

In contrast to the many soft and billowy perennials, sea hollies offer a stiff, sculptural look that borders on the artificial. In summer, a branched flowering stem rises from a rosette of 3- to 6-inch-long leaves; each branch bears at its tip a cone-shaped flower head sitting on a spiny starburst of bracts (modified leaves). Bracts are narrow and jagged in some species, broad and deeply cut in others. The usual flower and bract colors are silvery gray, steel blue, sea green—a palette that adds to the "fake flower" air!

Biennial Miss Willmott's ghost, *E. giganteum,* is a green-leafed plant to 4 feet or taller. Pale green to blue flower heads are surrounded by silvery white bracts; the whole inflorescence reaches about 4 inches across. The plant forms a foliage rosette in its first year from seed; the next year, it sends up flowering stems, blooms, and dies—but not before scattering seeds for a new generation of plants. By sowing seeds in two successive years, you can have flowering plants each year.

The remaining sea hollies discussed here are perennials. Despite its prickly appearance, *E. alpinum* is soft to the touch. Clumps of spiny-edged leaves give rise to 2½-foot, blue-tinted stems bearing 1½-inch-tall, silvery violet flower heads surrounded by intricately cut violet-blue bracts. Handsome *E. amethystinum* (Zones 1–24, 26, 28–45), another 2½-footer, has medium green leaves, silvery blue stems, and violet, 1-inch-tall flower heads encircled by a spiny ruff of silvery blue bracts.

Surrounded by spiky blue-green bracts, the light blue flower heads of many-branched, 3-foot-tall *E. planum* are only ¾ inch tall, but their profusion makes up for their small size. Foliage is deep green. Cultivars differ in flower color and/or plant height. Choices include 3- to 4-foot 'Silverstone', with creamy white flower heads; dark blue, 2-foot 'Flüela'; and 1½-foot 'Blue Diamond', also with deep blue blooms.

Hybrid *E.* × *zabelii* resembles its *E. alpinum* parent but has rounded flower heads and more deeply lobed leaves; 'Jewel' is a selection in dark steel blue.

CULTURE. Because sea hollies have long taproots, they are best planted in deep, fairly light soils; a sandy or gravelly soil that is not too fertile suits them well. All do well with moderate watering except *E. giganteum,* which prefers regular moisture. Clumps prefer to be left undisturbed, though you can take root cuttings in late winter to get new plants of perennial species (or grow them from seed). Plant seeds of biennial *E. giganteum* in fall or early spring, in the location where you want the plants to grow.

ESCHSCHOLZIA californica

CALIFORNIA POPPY

Papaveraceae

PERENNIAL OFTEN GROWN AS
    COOL-SEASON ANNUAL

ZONES 1–45; H1

FULL SUN

LITTLE TO REGULAR WATER

✿ ❀ ✿ ✿ ✿ FLOWERS IN LATE WINTER
    AND SPRING, EXCEPT AS NOTED

In its native western states, California poppy blooms from late winter through spring, adorning grassy hillsides and fields with patches of blazing orange and yellow. Each plant forms a foot-high clump (branching from the base) of green to silvery bluish green leaves that are divided into fine, nearly threadlike segments. Tapered buds open to four-petaled, satiny, 2-inch flowers on stems to 2 feet high. The typical colors are orange and orange-centered yellow, but cream to white variants also appear in the wild. Seed strains include a much wider range of colors; some also offer semidouble and double blossoms. Among widely available strains offering the full range of colors are **Sunset;** semidouble **Mission Bells;** semidouble **Ballerina,** with fluted petals; and **Thai Silk,** with semidouble, fluted-looking blooms and bronze-tinted foliage.

Named selections feature specific colors. Semidouble 'Apricot Flambeau' has fluted pale yellow petals tipped in coral orange; 'Carmine King' bears creamy white blooms heavily brushed with deep rosy red. 'Dalli' has orange-red flowers (some with yellow centers); 'Inferno' is solid scarlet orange. Other choices include 'Cherry Ripe', 'Milky White', and 'Purple Cup'. 'Golden Tears' has trailing, 2-foot stems.

CULTURE. In nature, this plant's seed capsules scatter copious amounts of seed with the onset of summer heat, after which the taprooted plant becomes semidormant. With the arrival of fall and winter rains, the seeds germinate and the parent plant resumes growth to flower the next year. In the garden, however, California poppy is usually treated as an annual, enjoyed for its flashy blooms in spring (in summer, in cold-winter regions), then discarded after it sets seed. Except in cool-summer climates, second-year plants rarely perform as well as new seedlings.

California poppy grows best in average, well-drained soil loose enough to let its taproot penetrate easily. It tolerates drought but performs best with moderate to regular water during growth and bloom. Sow seed in fall where winters are mild, in early spring in regions where temperatures dip to 0°F/−18°C or lower. If you remove spent flowers, the bloom period will last longer, but you'll want to let some flowers set seed to provide new plants for the next year. In mild-winter regions, let plants self-sow; in colder areas, collect seeds and sow them the following year.

Eschscholzia californica

EUPATORIUM
Asteraceae (Compositae)
PERENNIALS
ZONES VARY
FULL SUN OR LIGHT SHADE
REGULAR TO AMPLE WATER
✿ ✿ ✿ ✿ FLOWERS IN SUMMER, FALL

Their bulk, density, and large leaves give these perennials a shrublike appearance that doesn't quite match their summer-to-fall blossoms: the flowers are tiny, carried in large, loose clusters that suggest puffs of smoke. Stems are strong and erect, bearing whorls of lance-shaped leaves.

Known as hardy ageratum, **E. coelestinum** (**Conoclinium coelestinum;** Zones 1–9, 14–17, 25–43) bears broad clusters of fluffy blue blossoms resembling those of floss flower *(Ageratum)*. The many-branched plant reaches 3 feet high; dark green, 4-inch leaves are carried in opposite pairs. Smaller cultivars include pure blue, 2-foot-tall **'Cori'**, blooming later than the species; white **'Album'**, also 2 feet high; and blue **'Wayside Variety'**, reaching a compact 15 inches.

Joe Pye weed, **E. purpureum** (Zones 1–9, 14–17, 28–45), is a giant that can reach 9 feet high. Its hollow, upright stems are clothed in dark green, foot-long leaves and topped with domes of pale purple blossoms. Spotted Joe Pye weed, **E. p. maculatum**, is similar but shorter (6 to 7 feet high), with smaller leaves and purple-mottled stems. **'Atropurpureum'** has purple stems and leaf veins; **'Gateway'** (sometimes listed as a form of *E. fistulosum*) bears dusky rose flowers atop stems only 4 to 5 feet tall.

White snakeroot, **E. rugosum** (Zones 1–10, 14–17, 28–45), reaches 3 to 5 feet and bears fluffy white flower clusters; both the stems and the 5-inch leaves are heavily marked in brownish red. **'Chocolate'** has bronze to dark maroon leaves and stems.

CULTURE. Native to moist meadows, these plants are at their luxuriant best in good soil with plenty of water. *E. coelestinum* spreads to form broad clumps; dig and divide every 3 to 4 years in early spring. The remaining species can remain undisturbed for many years. For all species, it's wise to remove spent flower heads to prevent self-sowing.

Eupatorium purpureum maculatum 'Gateway'

EUPHORBIA
SPURGE
Euphorbiaceae
PERENNIALS AND WARM-SEASON ANNUALS
ZONES VARY
FULL SUN, EXCEPT AS NOTED
MODERATE WATER
✿ ✿ ✿ ✿ FLOWERS IN WINTER, SPRING, SUMMER

This amazingly varied group of plants includes lush, tropical-looking individuals (like the familiar holiday poinsettia) as well as desert natives that resemble cacti. What unites them is their floral structure: all have petal-like bracts (modified leaves), often quite colorful and showy, surrounding insignificant true flowers. Another common feature is a milky sap which can irritate the eyes and skin.

Annual snow-on-the-mountain, **E. marginata** (Zones 1–45), a slender plant to about 2 feet high, is an old-fashioned favorite for the summer garden. Along the upper parts of the stems, the oval light green leaves are margined and striped white—and may sometimes be solid white. Even the bract clusters are white and green. **'Summer Icicle'** is shorter, just 1½ feet high. Plant close together for good mass effect (stems become bare at the base, so use shorter annuals in the foreground). Listing continues>

Euphorbia marginata

Euphorbia × martinii

The following five evergreen species and hybrids (and their subspecies and cultivars) all have unbranched stems, domelike clusters of typically chartreuse to lime green bracts in late winter and early spring, and narrowly elliptical leaves that are usually bluish green. In 3-foot-tall *E. amygdaloides* (Zones 2b–24, 31–41), leaves have red undersides and stems are red tinged; the red shades intensify in winter. (For leaves and stems in solid reddish bronze, look for the cultivar 'Purpurea'.) Showy *E. characias* (Zones 4–24, 31, warmer parts of 32) forms an upright, shrubby clump to 4 feet high and has dark-centered bract clusters; more commonly grown is *E. c. wulfenii* **(E. veneta)**, with broader clusters of bracts that lack a dark center. *E. c.* 'Portuguese Velvet' has shorter leaves on a shorter plant (2 to 3 feet high) and features coppery gold bracts. *E. × martinii* (Zones 3–24, 31, 32), to 2½ feet tall, has bronze-tinted leaves and brown-centered bract clusters.

Trailing stems of *E. myrsinites* (Zones 2–24, 31–41) look something like bottlebrushes: they're thickly clothed in leaves and turn up just at the tips to bear flattish bract clusters. The plant grows about 6 inches tall and spreads to a foot wide. *E. rigida* **(E. biglandulosa;** Zones 4–24, 31) is another species with "bottlebrush" branches: its gray-green leaves sit directly on the stems and spiral around them. The stems sprawl outward, then turn upright to produce a clump 3 to 5 feet across but just 2 feet high.

Unlike the preceding spurges, the following three have branching stems. All are deciduous. *E. dulcis* 'Chameleon' (Zones 2b–24, 31–34), a mounding plant just 1 to 2 feet high and wide, has leaves that emerge purple in spring and mature to bronzed green by summer; in fall, all parts of the plant turn a rich purple. Purple-tinged, greenish yellow bract clusters appear at stem ends in summer. Another summer bloomer is *E. griffithii* (Zones 2–10, 14–24, 28–41), which forms clumps that expand by creeping rhizomes; its stems grow upright to 3 feet. The species has lance-shaped medium green leaves with pink midribs and bears open, branching clusters of orange-red bracts. 'Fireglow' has brick red bracts; 'Dixter' offers orange bracts and red-flushed foliage. A fine choice for borders is cushion spurge, *E. polychroma* **(E. epithymoides;** Zones A2, A3, 1–24, 26, 28–45). Dense, rounded foliage clumps to 1½ feet high and wide are covered from late spring into summer with flattened clusters of greenish yellow bracts. The dark green leaves turn red in autumn.

CULTURE. Sun, well-drained average soil, and moderate watering satisfy the spurges. *E. amygdaloides* and *E. griffithii* also take light shade; *E. polychroma* needs some shade in the hottest regions. When perennials' bract clusters turn brown, cut out the entire stem (by then, new stems will have grown from the base). Only *E. griffithii* needs periodic dividing or curbing; all the others form discrete clumps. Many self-sow.

Sow seed of annual *E. marginata* after the danger of frost has passed, in the spot where plants are to grow.

FILIPENDULA
MEADOWSWEET
Rosaceae
PERENNIALS
ZONES VARY
LIGHT SHADE, EXCEPT AS NOTED
REGULAR TO AMPLE WATER,
 EXCEPT AS NOTED
✿ ✿ FLOWERS IN SUMMER

Their dense plumes of tiny summer flowers floating above handsome clumps of large, jagged-lobed leaves, the meadowsweets look like pumped-up versions of their astilbe relatives. Their size puts them at the back of the border; their love of moisture recommends them for planting beside pools and streams.

Siberian meadowsweet, *F. palmata* (Zones A2, A3; 1–9, 14–17, 31–45), features pale pink blossoms on 3- to 4-foot stems that rise above coarse, palmately lobed leaves. Its selection 'Nana' is much smaller, reaching just 8 to 10 inches. Japanese meadowsweet, *F. purpurea* (Zones 3b–9, 14–17, 31–34, 39), forms broad clumps of maplelike leaves that send up reddish, 4-foot stems topped with dark pink blossom plumes. 'Elegans' has white blossoms accented by red stamens.

North American native queen of the prairie, *F. rubra* (Zones A1–A3; 1–9, 14–17, 31–45), is the most imposing species: it reaches 6 to 8 feet if given ample moisture. Leaves are deeply lobed, with jagged edges. The species has bright pink flowers; 'Venusta' bears darker, purplish pink blossoms on a smaller plant (4 to 6 feet). 'Alba', also growing 4 to 6 feet high, has white blooms.

Queen of the meadow, *F. ulmaria* (Zones 1–9, 14–17, 31–45), is a European native that resembles *F. rubra* but grows a little shorter (to 6 feet tall) and has creamy white blossoms. A bit showier is its 3-foot-tall, double-flowered selection 'Flore Pleno'. 'Variegata' has leaves margined in light yellow. 'Aurea' has solid bright yellow foliage; its flowers are insignificant.

Standing apart from the other species in appearance and cultural needs is drop-wort, *F. vulgaris* (*F. hexapetala*; Zones A1–A3, 1–9, 14–17, 31–45). Leaves are fine textured, almost fernlike, in low, spreading mounds. Slender stems rise 2 to 3 feet high, bearing branched sprays of white blossoms. 'Flore Pleno' has double flowers resembling small roses.

CULTURE. With the exception of *F. vulgaris*, the meadowsweets need good, organically enriched soil and a steady water supply; they prefer partial or light shade in most regions, though they can take full sun in northern latitudes and cool-summer areas. Plant *F. vulgaris* in full sun except in the warmest regions (where it needs light shade). It tolerates dry soils but looks better with moderate watering.

You can propagate all meadowsweets by dividing the clumps in early spring.

Filipendula ulmaria 'Flore Pleno'

These showy, easy-to-grow daisies feature warm, bright colors and a tough constitution. Native to the central and western U. S., they're unfazed by heat, wind, and capricious watering.

Annual *G. pulchella* blooms in summer, producing 2-inch-wide blossoms on long, whiplike stems that rise as high as 2 feet above a clump of narrow, deeply cut, downy gray-green leaves. Flower colors range from cream and yellow through orange and red, and there are bicolor combinations as well. Blossoms are typically single to semidouble, but double-flowered types are available, including 'Red Plume' and 'Yellow Plume' (both just 12 to 14 inches high).

Perennial *G. × grandiflora* blooms from early summer until frost, flaunting single or semidouble, 3- to 4-inch flowers on slender stems above clumps of gray-green, dandelionlike foliage. Flowers may be solid colored or bicolored; they typically have a dark center surrounded by red, maroon, or bronze petals tipped in yellow. Named selections vary in flower color and plant height. Among types reaching 2 to 3 feet in bloom are 'Dazzler', with yellow petals tipped in crimson; 'Torchlight', bearing yellow blossoms bordered with red; pure orange 'Tokajer'; 'Mandarin', with orange petals and a maroon center; wine red 'Burgundy'; and solid yellow 'Yellow Queen'. For front-of-the-border plants, look for foot-tall 'Goblin', with yellow-bordered red petals, and its all-yellow counterpart 'Goblin Yellow'. Shortest of all (to about 8 inches) is red-and-yellow 'Baby Cole'.

CULTURE. Blanket flowers need well-drained, preferably sandy to loam soil; in heavier, claylike soils, perennial kinds may rot over winter. To start either annuals or perennials from seed, sow indoors 4 to 6 weeks before the usual last-frost date. You also can sow seeds directly in the garden as soon as soil is workable in spring. Nursery plants of *G. × grandiflora* can be set out in early spring; when established clumps become crowded or show bare centers, divide in early spring. Or start new plants from stem cuttings taken in spring and early summer.

GAILLARDIA
BLANKET FLOWER
Asteraceae (Compositae)
PERENNIALS AND WARM-SEASON ANNUALS
ZONES 1–45; H1, H2
FULL SUN
MODERATE WATER
❀ ✿ ✿ ✿ FLOWERS IN SUMMER, FALL

Gaillardia × grandiflora 'Goblin'

GAURA lindheimeri

Onagraceae

PERENNIAL

ZONES 2B–35, 37, 38 (COASTAL), 39

FULL SUN

MODERATE WATER

❀ ✿ FLOWERS IN SPRING,
SUMMER, FALL

Gaura lindheimeri
'Siskiyou Pink'

Gaura doesn't put on a traffic-stopping display—but its grace, prolific spring-to-fall bloom, and toughness make it deserving of a spot in the garden. Numerous slender stems clothed in narrow, 3-inch leaves rise from a carrotlike taproot, forming a shrubby, vase-shaped plant 2 to 4 feet high and 3 feet across. In late spring, flower spikes rise above the foliage, bearing pink buds that open to starry white, 1-inch blossoms. Spikes open just a few flowers at a time, so established plants will give you the best show. Among selected forms, 3-foot-high **'Whirling Butterflies'** offers spikes of slightly larger, showier blossoms; **'Siskiyou Pink'** features maroon-mottled leaves and pink blooms that open from maroon buds; and 2½-foot **'Corrie's Gold'** has leaves conspicuously edged in gold.

CULTURE. Hailing from the dry Southwest, gaura handles adversity well. Give it deep, well-drained, preferably sandy to loam soil. (Where summers are hot, humid, and rainy, good drainage is essential.) This plant self-sows, sometimes to the point of being a nuisance; to curb this tendency, cut out spent flower stems. Gaura can remain in place indefinitely, and the deep taproot makes division difficult in any case. For additional plants, count on volunteer seedlings; or, to propagate named selections, take stem cuttings in summer.

GERANIUM

GERANIUM, CRANESBILL

Geraniaceae

PERENNIALS

ZONES VARY

FULL SUN OR LIGHT SHADE, EXCEPT
AS NOTED

REGULAR WATER

✿ ✿ ❀ ✿ FLOWERS IN SPRING,
SUMMER, FALL

Geranium × cantabrigiense
'Biokovo'

Not to be confused with *Pelargonium* (the well-known common and Martha Washington "geraniums"), these hardy true geraniums encompass an assortment of modestly pretty to frankly showy plants that remain attractive from spring through fall. In size and habit, they vary from ground-hugging spreaders to bushy 4-footers, but all have similar features: lobed, maplelike to finely cut leaves carried on long stalks; five-petaled flowers, circular in outline; and beaklike fruits that account for the common name "cranesbill." Flower colors range from subtle to vibrant; leaves of some species turn a striking orange to red in autumn. Specialty nurseries offer a great many species and named hybrids; those described below are among the most widely sold.

Among the lowest-growing geraniums is *G.* × *cantabrigiense* (Zones 1–24, 31–43), best known through two selections with ¾- to 1-inch-wide flowers: pink-tinged white **'Biokovo'** and bright bluish pink **'Cambridge'**. Both bloom from late spring to early summer. The dark green plants reach just 6 inches high but eventually spread widely, making a good small-scale ground cover. Another low, wide spreader is *G. cinereum* (Zones 1–24, 31–43), forming a dense, 8- to 12-inch-high mat of gray-green, deeply cut leaves. Appearing in early to midsummer, the pale pink, dark-veined flowers reach 1½ inches across; **'Ballerina'** has a longer season, bearing dark-centered lilac blossoms throughout summer and on into fall. *G. macrorrhizum* (Zones 1–24, 30–43) grows 8 to 10 inches high and spreads into sizable patches; lobed, pale green, 3- to 4-inch leaves offer good color in fall. Inch-wide white, pink, or magenta flowers bloom from spring through early summer. Selections include pink-flushed white **'Album'**, vibrant deep magenta **'Bevan's Variety'**, and soft lilac-pink **'Ingwersen's Variety'**.

The following three geraniums are all about 1 foot high. The hybrid *G.* **'Ann Folkard'** (Zones 2b–9, 14–24, 31–41) is a billowing, spreading plant to 5 feet across. Showy, 1½-inch magenta-purple flowers with black veins and centers bloom from spring into fall, set off nicely by the chartreuse to light green leaves. *G. himalayense* (*G. grandiflorum;* Zones 1–24, 31–43) is a spreading plant with deeply lobed medium green leaves that turn rich red in fall. It blooms from late spring into summer. The species has red-veined blue blossoms to about 2 inches in diameter; **'Plenum'**

('**Birch Double**') has lavender-blue double flowers. Hybrid **G. × *riversleaianum*** (Zones 2b–9, 14–24, 31–41) makes a broadly spreading, silvery green carpet dotted with ¾-inch flowers from late spring into fall. Two popular selections are soft pink **'Mavis Simpson'** and magenta **'Russell Prichard'**.

Geranium 'Johnson's Blue'

The remaining geraniums described here range from about 1½ feet high to as tall as 4 feet. **G. *clarkei* 'Kashmir White'** (Zones 2b–9, 14–24, 31–41) is a 2-footer with medium green, long-stalked leaves to 6 inches wide; it spreads widely by rhizomes. Pink-veined white, 1½-inch-wide flowers bloom from late spring into summer. **G. *endressii*** (Zones 1–9, 14–24, 31–43) is best known through its selection **'Wargrave Pink'**—a dense, bushy, 1½-foot-tall, mounding plant with soft light green leaves and vivid warm pink, 1½-inch flowers. It blooms from late spring into fall where summers are cool, from spring into early summer in hot-summer areas. The **G. *himalayense*** hybrid **G. 'Johnson's Blue'** (Zones 2–9, 14–24, 30–41) produces intense violet-blue, 2-inch flowers from spring to fall on a mounding, 1½-foot plant with deeply cut medium green leaves that, like those of the parent, turn vibrant red in autumn. Vigorous **G. × *oxonianum*** (Zones 2–9, 14–24, 30–41) is a *G. endressii* hybrid; best known is its selection **'Claridge Druce'**, a 2- to 3-foot plant with deeply cut gray-green leaves and cool lilac-pink, 1½-inch flowers in spring and early summer.

Mourning widow, **G. *phaeum*** (Zones 2b–9, 14–24, 32–41), is a bushy 2-footer bearing clusters of dark maroon or purple, ¾- to 1-inch blossoms from spring to fall; **'Samobor'** features white-centered maroon flowers and leaves with brown markings. **G. 'Philippe Vapelle'** (Zones 3–9, 14–24, 31–39), a rounded plant growing 1 to 1½ feet high, has gray-green foliage and blue-purple, 1¾-inch flowers from spring to midsummer. Meadow cranesbill, **G. *pratense*** (Zones 2–7, 14–24, 32–41), forms a bushy dark green clump to 2 feet high and 3 feet across. Blue, inch-wide flowers with red veins bloom in spring and early summer; fine selections are white **'Galactic'** and light blue **'Mrs. Kendall Clark'**. Reaching 4 feet high and wide, **G. *psilostemon*** (**G. *armeneum*;** Zones 2b–9, 14–24, 30–41) could fill in for a small shrub! The deep green leaves sometimes reach 8 inches across and turn flaming red in fall. Black-centered magenta, 1- to 1½-inch blossoms appear in early summer.

Geranium psilostemon

Geranium sanguineum striatum

Adaptable and easy-to-grow bloody cranesbill, **G. *sanguineum*** (Zones A2, A3; 1–9, 14–24, 30–45), reaches 2½ feet high and can spread to 3 feet or more; the deeply lobed dark green leaves turn bright red in fall. Blossoms about 1½ inches wide appear from spring into summer. Good selections include white **'Album'**, dark-veined pink **'John Elsley'**, red-purple **'Max Frei'**, and dark purple **'New Hampshire'**. A much lower version is **G. s. striatum (G. s. lancastriense);** it forms a spreading, 8-inch-high carpet decorated with salmon pink flowers.

CULTURE. These geraniums grow best where summers are cool to just mildly warm; in these climates, they'll thrive in full sun or light shade. For success in hotter-summer regions, be sure plants get filtered sunlight or light shade. They prefer moist, well drained, average to good soil. Set out plants in early to midspring—even late winter in mild-winter areas. Most can remain in place for many years before they become over-crowded and start to decline. When this occurs, dig, divide, and replant in early spring. If you want to increase an established planting, dig and transplant rooted portions from the edge of the clump.

ANNUAL AND PERENNIAL ORNAMENTAL GRASSES

Texture, color, height, graceful motion—when you plant ornamental grasses, you add all of these features to your garden. These plants highlight and enliven groups of more traditional annuals and perennials. And because their size range is so great (they vary from low tufts to giants reaching 8 feet or more), you'll find choices to use as edgings, combine with medium-size plants in a border, or plant as accents or focal points. Most are excellent for containers and cutting, as well. Many have variegated or colored foliage in addition to interesting flower heads; foliage and flowering stems often persist into autumn and winter, adding interest to the garden at a typically stark time of year.

Annual species complete their life cycle in a single year and require little maintenance. Perennial species need a bit more attention. Tidy up clumps in early spring before new growth begins, cutting back dead foliage; this is also the best time to divide crowded clumps and to set out new plants.

Note that a few annual and perennial ornamental grasses can be invasive, both in the garden and in nearby wild lands. Before trying a species new to you, ask suppliers whether it could cause problems in this regard.

ANNUAL GRASSES

Delicate, graceful rattlesnake or quaking grass, ***Briza maxima*** (Zones 1–45), grows 1 to 2 feet tall and has ¼-inchwide leaves to 6 inches long. It blooms in summer, bearing clusters of nodding, heart-shaped green spikelets that somewhat resemble rattlesnake rattles; they dangle from threadlike stems and quake in the lightest breeze. As the spikelets mature, they develop a purplish tinge, then eventually turn straw colored. Rattlesnake grass is valued for dried arrangements; cut the stems when green and hang them to dry, or cut them after they have dried on the plant.

Sow seed in place in the garden in spring, after the last-frost date. Choose a sunny spot with average, well-drained soil. Thin seedlings to stand a foot apart.

Two species of Natal ruby grass, ***Rhynchelytrum (Melinis)***, are usually grown as annuals. They succeed in all zones and may become perennials in mild-winter climates. Both form 1- by 1-foot clumps of narrow blue-green leaves that are erect, then arching. At bloom time, the clumps send up 2-foot spikes of flowers that open deep pink to purplish red, then gradually fade to light pinkish tan. A selection of ***R. nerviglume*** is sold as **'Pink Crystals'**; it blooms in late summer. ***R. repens*** is similar; it flowers in summer or early autumn (and may continue throughout winter in mild climates).

Sow seed indoors 6 to 8 weeks before the last frost. Set out seedlings in a full-sun location; soil type is not important, but drainage must be good. In the warm-winter climates where this grass is a perennial, plants are sometimes available in nurseries. Once these have put on some size, they can be divided in early spring to increase your plantings.

An annual grasslike plant popular in Victorian times is striped maize, ***Zea mays japonica*** (all zones). **'Variegata'**, with green leaves boldly striped in white, grows about 3 feet tall. **'Harlequin'**, to 4 feet high, has even showier foliage—it's striped in green, red (or pink), and cream. Both varieties

Briza maxima

Rhynchelytrum nerviglume
'Pink Crystals'   *Zea mays japonica*

are striking at the back of a border or massed as a focal point in a large bed of annuals.

Sow seed outdoors after the danger of frost has passed. Or sow indoors 6 weeks before the last-frost date, using individual peat pots to avoid root disturbance. Give plants full sun and well-drained soil enriched with organic matter. The plants may produce ears of corn; these are not edible, but they can be dried and used as decorations.

PERENNIAL GRASSES

Feather reed grass, *Calamagrostis × acutiflora,* succeeds in Zones 2b–24, 29–41. The well-known selection **'Karl Foerster'** (**'Stricta'**) has a strong vertical form, with narrow, reedlike, 1½- to 4-foot stems rising over lustrous deep green foliage. Flowering stems appear in early summer, growing to 6 feet high; they bear feathery purplish plumes that age to buff and remain attractive for much of the winter. **'Overdam'** is similar but has variegated foliage: each leaf has a central creamy white stripe. Clumps are compact and expand gradually. Feather reed grass is evergreen in milder climates, partially evergreen in colder regions. It rarely produces volunteer seedlings.

Calamagrostis × acutiflora 'Karl Foerster'

Choose a location in sun or partial shade. Performance is best with good soil and regular watering, but the plants will also grow in soil that is heavy, damp, and poorly drained.

Though members of the genus *Carex* are sedges rather than true grasses, their long, narrow leaves give them a grasslike appearance. Some species have striped or unusually colored foliage. Of the plants described here, all but *C. elata* 'Aurea' are evergreen. Leather leaf sedge, *C. buchananii* (Zones 2b–9, 14–24, 28–41), forms an upright, 2- to 3-foot clump of arching leaves that are slightly curled at the tips; foliage is a striking reddish bronze, offering a fine-textured color contrast to other plants. It needs moderate water. Bowles' golden sedge, *C. elata* **'Aurea'** (**'Bowles Golden'**; Zones 2–9, 14–24, 28–43), is just 2 feet tall, with an upright yet fountainlike habit. Its narrow leaves are brilliant yellow from spring well into summer, then turn green

Carex morrowii 'Variegata'

for the remainder of the season. Give it ample moisture. Variegated Japanese sedge, *C. morrowii* **'Variegata'** (Zones 3–9, 14–24, 28–32, warmer parts of 33), forms a 1-foot mound of drooping, green-and-white striped leaves. It does best with regular water.

Where summers are cool, grow these plants in full sun; in warmer areas, give them partial shade.

Tufted hair grass, *Deschampsia cespitosa* (Zones 2–24, 28–41), forms a 1- to 2-foot clump of narrow dark green leaves; it's evergreen in mild regions but goes dormant in colder climates. Delicate, arching, 3-foot stems bearing clouds of airy, green to greenish gold flower heads appear in early summer; the flowers persist into winter, turning straw colored as weather cools. Tufted hair grass prefers partial shade but will tolerate full sun where summers are cool. Provide regular moisture for the best performance.

The fescues form tight, tufted, evergreen clumps of narrow foliage. Nomenclature is confusing; you many find the following plants sold under different botanical names. Large blue fescue, *Festuca amethystina* (Zones 2–10, 14–24, 29–45), forms a clump of foot-tall, threadlike bluish green foliage; drooping flowering stems reach 2 feet high. The selection **'Superba'** has attractive amethyst pink flowers. Common blue fescue, *F. glauca* (*F. cinerea, F. ovina glauca;* Zones 1–24, 29–45), is available in a number of similar selections with foliage in various shades of blue; they grow from 8 to 12 inches tall, with the flowering stems reaching slightly higher.

Fescues tolerate partial shade in all regions and require it where summers are hot. Plant them in average, well-drained soil and provide moderate water.

TOP: *Deschampsia cespitosa*
BOTTOM: *Festuca glauca*

Miscanthus sinensis 'Cabaret'

Hakonechloa macra
'Aureola'

Japanese forest grass, ***Hakonechloa macra*** (Zones 2b–9, 14–24, 31–41), somewhat resembles a tiny bamboo. The widely grown variety '**Aureola**' has graceful, slender, lax or arching green leaves striped with gold; they reach about 1½ feet long. Foliage of '**All Gold**' is solid yellow. These grasses spread slowly by underground runners; they are dormant in winter. Plant in partial shade, in well-drained soil enriched with organic matter. Water regularly.

Blue oat grass, ***Helictotrichon sempervirens*** (Zones 1–24, 30–41), forms a 2- to 3-foot, evergreen fountain of narrow foliage in a bright blue gray. Small, straw-colored flower plumes appear in late spring, held a foot or two above the leaves on slim stems. This grass is clump forming and does not spread. Provide a full-sun location and well-drained, average to good soil; give

Helictotrichon sempervirens

moderate water. Poor drainage during the winter months can cause root rot.

Japanese blood grass, ***Imperata cylindrica*** '**Red Baron**' ('**Rubra**'), Zones 2b–24, 26, 28, 31–34, 39, is one of the most colorful ornamental grasses. Clumps of upright leaves grow 1 to 2 feet high; the top half of each leaf blade is red. The color is most intense in full sun and is especially striking if plants are located where sunlight can shine through the blades. Japanese blood grass

Imperata cylindrica
'Red Baron'

spreads slowly by underground runners. It is dormant in winter. Provide average to good soil; give moderate to regular water.

Eulalia grass, ***Miscanthus sinensis*,** grows in Zones 2–24, 29–41. The species and its many named selections all form tall, robust yet graceful clumps with stately flowering stems that rise well above the foliage in late summer or fall. Leaves and stems turn golden tan in winter, providing interest until you cut them down at cleanup time in early spring. One of the most compact selections is '**Yaku Jima**', a 2- to 3-footer with narrow green leaves and tan flower heads. '**Malepartus**', to 3 feet, has rose pink flower plumes borne on 6- to 7-foot stems; they appear earlier in the season than those of most selections. '**Strictus**', also known as porcupine grass, grows upright to 6 feet; it has coppery plumes and green leaves horizontally striped in white. '**Cabaret**' grows 6 to 7 feet tall and bears pink blossoms and broad green leaves with a creamy central stripe.

Whether planted in sun or light shade, eulalia grasses make dense clumps. Given moderate to regular water, they'll grow in any well-drained soil. The tallest varieties may need staking if grown in rich soil. In warm, moist regions with long growing seasons, varieties selected for early bloom may self-sow aggressively.

Purple moor grass, ***Molinia caerulea*** (Zones 1–9, 14–17, 32–41), forms a neat, dense, 1- to 2-foot-high clump. Narrow, spike-like clusters of yellowish to purplish flowers bloom in summer, rising 1 to 2 feet or more above the green foliage; the flowering stems are quite numerous, but they have a narrow structure that gives the clump an unusual see-through quality. The blossom clusters turn tan in fall and last until

Molinia caerulea arundinacea
'Skyracer'

late in the season, when both they and the leaves break off and blow away. A favorite selection of the subspecies **M. c. arundinacea** is **'Skyracer'**, with foliage clumps to 3 feet high and upright flowering stems reaching 7 to 8 feet.

Native to wet moorlands, these grasses prefer regular water and neutral to acid soil enriched with organic matter. Plant in full sun or light shade. They are long lived but slow growing, taking a few years to reach their full potential.

Native to the southern U. S. and Mexico, grasses in the genus **Muhlenbergia** are drought tolerant and sun loving.

Pennisetum orientale   *Stipa gigantea*

Muhlenbergia emersleyi

Most are large and showy, standing out in the garden whether used as specimens or planted in groups. They are evergreen in mild winters, though they turn tan or brown with hard freezes. Bull grass, **M. emersleyi** (Zones 2–24, 30, 33, 35), forms a 1½-foot-tall, 3-foot-wide mound of glossy green leaves; in summer and fall, spikes of purplish or reddish flowers rise 2 to 3 feet above the foliage. Purple muhly, **M. rigida** (Zones 6–24, 30, 33), forms a clump 2 feet high and wide; its 3-foot spikes of brownish to deep purple flowers appear in late summer and fall. Plant these grasses in well-drained, average soil. They will survive in dry conditions but look better and grow larger if given supplemental water.

Panicum virgatum

Switch grass, **Panicum virgatum** (Zones 1–11, 14–23, 28–43), native to the tall grass prairie of the Midwest, forms an upright clump of narrow leaves. In summer, the foliage clump is topped by slender flower clusters opening into loose, airy clouds of pinkish blossoms that age to

white and finally to brown. Clumps reach 4 to 7 feet when in bloom. Foliage turns yellow in fall, gradually fading to beige. Both foliage and flowers persist all winter. The 4-foot-tall selection **'Hänse Herms'** is grown for its red fall foliage; **'Heavy Metal'**, with metallic blue foliage, forms a stiffly upright clump to 5 feet high. Switch grasses are easy to grow, tolerating wet or dry soil and flourishing in both full sun and partial shade.

The fountain grasses, belonging to the genus **Pennisetum**, form graceful clumps of gently arching leaves; slender stems carrying furry, foxtail-like flower plumes rise above the foliage in summer. Hardiest is 4-foot-tall **P. alopecuroides** (Zones 2b–24, 31–35, 37, 39), with bright green leaves and pinkish plumes. Its leaves turn yellow in fall, brown in winter. The selection **'Hameln'** is more compact (to just 1 to 1½ feet); its white plumes are carried on stems to 3 feet tall. **'Moudry'** bears dramatic black plumes that rise to about 3 feet, held above a 2-foot clump of glossy foliage. *P. alopecuroides* and its varieties may self-sow to some extent, but they are usually not weedy—with the exception of 'Moudry', which self-seeds heavily and can be weedy.

Oriental fountain grass, **P. orientale** (Zones 3–10, 14–24, 31–35, 37, 39), forms a dense, rounded, 1½-foot clump of narrow gray-green leaves that turn straw colored in fall. The fuzzy pink flowers arch a foot or more above the foliage.

Plant fountain grasses in sun or light shade, in average soil; provide regular water.

Giant feather grass, **Stipa gigantea** (Zones 4–9, 14–24, 29–34, 39), forms 2- to 3-foot-tall clumps of narrow, arching leaves. During the summer bloom season, it lives up to its name, producing stems up to 6 feet high that carry large, open, airy sheaves of yellowish flowers that shimmer in the breeze. This stately grass is evergreen in mild climates. Give it full sun and good soil. Water regularly when young; established plants will take some drought.

GOMPHRENA

GLOBE AMARANTH

Amaranthaceae

WARM-SEASON ANNUALS AND PERENNIALS
GROWN AS ANNUALS

ZONES 1–45; H1, H2

FULL SUN OR PARTIAL SHADE

MODERATE WATER

✿❀✿✿✿ FLOWERS IN
SUMMER, FALL

Reveling in the heat of summer and early fall, globe amaranths make a bright splash—both in garden beds and in containers. They're also good cut flowers for fresh as well as dried arrangements. The more common species is **G. globosa,** an upright 2-footer with narrowly oval, 2- to 4-inch leaves and ½-inch flower heads that look like clover. Colors include purple, red, pink, lavender, and white. You can buy seeds of specific colors as well as named selections such as **'Lavender Lady'** and red **'Strawberry Fields'.** Dwarf selections, growing just 8 to 10 inches high, include purple **'Buddy',** white **'Cissy',** and rosy purple **'Gnome'.**

Technically a perennial but generally grown as an annual, **G. haageana** produces orange-and-yellow flowers resembling inchwide pinecones; selections with flowers in red and apricot are sometimes available. Like *G. globosa,* this species is an upright, 2-foot-tall plant.

CULTURE. Globe amaranths prefer well-drained, sandy to loam soil. Sow seeds in place after all danger of frost is past. For an earlier start, sow indoors 4 to 6 weeks before the last-frost date.

Gomphrena globosa
'Lavender Lady'

GYPSOPHILA paniculata

BABY'S BREATH

Caryophyllaceae

PERENNIAL

ZONES A2, A3; 1–10, 14–16, 18–21,
31–45; H1

FULL SUN

MODERATE WATER

❀✿ FLOWERS IN SUMMER

Bearing a summertime froth of small flowers that almost appear to float in midair, baby's breath is a much-branched, rounded plant reminiscent of a tumbleweed, its stems set rather sparsely with narrow leaves. In the garden, it's used as an airy filler—the role it also plays in bouquets. The basic species grows about 3 feet high and wide, with white, ⅛-inch single flowers. More popular are a number of showier cultivars. **'Bristol Fairy',** reaching 3 to 4 feet, is the classic double-flowered white baby's breath, bearing flowers about ¼ inch wide. **'Perfecta',** the florists' favorite, is about the same size but features ½-inch double blossoms. **'Compacta Plena'** is a double-flowered white form just 1½ feet tall. Other short cultivars, all with double pink flowers, include **'Pink Fairy'** (1½ to 2 feet high and wide), **'Pink Star'** (to 1½ feet), and **'Viette's Dwarf'** (12 to 15 inches). **Double Snowflake** and **Early Snowball** are seed strains that produce 3-foot plants with double white flowers.

CULTURE. This taprooted plant needs deep, well-drained, nonacid soil; if soil is acid, add lime to neutralize it (the name *Gypsophila* can be roughly translated as "lime loving"). If you want the plant to remain spherical, provide some sort of support (see page 73) to counteract the flattening effects of overhead watering, rain, and wind. Once planted, baby's breath is a permanent plant that never needs dividing or replanting.

Note: In coastal parts of the Great Lakes region, baby's breath has naturalized and become invasive, crowding out native vegetation. If you live in this area, check with your Cooperative Extension Office or a local nursery before you plant.

Gypsophila paniculata 'Bristol Fairy'

HELENIUM

SNEEZEWEED

Asteraceae (Compositae)

PERENNIAL

ZONES 1–45

FULL SUN

REGULAR WATER

✿✿✿ FLOWERS IN SUMMER, FALL

Bright daisies in autumnal colors light up the garden from midsummer well into fall—a time when many other flowers are on the wane. Each 1- to 2-inch blossom has a nearly spherical yellow or brown center that sits on a "wheel" of notched petals. Most widely available are hybrids (often sold—incorrectly—as selections of **H. autumnale**). These are available in specific colors and in sizes ranging from 2 to nearly 5 feet; all are upright, branching plants with narrow, linear leaves. At the short end of the height scale is **'Crimson Beauty',** with bronzy red flowers on a 2- to 3-foot plant. Reaching 3 feet or a bit taller are **'Butterpat',** with solid yellow blooms; dark-centered mahogany **'Moerheim Beauty';** and brown-centered yellow **'Wyndley'.** Taller cultivars (4 to 5 feet high) are **'Baudirektor Linne'** (brownish red with brown center), **'Riverton Beauty'** (tawny gold with brown center), and **'Waldtraut'** (coppery brown with dark center).

CULTURE. Sneezeweeds turn in their best performance in hot-summer climates, with average soil and regular watering. They bloom more profusely if you're stingy with fertilizer. Taller kinds may need staking. Clumps become crowded fairly quickly; dig and divide every 2 or 3 years in early spring.

Helenium 'Moerheim Beauty'

HELIANTHUS
SUNFLOWER
Asteraceae (Compositae)
PERENNIALS AND WARM-SEASON ANNUALS
ZONES VARY
FULL SUN
REGULAR WATER
❀ ✿ ✿ ✿ FLOWERS IN SUMMER, FALL

The annual sunflower is recognized all around the world: a big, dark disk surrounded by a single row of yellow petals. Native to central North America, it is grown worldwide for its edible seeds and the oil they produce. Both the familiar annual species and the perennial types have the same general appearance: brash blossoms on coarse, upright plants with oval, sandpapery leaves. All bloom in summer and autumn.

The classic yellow annual sunflower, *H. annuus* (all zones), includes the familiar yellow-flowered plants of towering size—traditional seed-producing sunflowers such as **'Kong'**, **'Mammoth Russian'**, and **'Russian Giant'**, all reaching at least 10 feet high and bearing foot-wide (or larger!) blossoms with short petals and broad disks. (**'Sunspot'** is a much shorter version, with 10-inch flowers on a plant just 2 to 2½ feet tall.)

Plant breeders have also produced an assortment of smaller cultivars in a wider color range, intended more for simple garden ornament and cut flowers than for seed crops. Among these, most of the following bear 4- to 8-inch-wide flowers. Pollenless kinds (generally classed as *H. × hybridus*) are better for cutting, since they won't shed pollen on furniture. The **Large Flowered Mix** features yellow, red, and bronze flowers on 6- to 10-foot plants. Among named cultivars are 4- to 7-foot **'Bright Bandolier'** (yellow-and-mahogany bicolor), 5- to 7-foot **'Cinnamon Sun'** (rosy bronze), and 6- to 8-foot **'Velvet Queen'** (bicolor combination of brown and wine red). Deep garnet **'Prado Red'** reaches only 4 feet; light yellow **'Valentine'** grows no more than 5 feet tall.

In the pollen-bearing category of *H. annuus*, **Parasol Mix** gives yellow, orange, red, and bicolored blossoms on 4- to 5-foot plants; **'Soraya'**, to 6 feet, has dark-centered orange blooms. For pale colors, try 5-foot **'Italian White'** (cream to nearly white), 4-foot **'Moonshadow'** (pale yellow to cream), and 4- to 6-foot **'Lemon Eclair'** (light yellow). **'Indian Blanket'** grows 4 to 5 feet tall and bears blossoms with yellow-tipped red petals. **'Pacino'**, reaching only 2½ feet high, bears 8-inch-wide yellow flowers with yellow centers. **'Teddy Bear'** is smaller still, with fully double, bright yellow, 6-inch-wide flowers on 1½-foot plants.

Perennial sunflowers may have single, semidouble, or double blossoms, but the color is always yellow. Best known is *H. × multiflorus* (Zones 1–24, 28–43), a hybrid group of narrow, bushy plants to about 5 feet high. **'Loddon Gold'** (**'Flore Pleno'**) has fully double, 4-inch blossoms. Lemon yellow **'Capenoch Star'** has 4-inch-wide single blooms—but its disk flowers are rolled into tubes, giving the blossom's center a pincushionlike look. (Nurseries sometimes offer the above as selections of *H. decapetalus*.) Another noteworthy perennial is 8-foot-tall willowleaf sunflower, *H. salicifolius* (*H. orgyalis;* Zones 1–24, 28–43), with narrow, 8-inch, gracefully drooping leaves and dark-centered, 2-inch flowers in branched clusters.

CULTURE. All sunflowers perform best with good soil and regular watering. Plant the large seeds of annual sunflower directly in the garden after all danger of frost is past. Thin plants to 1½ feet apart; stake the tallest, seed-producing kinds as flower heads form. Set out young perennial plants in early spring. They increase fairly rapidly; you'll need to dig and divide clumps every 3 to 4 years in early spring.

TOP: *Helianthus* 'Velvet Queen'
BOTTOM: *Helianthus* × *multiflorus*
'Capenoch Star'

Helichrysum bracteatum

HELICHRYSUM
Asteraceae (Compositae)
WARM-SEASON ANNUALS AND PERENNIALS
USUALLY TREATED AS ANNUALS
ZONES VARY
FULL SUN
MODERATE WATER
✿ ❀ ✿ ✿ ✿ FLOWERS IN SUMMER, FALL

Helichrysum petiolare 'Limelight'

The two helichrysums discussed here are strikingly different plants—one is a staple for dried flower arrangements, the other an invaluable filler for container plantings.

Annual strawflower, **H. bracteatum** (all zones), is probably the most popular flower for use in everlasting arrangements. What appear to be petals are actually papery bracts (modified leaves) surrounding a central disk of true flowers; the flower head resembles a prickly, pompomlike double daisy with flat to incurved petals. The plant grows upright to 3 feet tall and 1 foot wide, with medium green, straplike leaves to 5 inches long. About 2½-inch-wide flowers in a range of bright colors bloom from summer until frost. Though fine in fresh bouquets, they're much more widely used in their dried form—in which they can remain "fresh" for well over a year. Various named strains are available, featuring mixed pastels, mixed bright colors, and individual colors. Dwarf types, such as **Bright Bikini** and **Dwarf Spangle**, reach just 1 foot high.

Licorice plant, **H. petiolare,** can be perennial in Zones 16, 17, 22–24, but it grows so rapidly it is usually treated as an annual in all zones. Lax stems bear rounded, inch-long grayish green leaves with a woolly white coating; tiny flowers are inconspicuous. Where the growing season is long, the plant can reach 1½ to 3 feet high and spread to 4 feet. It's most often used in combination with other plants; you'll see it spilling from mixed container plantings or meandering through the foreground of a border. Several cultivars vary in foliage color, though all retain the woolly white coating. **'Limelight'** has light chartreuse leaves; **'Licorice Splash'** is variegated in yellow and green; **'Variegatum'** has green-and-white variegation.

CULTURE. Both species need well-drained, light to medium soil and moderate watering. Set out plants of *H. petiolare* after danger of frost is past. Where plants will be killed by frosts, take stem cuttings in late summer; then overwinter the started plants indoors for planting out the next year. To grow *H. bracteatum* in mild-winter regions, sow seeds outdoors at any time after the danger of frost is past. In colder regions, sow outdoors after weather has warmed; or sow indoors 6 to 8 weeks before the last-frost date, preferably at a temperature of 65 to 70°F/18 to 21°C. Indoors or out, simply press seeds onto the soil surface, but do not cover them; they need light for germination. Tall kinds may need staking to remain upright.

HELLEBORUS
HELLEBORE
Ranunculaceae
PERENNIALS
ZONES VARY
PARTIAL TO FULL SHADE, EXCEPT AS NOTED
REGULAR WATER, EXCEPT AS NOTED
✿ ❀ ✿ ✿ ✿ FLOWERS IN WINTER,
EARLY SPRING

Elegant plants with an air of understated sophistication, the hellebores flower in winter and early spring—a time when not much else is in bloom, and their beauty is especially appreciated. All bear blossoms consisting of five petal-like sepals surrounding a large cluster of stamens; they look a bit like single roses, a fact reflected in the common names of several species. Each long-stalked leaf is composed of large, leathery leaflets grouped together like fingers on an outstretched hand.

Two growth habits are possible. Most hellebores form tight clumps with leafstalks seeming to rise directly from the ground; separate (typically leafless) flower stems arise from the same growing points. These are the *acaulescent* types. A few species and hybrids—the *caulescent* types—form clumps of stems set with leaves all along their length; the stems produce dome-shaped flower clusters at their tips, then die back as new stems rise from the ground.

The caulescent group includes the largest species: Corsican hellebore, **H. argutifolius (H. corsicus;** Zones 3b–9, 14–24, 31, 32), an almost shrublike plant with numerous stems rising to as high as 3 feet. Each pale blue-green leaf has three leaflets with sharply toothed edges. In milder zones, the light chartreuse, 2-inch flowers may appear in late fall or winter; in colder areas, bloom comes in early spring. Unlike the other hellebores, this one will take some sun; it is also fairly drought-tolerant once established. Bear's-foot hellebore, **H. foetidus** (Zones 2b–9, 14–24, 30–34, 39), bears the most graceful foliage of the group, with each leafstalk carrying 7 to 11 narrow, blackish green leaflets. In late winter and early spring, clusters of inch-wide, purple-marked green flowers appear atop leafy, 1½-foot stems. In the **Wester Flisk** strain, all plant parts are strikingly infused with red. **H. × sternii** (Zones 4–9, 14–24, 31, 32) is a hybrid group derived from *H. argutifolius* and another, similar species. Plants have bluish green leaves netted with white or cream; pink-tinted greenish flowers to 2 inches wide come in winter to early spring, carried on stems to about 2 feet tall.

Helleborus argutifolius

Among the acaulescent types, Christmas rose, **H. niger** (Zones 1–7, 14–17, 32–45), is the first to bloom. Depending on the severity of the winter, flowers can appear from early winter to early spring. Each leafless, 1½-foot stem usually holds one upward-facing flower to 2 inches across; the blossoms open white, then age to purplish pink. Dark green, lusterless leaves have seven to nine leaflets. Blooms of **'Potter's Wheel'** have a conspicuous green center; **'White Magic'** has white flowers that blush pink with age. **Sunrise** (with pink-infused flowers) and **Sunset** (near-red) are two seed strains available as both seeds and plants.

Lenten rose, **h. orientalis** (Zones 2b–10, 14–24, 31–41), is an easy-to-grow plant that resembles *H. niger* but blooms a bit later, from the end of winter into spring. Each 1- to 1½-foot stem bears a few modified leaves and branched clusters of nodding, 2- to 3-inch, downward-facing flowers. Colors range from greenish or buff-tinted white through pinkish tones to maroon and liver purple; blossoms frequently show dark spots in the center or a freckling of spots overall. Leaves have 5 to 11 broad, glossy leaflets. Many plants sold as *H. orientalis* actually are hybrids—derived in large part from *H. orientalis* but also involving other, similar species. In plant, flower, and zone adaptation, these hybrids are similar to *H. orientalis,* but they have a wider range of blossom colors and patterns, including near-yellow, blackish red, mauve gray, and various color combinations with contrasting dotting.

Helleborus foetidus

CULTURE. Though established plants of *H. argutifolius* and *H. foetidus* withstand some drought and prosper with just moderate water, all hellebores appreciate good, organically enriched soil and regular watering. Choose a planting spot in filtered sun to partial or full shade (*H. argutifolius* will also take full sun). Clumps can remain in place indefinitely with no need for division. You can, however, divide clumps in early spring—but divisions reestablish slowly, and some of them may not survive. An easier way to increase a planting is to transplant volunteer seedlings. Keep in mind that seedlings' flowers may differ somewhat from those of the parent plants.

In the hands of dedicated amateur and professional breeders, the old yellow or orange daylily has been transformed: today's hybrids offer a dazzling color array (including patterns of two or more colors), increased petal width and thickness, and, in some cases, blossoms that remain open well into the evening or even overnight. In size, plants range from foot-high miniatures to giants that can hit 6 feet when in bloom. But all produce linear, arching leaves in flat sprays that account for another of this plant's common names—"corn lily."

Daylilies may be deciduous, semievergreen, or evergreen. Deciduous types die back completely in winter and are the hardiest, withstanding −35°F/−37°C with little

HEMEROCALLIS
DAYLILY
Liliaceae
PERENNIALS
ZONES 1–45; H1, H2
FULL SUN, EXCEPT AS NOTED
REGULAR WATER
✿✿✿✿✿ FLOWERS IN SPRING, SUMMER, FALL

TOP: *Hemerocallis* 'Oodnadatta'
BOTTOM: *Hemerocallis* 'Black-eyed Stella'

or no snow protection; in mild-winter regions, however, they may not get enough chill for top performance. Evergreen kinds grow well in both mild and cold regions but need a protective winter mulch where temperatures normally dip below −20°F/−29°C. Semievergreen types are intermediate between the other two in hardiness; some perform better than others where winters are mild.

The majority of daylily hybrids reach 2½ to 4 feet high in bloom. Carried on stems that branch near the top, the blossoms are lily or chalice shaped, in widths ranging from 3 to 8 inches (1½ to 3 inches in smaller and miniature types). A typical flower has six overlapping, petal-like segments, but there are also double kinds (with an indeterminate number of segments) and spider types with long, narrow segments that are frequently twisted. Though each flower lasts just one day, stems produce many buds that open sequentially over a long period. Flowering typically runs from midspring into early summer—but cultivars bloom at the beginning, middle, or end of this period, so if you choose carefully, you can enjoy an extended display. Scattered bloom may also come in summer, and some cultivars reliably rebloom in fall. A few types flower throughout the growing season, notably the 2-foot-tall **'Stella de Oro'** and **'Happy Returns'** (both yellow), **'Black-eyed Stella'** (yellow with red eye), and **'Pardon Me'** (red).

A few daylilies are fragrant. The old favorite **'Hyperion'**, a 4-footer with yellow blooms, is notably sweet scented, as is **_H. lilioasphodelus (H. flavus)_**, the lemon daylily, with 3-foot stems and pure yellow blossoms.

CULTURE. Few perennials are as easy to grow as daylilies, but extra attention reaps rewards. Plant in well-drained, organically amended, average to good soil. Full sun is best, but partial shade is a good idea where summers are hot and dry. Set out bare-root plants in fall or early spring, or plant from containers at any time during the growing season. Water regularly throughout the growing season. Divide clumps when they become crowded—usually every 3 to 6 years, though reblooming types should be divided every 2 or 3 years. In hot-summer regions, do the job in fall or early spring; in areas with cool summers or a short growing season, divide in summer.

HEUCHERA
(and × HEUCHERELLA)
CORAL BELLS, ALUM ROOT
Saxifragaceae
PERENNIALS
ZONES VARY
FULL SUN, EXCEPT AS NOTED
MODERATE TO REGULAR WATER
❀✿✿ FLOWERS IN SPRING, SUMMER, FALL

Heuchera sanguinea

Coral bells are old-fashioned favorites, long prized for their good-looking foliage and graceful spikes of showy flowers. And in recent years, hybrids and selections of species with quite understated blossoms have become popular for their strikingly attractive leaves. Whether grown for flowers, foliage, or both, all kinds have nearly round to heart-shaped leaves on long leafstalks and form low, mounded clumps that gradually spread as the woody rootstocks branch and elongate. Leaves are typically hairy and may have scalloped margins and decorative dark or silvery mottling. Wiry, branching stems rise above the leaves, bearing open clusters of small, bell-shaped blossoms.

Of the showy-flowered kinds, the hybrid **_H. × brizoides_** (Zones 1–10, 14–24, 31–45) has spawned a number of named cultivars. The rounded leaves are shallowly lobed, with scalloped edges; flowers in white, pink shades, and red come in spring or summer on 1- to 2½-foot-tall stems. Representative are **'Firefly' ('Leuchtkäfer')**, with fragrant scarlet flowers; rosy pink **'Freedom'**; white **'June Bride'**; and **'Snowstorm'**, with reddish pink flowers and white-variegated leaves. The seed-grown **Bressingham Hybrids** offer the full color range of white through pink to red; some have been named, including **'Bressingham White'**.

H. sanguinea (Zones A1–A3; 1–11, 14–24, 31–45) is a favorite from times past. Round, scallop-edged green leaves are 1 to 2 inches across; nodding bells in bright red to coral pink bloom from spring into summer, carried on stems that reach 1 to 2 feet high. Selections are available with blooms in white, pure pink, and red shades. Two red-flowered varieties are **'Cherry Splash'**, with foliage variegated in white and gold, and **'Frosty'**, with silver leaf variegation.

Good choices for gardeners in the western U.S. are hybrids of *H. sanguinea* with Western native species. The following three succeed in Zones 14–24. All bloom from spring through summer and into fall and are somewhat drought tolerant. **'Santa Ana Cardinal'** has light green, 3- to 4-inch leaves that make a sizable foliage mound; massive clusters of bright rosy red flowers come on 2- to 3-foot stems. **'Genevieve'** has pink-centered white bells and gray-mottled, 2- to 3-inch leaves, while **'Wendy'** has peachy pink blossoms and lightly mottled light green leaves 3 to 4 inches wide.

H. sanguinea hybrids belonging to the spring-blooming **Canyon Series** grow in Zones 2–11, 14–24. Medium green, 1½-inch leaves form matlike mounds to 6 inches high and 2 feet across. Red **'Canyon Belle'**, rosy **'Canyon Delight'**, and **'Canyon Pink'** have 20-inch stems; smaller overall, with 1-foot stems, are **'Canyon Chimes'**, **'Canyon Duet'**, and **'Canyon Melody'**, all with pink-and-white blossoms.

Two species account for the growing number of coral bells with showy foliage. **H. americana** (Zones 1–9, 14–24, 32–43), a mounding plant to 2 feet high, has green leaves to 4 inches across with attractive silver-and-white veining and mottling. Tiny greenish white flowers appear in early summer on thread-thin stems to 3 feet tall. Many of this species' cultivars feature purple leaves variously flushed and veined in silver; these include **'Chocolate Veil'**, **'Persian Carpet'**, **'Pewter Veil'**, **'Plum Pudding'**, and **'Ruby Veil'**. **'Ring of Fire'** has maroon-veined silver leaves that turn red at the edges in cold weather. **'Chocolate Ruffles'** (chocolate above, wine red beneath) and **'Velvet Night'** (bluish purple) are dramatic solid-colored choices.

H. micrantha (Zones 1–10, 14–24, 31–43) is best known in its form (or hybrid) **'Palace Purple'**, with maplelike, brownish to purplish, 3-inch leaves that color best in sun. This is now a seed strain, so color saturation will vary. In late spring and early summer, tiny greenish white flowers come on red-tinged 2-foot stems.

The plants known as × **Heucherella** (Zones 1–10, 14–24, 31–45) are a group of hybrids between *Heuchera* × *brizoides* and related *Tiarella* species. All form mounded, foot-wide clumps of heart-shaped to maplelike, hairy leaves that send up wiry spikes of tiny, starlike pink flowers. Widely available × **H. alba 'Bridget Bloom'**, to 16 inches high, flowers from spring to midsummer. **'Pink Frost'**, to 2 feet, blooms from spring to fall.

CULTURE. Give *Heuchera* and × *Heucherella* well-drained soil enriched with organic matter. Plants prefer full sun except where summers are hot and dry; in those areas, they need light or partial shade, especially in the afternoon. Moderate to regular watering is suitable for *Heuchera*; × *Heucherella* does best with regular moisture. Clumps become crowded after 3 or 4 years, with the foliage clustered at the ends of short, thick, woody stalks. Divide crowded clumps in early spring (in fall, where winters are mild), replanting divisions so crowns are even with the soil surface.

Heuchera × *brizoides*

× *Heucherella alba* 'Bridget Bloom'

Flamboyant rose-mallow brings a touch of the tropics to temperate gardens. Blossoms reminiscent of giant morning glories (up to a foot wide) decorate upright, shrubby plants that can reach as tall as 8 feet in the basic species. The oval leaves, dark green above and nearly white beneath, are correspondingly large—to 10 inches long and 4 inches wide. Bloom begins in early summer and continues until frost, after which stems die to the ground.

Named cultivars come in specific colors. The following choices are all about 4 feet tall. Sporting 10-inch flowers are pure white **'Blue River'**, **'George Riegel'** (ruffled

HIBISCUS moscheutos
ROSE-MALLOW
Malvaceae
PERENNIAL
ZONES 2–24, 26–41; H1
FULL SUN, EXCEPT AS NOTED
REGULAR WATER
❀✿✿ FLOWERS IN SUMMER, FALL

Hibiscus moscheutos

HOSTA

HOSTA, PLANTAIN LILY
Liliaceae
PERENNIALS
ZONES 1–10, 14–21, 28, 31–45,
  EXCEPT AS NOTED
PARTIAL TO FULL SHADE, EXCEPT AS NOTED
REGULAR WATER
✿ ❀ FLOWERS IN LATE SPRING, SUMMER;
  MOST ARE GROWN PRIMARILY FOR
  FOLIAGE IN BLUE, GREEN, YELLOW, AND
  VARIEGATED COMBINATIONS

Hosta fortunei

pink with red center), and dark red **'Lord Baltimore'**. **'Turn of the Century'** boasts 5- to 10-inch pink-and-white flowers with red centers; **'Lady Baltimore'** and **'The Clown'** have 8-inch-wide pink blossoms centered in red.

Seed strains offer shorter plants with 8- to 12-inch-wide flowers in white, pink, and red, often with red centers. **Southern Belle** grows 4 feet high; **Disco Belle, Frisbee,** and **Rio Carnival** reach only 2½ feet. You can sometimes find specific color selections of these; Disco Belle, for example, is available in white and pink.

CULTURE. Rich soil and plenty of water help these plants achieve full magnificence. Liberally amend the soil with organic matter before planting; mulch to conserve moisture. Avoid planting in windswept locations where leaves and flowers will burn. Where summers are hot and dry, give plants a bit of afternoon shade to prevent wilting. Fertilize plants every 6 to 8 weeks during the growing season. Clumps gradually increase in size but do not need division for good performance. You can start new plants from stem cuttings taken in summer. To raise from seed, sow indoors 6 to 8 weeks before the last-frost date; plants may flower the first year from seed.

Though hostas bear spikes of modest trumpet-shaped flowers in spring and summer, the blossoms pale in significance when weighed against the season-long show of exceptionally handsome foliage. Named cultivars and species offer a bewildering assortment of colors, markings, and shapes. Leaves may be lance shaped, heart shaped, oval, or nearly round, with smooth or gracefully undulating margins; the surface may be smooth, quilted looking, or puckered, either glossy or dusted with a grayish bloom like that on the skin of a plum. Colors range from light to dark green to chartreuse, near-yellow, and virtually blue; you will also find color combinations, including variegations with white, cream, or yellow.

The leaves are carried on long stalks that rise from the ground, radiating from a central point; plants increase to form tight clumps. In some hostas, the clump has an elegant vase shape, but most make mounds of leaves that overlap like shingles. In size, plants range from demure 4- to 6-inch specimens to showpiece types that can reach 3 to 4 feet high with equal or greater spread. Flowers come in white or purple shades; they rise well above the foliage in some kinds but barely show in others. Some are pleasantly fragrant.

Hosta specialists offer a dazzling array of cultivars, and even well-stocked nurseries may carry quite a range of sizes and colors. Even so, there are a number of tried-and-true, widely available plants that are good, inexpensive choices for the neophyte. One word of caution: the names of many hosta species have been changed over the years, with the result that the same plant may go by one name in older references, by another in more recent ones.

Hosta species. The following six species are long-time garden favorites; they and their selected forms offer a sampler of these plants' variability.

Plants sold as ***H. fortunei*** (Zones A1–A3; 1–10, 14–21, 28, 31–45) may actually be hybrids involving *H. sieboldiana* (see facing page). Many named selections are sold, in colors ranging from gray green to yellow green to variegated combinations. Leaves are typically broadly heart shaped, up to a foot long; they form clumps to 2 feet high and somewhat wider. Lilac flowers bloom on stems to 3 feet tall. **'Albo-marginata'** has dark green leaves with a creamy white margin; ***H. f. hyacinthina*** features slightly puckered gray-green leaves thinly edged in white.

As the name indicates, ***H. lancifolia*** has narrow leaves—dark green, about 6 inches long, tapering to long leafstalks. The entire clump mounds to about 1 foot.

Outward-facing lavender flowers come on 2-foot stalks. Fragrant plantain lily, **H. plantaginea,** offers scented, 4-inch white flowers on short spikes rising just above a 2-foot-high foliage mound. Leaves are typically quilted-looking, bright apple green ovals to 10 inches long.

H. sieboldiana (H. glauca) is a big plant with puckered, broadly heart-shaped blue-green leaves that can reach 15 inches long; an established clump may reach 2½ feet high, 4 feet or more wide. The small flowers are palest lavender, barely showing above the leaves. **'Elegans'** has foliage covered with a gray-blue bloom; its sport **'Frances Williams'** adds a broad chartreuse edge to the leaves, while another sport, **'Great Expectations'**, features a creamy flame pattern in the center of each leaf.

The appropriately named **H. undulata** has narrow, oval, 8-inch leaves with undulating margins; it forms lively-looking clumps about 1½ feet high. The species has green leaves with a white central stripe; **H. u. albo-marginata** has green leaves with a white margin, while **H. u. erromena** features solid green foliage. Blue plantain lily, **H. ventricosa,** forms a mound to 2 feet tall of deep green, 8-inch-long, deeply veined leaves with a broad heart shape. Showy blue-violet blossoms are carried on 3-foot stems above the foliage. **'Aureomarginata'** has leaves margined in creamy white.

Hosta hybrids. The majority of available named hostas fall into this group. Among proven performers, **'Blue Angel'** makes an impressive clump to 4 feet high and 5 feet wide; the broadly heart-shaped, steel blue leaves have a veined, corrugated surface. White flowers come on 4- to 5-foot stems. **'Francee'**, forming a clump to 1½ feet high, has rich green, broadly oval leaves with a crisp white margin; light lavender blossoms appear above the foliage. In its sport **'Patriot'**, the white leaf margins are much wider. **'Ginko Craig'** forms a 7- to 12-inch mound of narrow dark green leaves edged in white; lavender flowers are held above the foliage. **'Halcyon'** has foliage in a fetching silvery blue, the heart-shaped and deeply veined leaves making an arching clump to about 15 inches high. Bluish lilac blossoms are carried several inches above the foliage.

'Honeybells' has deeply veined, wavy-edged, oval bright green leaves in a clump to 2½ feet high; pale lilac blooms come on 3-foot stems. **'Krossa Regal'** is an elegant vase-shaped plant to about 2½ feet high, with lance-shaped, powdery blue gray leaves on long stalks; spikes of lavender flowers can rise to 5 feet. **'Sum and Substance'** forms a massive mound—to 3 feet high and 5 feet across—of chartreuse, very broadly heart-shaped leaves to 20 inches long. Lavender blossoms appear just above the foliage.

CULTURE. All hostas grow most luxuriantly in good, organically enriched soil, with regular moisture and periodic feeding during the growing season. They are, however, tough and durable enough to take leaner diets and occasional lapses in watering, though growth in such conditions will of course be less impressive. They perform best in regions with frosty or freezing winters followed by humid summers.

In general, hostas prefer a spot in partial or even full shade, though they'll also take sun where summers are cool and humid. Plants with a considerable amount of white or yellow in their leaves tend to be the most sun sensitive. The more sun a hosta receives, the more compact it will be and the more flowers it will produce; grown in shade, the same plant is likely to be taller and broader.

Watch for snails and slugs, which zero in on hosta leaves, especially emerging new growth. Cultivars with a waxy "bloom" on the leaves are more resistant to slug and snail damage. Foliage of all hostas collapses and withers after frosts.

Hostas are permanent perennials, remaining vigorous without periodic division—and in fact, they gain in beauty as they put on size. To increase your supply of a favorite plant, carefully remove rooted pieces from the clump's perimeter; or cut a wedge-shaped piece from the clump and transplant it (the resulting gap will fill in quickly).

Hosta sieboldiana 'Frances Williams'

Hosta sieboldiana 'Elegans'

Hosta 'Ginko Craig'

IBERIS
CANDYTUFT
Brassicaceae (Cruciferae)
PERENNIALS AND COOL-SEASON ANNUALS
ZONES VARY
FULL SUN, EXCEPT AS NOTED
REGULAR WATER
✿ ❀ ✿ ✿ FLOWERS IN SPRING, SUMMER, FALL

TOP: *Iberis umbellata,* Dwarf Fairy strain
BOTTOM: *Iberis sempervirens*

Both annual and perennial candytufts are dense, low-growing plants that bear small flowers massed together in tight clusters. Profuse bloom and overall charm make them delightful front-of-the-border plants; many are good cut flowers as well.

Two annual species grow in Zones 1–45. Both flower in spring and summer, performing best with moderate daytime temperatures and cool nights. Hyacinth-flowered candytuft, *I. amara,* is accurately described by its common name: the fragrant white flowers are borne in a tight, domed cluster that eventually elongates into a hyacinthlike spike. The plant grows upright to 15 inches high but just 6 inches wide; leaves are narrow and slightly fuzzy. Globe candytuft, *I. umbellata,* is a bushy plant to 15 inches tall and about 9 inches wide. Blossoms are borne in clusters shaped like flattened cones; colors include white, pink shades, rosy red, purple, and lavender. Low-growing strains **Dwarf Fairy** and **Magic Carpet** offer the full color range on 6-inch plants; **Flash** is a few inches taller.

Perennial evergreen candytuft, *I. sempervirens* (Zones 1–24, 31–45), smothers itself in 2-inch clusters of sparkling white flowers from early to late spring. Even when not in bloom, the plants are attractive, their narrow, glossy dark green leaves forming dense mounds to 1 foot high, up to 2 feet wide. Named cultivars are lower and more compact. **'Little Gem'** grows just 4 to 6 inches high; **'Alexander's White'** (with very narrow leaves) and **'Kingwood Compact'** top out at 6 inches. **'Purity'** ranges from 4 to 12 inches high and spreads widely. **'Snowflake'** offers larger-than-normal flowers and broader leaves on a plant 4 to 12 inches high and up to 3 feet wide; it blooms sporadically throughout the year where summers and winters are mild. **'Autumnale'** and **'Autumn Snow'** reliably rebloom in fall.

CULTURE. Both annual and perennial candytufts need well-drained soil. Plant them in full sun except in hot-summer regions; in those areas, they'll benefit from a little afternoon shade. In all regions, you can plant *I. sempervirens* in spring; where winters are fairly mild, plants set out in fall will get established over winter and come into bloom earlier the following spring. After the main flowering burst, cut or shear back plants to encourage compactness. You can start new plants from stem cuttings taken in summer.

Sow seeds of annual *I. amara* and *I. umbellata* in place in the garden—in early spring in cold-winter climates, in late fall where winters are mild. Or sow indoors 6 to 8 weeks before the last-frost date.

IMPATIENS
Balsaminaceae
PERENNIALS USUALLY GROWN AS
  WARM-SEASON ANNUALS
ALL ZONES
EXPOSURE NEEDS VARY
REGULAR WATER
✿ ❀ ✿ ✿ FLOWERS IN SPRING, SUMMER

Available in a range of brilliant and soft colors lacking only true blue and yellow, impatiens have become *the* premier summer bedding plants for lightly or partially shaded gardens. In frost-free areas, they'll live from one year to the next, self-sowing to ensure a permanent presence in the garden. In all other areas, plants die with a touch of frost. Even where they can live over, though, they are typically grown as annuals. Two kinds are sold almost everywhere: *I. walleriana* (sometimes called busy Lizzie) and the New Guinea Hybrids. Both are bushy, fleshy-leafed, succulent-stemmed plants that branch from the base. The flat, roughly circular flowers have petals that are not quite uniform in size; a slender spur projects from the blossom's back. Ripe seed capsules burst open at the slightest touch, scattering seeds in all directions.

I. walleriana includes plants in a range of sizes, from 6- to 12-inch dwarfs to 2-foot-tall strains. It has 1- to 2-inch flowers and semiglossy dark green, spade-shaped, 1- to 3-inch-long leaves set on light green stems. Plant breeders have developed many strains that offer particular flower characteristics or plant habits. Unless otherwise indicated, the following strains come in mixed colors and, usually, in individual colors as well (**Accent Coral**, for example).

Among the smallest strains are **Firefly,** with ½-inch flowers, and **Neon,** both on 6- to 8-inch plants. **Super Elfin** grows 8 to 10 inches high and offers blended colors—pink with a wash of red, for instance—in addition to mixed and single hues. Ten-inch-high choices include **Accent; Accent Star,** bearing blossoms with a white central blaze; and **Tempo,** especially good in hanging containers (flowers of **Tempo Butterfly** have a butterfly-shaped central marking in a contrasting color). Strains with plants in the 10- to 16-inch range are **Bruno** and **Pride,** with large (2½-inch) flowers; **Mosaic,** featuring rose and lilac tones irregularly splashed white; **Stardust,** in which flowers have a central white star; and **Swirl,** in pastel colors with darker picotee margins.

Double-flowered impatiens, with blossoms resembling small roses, include **Confection, Fiesta,** and **Tioga,** all growing 10 to 12 inches high. **'Victorian Rose'** is the same size; it bears frilled, rose pink semidouble flowers.

New Guinea Hybrids are as valued for foliage as they are for flowers. They grow larger than *I. walleriana*—usually 1 to 2 feet tall and wide—and bear dark green, lance-shaped leaves to as much as 8 inches long. Some have foliage with striking cream or red variegation, and a few have bronze leaves. Plants don't produce the mass of flowers that the *I. walleriana* types do, but the 2½-inch blossoms are showy nonetheless, in colors including pure lavender, purple, pink, salmon, orange, red, and white. A number of strains are sold, some available as seeds, some only as cutting-grown plants. **'Tango',** with glowing orange flowers and bronzy green leaves on a 2-foot plant, is sold as seeds; other seed strains are **Java,** with bronze foliage, and **Spectra (Firelake),** with cream- or white-variegated leaves. **Paradise** and **Pure Beauty** are sold as cutting-grown plants, as is **Celebration,** with 3-inch flowers.

CULTURE. All impatiens appreciate plenty of water, especially during hot weather. These are premier container plants, needing a highly organic potting mix that is moisture retentive but fast draining. Plants also can be grown in lightly shaded borders, given soil liberally amended with organic matter. Though *I. walleriana* will take morning sun in cool- and mild-summer regions, it's usually grown in light shade. New Guinea Hybrids are a bit more sun tolerant. Nursery plants of both kinds are readily available, but you can also grow them from seed sown indoors 4 to 6 weeks before the last-frost date. For best germination, keep the planted containers in a warm spot (70 to 75°F/21 to 24°C).

Impatiens walleriana

Impatiens, New Guinea Hybrid

The mainstays of the spring flower border, irises bear showy flowers that rise above fans of swordlike leaves. An iris blossom is composed of three true petals *(standards)* and three petal-like sepals *(falls);* standards may be upright, arching, or flaring to horizontal, while falls range from flaring to drooping. Popular garden irises are separated into two broad categories. *Bearded* irises have a caterpillarlike ridge of hairs on each fall; *beardless* irises lack this feature.

BEARDED IRISES

The various bearded irises (Zones 1–24, 30–45) are more widely grown than beardless types. Available in a dazzling array of colors, patterns, and color combinations, these hybrids typically bloom in spring, though the growing category of rebloomers (often called remontants) flowers a second time in summer, fall, or winter. Bearded irises are classified according to stem height—as tall, median, or miniature dwarf. Most familiar are the *tall bearded* kinds; these flower in midspring, bearing large blossoms on branching stems ranging from 28 inches to 4 feet tall. The flowers, many with elaborately ruffled or fringed petals, bloom in all colors but true red and green (and breeders are coming close to these).

Listing continues>

IRIS
Iridaceae
PERENNIALS
ZONES VARY
FULL SUN, EXCEPT
   AS NOTED
REGULAR WATER, EXCEPT
   AS NOTED
✿ ✿ ✿ ✿ ✿ ✿ FLOWERS
   IN SPRING, EXCEPT
   AS NOTED

Tall bearded iris 'Orange Harvest'

Median irises comprise four classes that cover the height range from 8 to 28 inches. *Border bearded* and *miniature tall bearded* irises flower at the same time as the tall beardeds, on stems from 15 to 28 inches tall; *standard dwarf bearded* irises are early-spring bloomers with 8- to 15-inch stems. *Intermediate bearded* irises bloom midway between the standard dwarf beardeds and tall beardeds; they have 15- to 28-inch stems.

Miniature dwarf bearded irises are at the low end of the size range: they are 2- to 8-inch-high plants that flower at the first breath of spring.

Given the huge number of named cultivars, choices can be bewildering. A great way to get an idea of what's available is to visit a commercial iris garden during the bloom season; lacking that opportunity, you can turn to mail-order catalogs, some of which have plenty of color photographs.

CULTURE. Bearded irises need good drainage, since the rhizomes may rot if kept too wet. They'll grow in a range of soils—sandy to claylike, somewhat acid to somewhat alkaline—but if you plant in clay, make planting ridges (or plant in raised beds) to assure good drainage. Amend any soil with organic matter before planting. In cool- and mild-summer climates, choose a full-sun location; in the hottest-summer regions, a bit of afternoon shade is beneficial (though too much shade reduces the amount of bloom). Plant in July or August in cold-winter areas, in September or October where summers are hot. Where both winters and summers are mild, plant at any time from July to October.

Set rhizomes with their tops barely beneath the soil surface. New growth proceeds from the leafy end of the rhizome, so place the foliage fan in the direction you want growth to proceed initially. Bearded irises grow best if watered regularly from the time growth begins until about 6 weeks after the blooms fade; during summer, they need less moisture, though the smaller types (with smaller, shallower root systems) need a little more attention than larger growers do. After 3 to 4 years, clumps become crowded and bloom decreases in quantity and quality. When this occurs, dig and divide at the best planting time for your climate.

BEARDLESS IRISES

Of the many classes among the beardless category, Japanese and Siberian irises are the most widely grown. Both types have long, narrow, almost grasslike leaves and slender rhizomes with fibrous roots (rather than the fleshy roots of bearded types). In other respects, they differ considerably from one another.

Japanese irises (Zones 1–10, 14–24, 32–45) are derived solely from *I. ensata* (formerly *I. kaempferi*). Slender stems up to 4 feet high rise above clumps of graceful foliage, bearing sumptuous, single to double, relatively flat flowers 4 to 12 inches across. Colors include purple, violet, pink, rose, red, and white, often with contrasting veins or edges. Japanese irises bloom later than most tall beardeds, typically in late spring or early summer.

CULTURE. Set out plants in fall or spring, being careful not to let roots dry out (soak newly received mail-order plants overnight in water). Plants need organically amended, acid to neutral soil. Plant them in a sunny spot where summers are cool, in dappled sun or light afternoon shade where summers are hot. They revel in plenty of moisture, so give them a well-watered garden bed—or grow them at pond margins or in containers sunk halfway to their rims in water during the growing season. Divide crowded clumps in late summer or early fall; replant immediately so roots remain moist.

Siberian irises (Zones 1–10, 14–23, 32–45) are, for the most part, named hybrids derived from *I. sanguinea* and *I. sibirica*. In midspring, slender stems 2 to 4 feet tall (depending on the cultivar) rise above clumps of grasslike foliage, each bearing two to

Japanese iris 'Caprician Butterfly'

Siberian iris

five blossoms with upright to splayed standards and flaring to drooping falls. Colors include white, light yellow, and various shades of blue, lavender, purple, wine red, and pink. Foliage turns an attractive tawny gold in autumn.

CULTURE. Plant in full sun or partial shade, in neutral to acid soil well amended with organic matter. In cold-winter regions, plant in early spring or late summer; in milder regions, plant in fall. Be sure to keep roots moist (see facing page, under Japanese iris culture). Water liberally from the time spring growth begins until several weeks after bloom ends; regular water will suffice for the rest of the growing season. Clumps may remain in place for many years but will eventually become hollow in the center; when this happens, dig and divide at the best planting time for your climate.

KNIPHOFIA
RED-HOT POKER
Liliaceae
PERENNIALS
ZONES 2–9, 14–24, 28–41
FULL SUN, EXCEPT AS NOTED
REGULAR WATER, EXCEPT AS NOTED
❁ ✿ ✿ ✿ ✿ FLOWERS IN SPRING, SUMMER

Thick, fountainlike clumps of coarse, narrow leaves give these plants a decidedly grassy appearance. At flowering time, though, they're far more flamboyant than even the most ornamental of grasses: spearlike stems rise above the foliage, each bearing a thick, bottlebrush-style "torch" of drooping tubular flowers.

Old-fashioned favorite **K. uvaria** forms a hefty clump that sends up flower spikes to 6 feet tall; blossoms at the bottom of each cluster are yellow, those closer to the top orange red. Bloom comes at some point during spring.

Modern selections and hybrids—with *K. uvaria* and other species in their ancestry—offer an expanded color palette and a greater range of plant sizes; they generally bloom in late spring or summer. At the short end of the scale are 2-foot **'Little Maid'**, with creamy white flowers above notably thin leaves; 2- to 2½-foot **'Vanilla'**, with yellow buds opening to cream blossoms; and 2½-foot **Flamenco**, a seed-grown strain that offers the full range of colors. In the 3-foot range are **'Bee's Sunset'** (yellow flowers opening from near-orange buds), **'Gold Mine'** (amber yellow), and **'Primrose Beauty'** (light yellow). At 4 to 5 feet are **'Border Ballet'** (coral pink and cream), **'Peaches and Cream'** (peach pink and cream), and **'Percy's Pride'** (color varies from greenish yellow to cream). **'Malibu Yellow'** is about the size of *K. uvaria* and produces bright yellow flowers from green buds.

CULTURE. Give red-hot pokers good, organically enriched, fast-draining soil. Water regularly in spring and summer; cut back later in the year. Be particularly careful not to overwater in winter, since plants cannot tolerate saturated soil then. Choose a spot in full sun except in hot-summer regions, where plants need afternoon shade. Where winter temperatures drop to 0°F/−18°C or lower, tie the leaves together over the clump to protect the growing points from freezes; in warmer regions, you can cut old foliage to the ground in fall. Clumps can remain in place indefinitely; to increase your planting, just dig and relocate young plants from the clump's edge.

Kniphofia uvaria

LATHYRUS odoratus
SWEET PEA
Fabaceae (Leguminosae)
COOL-SEASON ANNUAL
ALL ZONES
FULL SUN
REGULAR WATER
✿ ✿ ❁ ✿ ✿ FLOWERS IN LATE WINTER, SPRING, EARLY SUMMER

Sweet peas have been cherished for hundreds of years for their memorable fragrance and clean, fresh colors. In most climates, they flower from spring into summer, but in mild-winter regions they can be planted in late summer for bloom in winter and early spring.

Traditional vining sweet peas are described on page 181; here, we focus on the more recently introduced nonvining, bushy strains that can be used in borders and containers. All have the familiar banner-and-keel flower shape. The taller types may need some support to remain upright; brush staking, shown on page 73, is a simple solution.

Listing continues>

At 2 to 3 feet, **Jet Set** is potentially the tallest bush sweet pea. **Knee-Hi** reaches about 2½ feet in the open garden, though plants against a wall or fence will grow taller. Topping out at about 2 feet are **Explorer** and **Supersnoop. Snoopea** grows 12 to 15 inches high; **Bijou** reaches about 1 foot. Still shorter is the little **Little Sweethearts** strain, with rounded, bushy, mounding plants to 8 inches high and wide. Plants of the **Cupid** strain grow a mere 4 to 6 inches high and spread to about a foot; they're excellent for window boxes and hanging containers.

CULTURE. Sweet peas revel in the best "vegetable garden" treatment, flourishing with good soil and regular moisture. Dig soil thoroughly and deeply before planting, incorporating plenty of organic matter. If soil is on the heavy side, mound it a bit to ensure that water will drain away from the plants' bases.

Like their vining kin, bush sweet peas are cool-season performers, ending their run with the onset of hot weather. For this reason, your climate determines the time of year you should plant. Where winters are mild and summers are warm to hot, plant seeds at some point from late summer through early January; you'll get flowers as early as late winter and on into spring, depending on when you planted. Where winters are cool and summers warm to hot, plant seed as early as possible in spring for flowers in later spring and into summer. In cold-winter areas with cool or short summers, also plant as soon as soil is workable in spring.

To hasten germination, soak seeds in lukewarm water overnight before planting.

Lathyrus odoratus, Knee-Hi strain

LAVATERA trimestris
ANNUAL MALLOW
Malvaceae
WARM-SEASON ANNUAL
ALL ZONES
FULL SUN
REGULAR WATER
❀ ✿ FLOWERS IN
    SUMMER, FALL

Reaching 2 to 6 feet tall, these shrubby plants bear satiny, 2- to 4-inch-wide flowers that resemble smaller versions of tropical hibiscus. Quick to grow from seed, they will flower from midsummer until frost if you remove spent blossoms faithfully. Named selections and strains are the most widely sold annual mallows. Few of these reach the upper end of the height range; the tallest, at 3 to 4 feet, is deep rose **'Loveliness'.** Compact kinds (to about 2 feet) include white **'Mont Blanc'**, rose pink **'Mont Rose'**, soft pink **'Pink Beauty'**, bright pink **'Silver Cup'**, and **'Ruby Regis'**, in cerise pink with darker veins.

CULTURE. Give plants average soil; overly rich soil promotes foliage at the expense of flowers. Sow seeds in place, a little before the last-frost date (or in early spring, in mild-winter climates). In cold-winter areas, you also can sow indoors 6 to 8 weeks before the last-frost date.

Lavatera trimestris
'Mont Blanc'

LIATRIS
GAYFEATHER
Asteraceae (Compositae)
PERENNIALS
ZONES A2, A3; 1–10, 14–24, 26, 28–45
FULL SUN
MODERATE TO REGULAR WATER
✿ ❀ ✿ FLOWERS IN SUMMER

For relatives of chrysanthemum and perennial aster, the gayfeathers look amazingly un-daisylike. Rising in summer from tufts of grassy foliage, leafy stems bear spikes of small, tightly clustered blossoms with prominent stamens. An unusual feature is that the blossoms open from the top of the spike downward—rather than from the bottom up, as flowers in spikes usually do.

Two species produce stems up to 5 feet high. *L. ligulistylis* has dark red buds opening to reddish purple flowers. Kansas gayfeather, *L. pycnostachya*, has purplish pink blossoms; its variety **'Alba'** is pure white. The most widely sold species, light purple *L. spicata*, reaches about 4 feet high. Attractive variants are **'Floristan White'** and **'Floristan Violet'**, both 3 feet tall; 2- to 2½-foot **'Kobold'**, with bright rose pink blossoms; and 3-foot **'Silvertips'**, bearing silvery lilac blooms with white tips.

Liatris pycnostachya

CULTURE. The gayfeathers need moderately fertile soil and good drainage; their thick, almost tuberous roots are especially prone to rot if soil is soggy during the winter dormant period. Plants are moderately drought-tolerant but perform best with regular watering during the growing period. After a number of years, when performance declines, divide crowded clumps in early spring.

Given their preferred conditions of rich soil, ample water, and moist air, ligularias will reward you with bold clumps of handsome foliage, topped in summer by spikes or clusters of bright, daisylike flowers. Leaves are usually heart-shaped to nearly circular and a foot or more across, with margins that may be strongly toothed, wavy, or deeply dissected.

Dramatic foliage is the main selling point of **L. dentata** (Zones 1–9, 14–17, 32, 34, 36–43): its leathery, tooth-edged, rounded medium green leaves can reach 16 inches across. The foliage forms a clump to 2 feet high; at bloom time, 3- to 5-foot stems rise above the leaves, bearing orange, 4-inch flowers in branched clusters. **'Dark Beauty'** has leaves in a particularly dark purple; **'Desdemona'** and **'Othello'** have green leaves with purple stalks, veins, and undersides.

Elegant blossom spires adorn clumps of **L. stenocephala** (Zones A2, A3; 1–9, 14–17, 32, 34, 36–45), usually represented in catalogs by its selection (or hybrid) **'The Rocket'**. Heart-shaped, deeply toothed green leaves to 1 foot wide send up 5-foot-tall purple stems carrying yellow, 1½-inch daisies in foxtail-like spikes.

CULTURE. Ligularias grow best in good, organically enriched soil with plenty of moisture and some shade. They're ideal for shady pondside plantings. They don't take kindly to heat or dry air, and even with humidity and ample water, leaves may wilt somewhat during the warmest part of the day. Slugs and snails can ravage the foliage. Clumps can remain in place for many years, though you can divide for increase in early spring.

Tough and trouble free, the various species of statice give you garden color that can be cut and dried for everlasting bouquets. Though the plants do vary, all have similar blossoms: each consists of an outer, petal-like, papery envelope that surrounds the very tiny true flowers. The two parts often differ in color. Though individually small, the blossoms are carried in showy clusters or impressive, airy sprays.

Annual **L. sinuatum** (all zones) is a summer bloomer 1½ to 2 feet high, up to 1 foot wide. The basal leaves are deeply lobed, while the many-branched flower stems have distinctive leaflike "wings." Tight, flat-topped blossom clusters come in white and shades of blue, purple, yellow, orange, and pink; seeds are sold in both mixed and individual colors. **Pastel Shades** is a mixed-color strain; **Pacific, Soirée Improved,** and **Turbo** are all sold in mixed and single colors. **Forever Gold** has bright yellow flowers; **Sunset** offers blossoms in orange, yellow, apricot, peach, and rose.

Perennial species are taprooted plants that produce clumps of leathery leaves and multibranched blossom stalks bearing clouds of flowers. Summer-flowering **L. gmelinii** (Zones 1–10, 14–24, 32–43) forms clumps of oblong, 5-inch leaves and somewhat flattened sprays of tiny white-and-lavender flowers that float above the foliage like a haze of lavender baby's breath *(Gypsophila)*. On established plants, the flower "cloud"

LIGULARIA
Asteraceae (Compositae)
PERENNIALS
ZONES VARY
PARTIAL TO FULL SHADE
REGULAR TO AMPLE WATER
✿ ✿ FLOWERS IN SUMMER

Ligularia stenocephala 'The Rocket'

LIMONIUM
STATICE, SEA LAVENDER
Plumbaginaceae
PERENNIALS AND WARM-SEASON ANNUALS
ZONES VARY
FULL SUN
LITTLE TO MODERATE WATER
✿ ✿ ✿ ✿ ✿ FLOWERS IN SPRING, SUMMER

Limonium sinuatum

may reach 2 feet across. ***L. platyphyllum*** (***L. latifolium;*** Zones 1–10, 14–24, 26, 28, 31–43, H1) is essentially a larger version, with leaves to 10 inches long and a blossom cloud to 2 feet high and 3 feet across.

Blooming in spring and summer, ***L. perezii*** (Zones 13, 15–17, 20–27) grows quickly enough to be used as an annual in zones too cold for its year-round survival. Clumps of broad, wavy-edged leaves to 1 foot long are topped by dense clusters of purple-and-white flowers on wiry stems to 3 feet tall.

CULTURE. The perennial forms of statice need only average, well-drained soil. They withstand drought but bloom profusely with moderate water. Clumps may remain in place indefinitely; to increase a planting, take root cuttings in late winter or divide clumps in early spring. All can also be raised from seed sown indoors 6 to 8 weeks before the last-frost date.

Like its perennial kin, annual *L. sinuatum* performs well in average, well-drained soil, but it doesn't take drought and needs consistent moderate watering. Sow seeds outdoors after all danger of frost is past; or sow indoors 6 to 8 weeks before the last-frost date.

LOBELIA
Campanulaceae (Lobeliaceae)
PERENNIALS AND WARM-SEASON ANNUALS
ZONES VARY
PARTIAL SHADE, EXCEPT AS NOTED
WATER NEEDS VARY
✿ ✿ ❀ ✿ ✿ FLOWERS IN SUMMER,
  EXCEPT AS NOTED

Lobelia cardinalis

The lobelias are a varied group: there are perennials for perpetually damp soil and one that will colonize dry ground, plus an annual beloved for its abundant bloom. All bear tubular blossoms that flare into five unequal lobes—but beyond that, they can differ quite markedly.

Flowering during the hot times of year, annual ***L. erinus*** (all zones) is an invaluable source of cool blue color. The 3- to 6-inch-high plant consists of many slender, branching stems clothed in small green to bronze leaves; its dense foliage as well as its generous bloom make it a topnotch choice for borders and containers. Each ½-inch flower has the standard five unequal lobes and a dot of white or yellow in the throat; blue shades, white, and lilac pink are the basic colors. In mild-winter regions, the plant blooms from spring until frost; performance is best where summer nights are cool. In mild-winter desert zones, grow it for bloom in winter or early spring. Two old seed-grown cultivars still are popular. '**Cambridge Blue**' has lettuce green leaves and soft blue blossoms; '**Crystal Palace**' offers vivid deep blue blooms and bronzy green foliage. '**Rosamund**' provides a change of pace, bearing flowers in cherry red. The **Riviera** series features low, compact, mounded plants with flowers in various blue shades, white, and pink. Plants in the **Cascade** series are trailing, making them especially good for hanging baskets and window boxes; you'll find mixed as well as individual colors, including light and dark blue, white, pink, and purplish red.

The following moisture-loving perennial lobelias all form clumps of lance-shaped leaves that give rise in summer to flowering stems 2 to 5 feet high. Best known is cardinal flower, ***L. cardinalis*** (Zones 1–7, 14–17, upper half of 26, 28–45), with foliage rosettes sending up leafy, 3- to 4-foot stems bearing spikes of vivid red, 1½-inch blossoms. White and pink forms are sometimes available. *L. siphilitica* (Zones 1–9, 14–17, 31–45) resembles *L. cardinalis* but has flower stems just 2 to 3 feet high and bears rich blue to blue-violet blossoms. ***L. × gerardii*** (Zones 2–9, 14–17, 31–43), a hybrid between *L. cardinalis* and *L. siphilitica,* is available in several named cultivars. Red-flowered '**Ruby Queen**' reaches about 3 feet high; 4-foot '**Vedrariensis**' carries royal purple flowers above clumps of copper-infused leaves.

Breeding between various moisture-loving perennial species (including those discussed above) has produced a number of excellent plants in a range of colors. These may be offered as cultivars of ***L. × speciosa,*** though more often you'll find them simply listed by cultivar name. All flourish with ample water and succeed in Zones 2–9,

14–17, 31–43. Spectacular '**Bees Flame**' features beet red foliage and bright scarlet blooms on spikes to 5 feet. The **Compliment** series, available from seed, produces 2½-foot-tall plants with blooms in red, pink, or purple. Unusual '**Cotton Candy**', also about 2½ feet tall, has white flowers tinged with pink. '**Dark Crusader**', to 3 feet high, has deep magenta blossoms and dark purple leaves; another 3-footer, '**Tania**', produces magenta purple blossoms and silvery green foliage. '**Sparkle DeVine**' carries its blue-flushed fuchsia blooms on stems to 4 feet high.

Unlike the preceding plants, Southwestern native ***L. laxiflora*** (Zones 7–9, 12–24) is notable for its drought tolerance. Upright stems reach 2 feet high, set somewhat sparsely with dark green, very narrow leaves and topped by loose clusters of tubular orange-red flowers over a long summer season.

CULTURE. Annual *L. erinus* is rather slow growing after germination, taking about 2 months to reach planting-out size; for this reason, most gardeners prefer to buy nursery-grown young plants. To raise from seed, sow indoors 8 to 10 weeks before the last-frost date. Simply press seeds into the potting mix, being careful not to cover them; they need light to germinate. Give regular water; provide partial shade except in cool-summer areas, where the plant does well in a sunny spot.

Perennial lobelias (*L. laxiflora* excepted) need ample water, good soil liberally enriched with organic matter, and a location in partial shade (in all but cool-summer regions, where they'll take full sun). Left unattended, clumps will dwindle and disappear; divide them every couple of years to keep the plants vigorous. You also can take stem cuttings just after flowering or layer stems to start new plants. If soil is constantly damp, volunteer seedlings may appear. Where winter temperatures dip to −10°F/−23°C or lower, protect plants with a layer of mulch; remove it as weather warms in spring.

L. laxiflora takes full sun and thrives with little water; it is unparticular about soil quality, growing well even in poor soil. Clumps spread by underground stems and can become invasive, especially in good soil with moderate to regular water.

Lobelia siphilitica

Sweet alyssum blooms throughout the growing season, bearing its tiny, honey-scented flowers in dense, dome-shaped clusters that literally cover the plant. Leaves are very narrow, at most a little over 1 inch long; the plant is bushy and spreading, reaching 1 foot high and wide. Sweet alyssum is excellent as an edging or small-scale ground cover, for planting between paving stones, and as a filler in containers. The basic flower color is white, but you can find named selections in lilac pink ('**Pink Heather**' and '**Rosie O'Day**') and violet ('**Oriental Night**' and '**Violet Queen**'); these are compact plants that reach no higher than 6 inches. '**Pastel Carpet**' features a mixture of white, pink, lavender, violet, and cream flowers on spreading plants about 4 inches high. Low, compact white selections include '**Carpet of Snow**', '**Little Gem**', and '**Tiny Tim**'. At the other end of the size scale is foot-high '**Tetra Snowdrift**', featuring larger flowers on long stems.

CULTURE. Nothing is easier to grow than sweet alyssum. The simplest method is to sow seeds where you want plants to grow, then thin seedlings to about 8 inches apart. Sow seeds in fall (even winter, in mild-winter regions), pressing them onto the soil without covering them; they need light to germinate. You also can sow in spring, a few weeks before the last-frost date (while soil is still cool). After the first flush of bloom, shear plants back about halfway to promote compactness and another round of flowers.

Sweet alyssum self-sows freely. Where colored- and white-flowered types grow together, the first volunteer seedlings will be in white and in paler shades of the parents' colors; in years to come, white flowers will prevail. Even volunteers from all-colored plantings usually lack the color depth of the parent plants.

LOBULARIA maritima
SWEET ALYSSUM
Brassicaceae (Cruciferae)
WARM-SEASON ANNUAL
ALL ZONES
FULL SUN
REGULAR WATER
✿❀✿ FLOWERS IN SPRING, SUMMER, FALL

Lobularia maritima

LUPINUS

LUPINE

Fabaceae (Leguminosae)

PERENNIALS

ZONES A1–A3; 1–7, 14–17, 34, 36–45

FULL SUN, EXCEPT AS NOTED

REGULAR WATER

✿ ✿ ❀ ✿ ✿ ✿ ✿ FLOWERS IN SPRING, SUMMER

Lupinus, Russell Hybrids

Magnificent perennial lupines, their stately spires packed with colorful blossoms, evoke images of romantic cottage-garden plantings and Victorian perennial borders. Nonetheless, they derive from a number of species native to the western U.S.—though the original hybrids were developed in England during the early 20th century. These plants—the **Russell Hybrids**—set the standard for beauty and appearance. Some of them still are sold, but other, more recent hybrids have captured the Russell look in vigorous, more widely adapted plants that lack the Russell susceptibility to powdery mildew.

A typical lupine forms a bushy clump of attractive leaves that resemble, in both shape and size, a hand with fingers spread. At bloom time in spring and summer, vertical flower spikes rise to 4 to 5 feet, with sweet pea–shaped blossoms encircling each spike's upper portion. You'll find individual solid colors as well as lovely bicolor combinations; plants usually are sold as mixed colors, though some specialty nurseries offer named cultivars in specific colors. The **New Generation Hybrids** give you the Russell style and color range on sturdier, mildew-resistant, 4-foot-tall plants that need no staking. **Gallery, Little Lulu, Popsicle,** and **Minarette** are mixed-color strains that produce Russell-type flowers on plants to about 20 inches high.

CULTURE. Lupines grow best in regions with fairly cool summers, where they flourish in sunny locations. Where summers are warm and dry, they can be grown with some success if planted in light shade and kept moist. In regions with hot, humid summers, they are likely to fail even with shade and regular water. Set out plants in spring, in well-drained, neutral to acid soil enriched with organic matter. Clumps are not long lived, but you can revitalize them by division in early spring or start new plants from stem cuttings taken in spring. Or start from seed sown indoors 6 to 8 weeks before the last-frost date or outdoors 2 to 3 weeks before that time. To hasten germination, soak seeds overnight in lukewarm water before planting.

MALVA

MALLOW

Malvaceae

PERENNIALS

ZONES 1–9, 14–24, 31–45

FULL SUN, EXCEPT AS NOTED

REGULAR WATER

✿ ✿ ❀ ✿ FLOWERS IN SUMMER, FALL

Malva moschata 'Alba'

Several long-blooming, easy-to-grow mallows are popular in gardens. All offer deep green, rounded, lobed or cleft leaves and hollyhock-like, typically 2-inch-wide blossoms from summer into fall. **M. sylvestris,** an erect, bushy plant reaching 2 to 4 feet tall, is a short-lived perennial more often grown as a biennial. Often flowering until stopped by autumn frost, it bears rosy purple flowers with darker stripes on the petals. **'Zebrina'** has pale lavender blossoms with pronounced deep purple veins. Two 1½- to 2-foot-tall choices with 1¼-inch flowers are **'Primley Blue',** with soft blue, dark-veined flowers on a somewhat spreading plant, and **'Marina',** bearing dark-veined violet blooms on a less spreading plant.

Two other species are truly perennial. Neither is quite as large or tall as hollyhock (*Alcea*), but the plants are bushier and bloom more profusely. Hollyhock mallow, **M. alcea,** is usually represented by its cultivar **'Fastigiata':** an upright, narrow, many-branched plant 3 to 4 feet high, with deeply lobed leaves and dark pink blossoms. Musk mallow, **M. moschata,** is a broader plant—to around 3 feet high and 2 feet wide—with rose pink flowers and leaves cut into threadlike segments. **'Alba'** has blossoms in sparkling white.

CULTURE. The mallows don't demand good soil, but they do need good drainage. Give them full sun except in the hottest regions, where light shade is appreciated. Even the truly perennial sorts are fairly short lived, but volunteer seedlings usually provide replacement plants. All species are easy to grow from seed sown outdoors where plants are to grow, several weeks before the usual last-frost date. You can also start new plants from stem cuttings taken in summer.

A fragrance both sweet and spicy has endeared stock to generations of gardeners. With hints of clove and cinnamon, the perfume alone makes the plants worth growing—but fortunately, the flowers are as lovely as the scent. In the mildest climates, plants bloom from late winter into spring; in cooler ones, you can plant for flowers in summer.

The more widely grown species is *M. incana,* typically a bushy plant with narrow gray-green leaves. Carried in upright spikes at stem ends, the inch-wide, single or double flowers come in cream, white, and shades of pink, red, and purple. Many strains are available, ranging in size from under a foot to 3 feet tall. At the high end of the range, the **Giant Imperial** strain grows to 2½ feet; unbranched **Column** and **Double Giant Flowering** strains can reach 3 feet high. **Ten Weeks** (to 1½ feet) and the shorter **Dwarf Ten Weeks** (to 1 foot) flower in 10 weeks from seed; **Trysomic Seven Weeks** (to 15 inches) beats them into bloom by 3 weeks. Lower-growing strains abound, among them **Vintage** (to 15 inches high), **Brilliant Double Purpose** (1 foot), **Cinderella** (10 inches), and **Midget** (10 inches). Strains may be available as both mixed and single colors.

Foot-tall evening scented stock, *M. longipetala bicornis,* with lance-shaped green leaves and spikes of small lilac-purple flowers, is considerably less showy than *M. incana.* But its wonderful fragrance (most pronounced during the evening) is even more potent.

CULTURE. For success with stock, provide moderately rich, preferably neutral to slightly alkaline soil. Plants prefer cool weather and do not perform well where summers are hot or nights are warm. These preferences influence planting times. In regions where days are mild and nights are cool in summer, you can grow stock for summer flowers; sow seeds indoors 6 to 8 weeks before the last-frost date, or sow outdoors just after the last frost. Where spring is mild but summer is hot, grow stock for spring flowers, starting seeds indoors in winter for planting out in very early spring. In mild-winter areas, you can sow seeds in early fall for flowers in late winter and spring.

When sowing seeds, just press them onto the soil surface; they need light in order to germinate.

G reen leaves are commonplace, but green flowers are a rarity—one reason bells-of-Ireland has been a favorite with generations of flower arrangers. What look like petals are in fact prominent, white-veined apple green calyxes; these form a cup-shaped "flower" that surrounds the true flowers, which are tiny, white, and fragrant. Blossoms appear in whorls of six, stacked in tiers along the upper one-third of 2- to 3-foot stems. Leaves are rounded and coarsely toothed; by the time plants come into bloom, the lowest leaves will have started to shrivel. You can use bells-of-Ireland in fresh arrangements or dry the stems for use in everlasting bouquets.

CULTURE. Bells-of-Ireland prefers a well-drained soil but doesn't need a particularly fertile one. The best way to grow this plant is to sow seeds in place in the garden, then thin seedlings to about a foot apart. The seeds need chilling to germinate well. Where winters are moderately cold (to about −10°F/−23°C), sow seeds outdoors several weeks before the normal last-frost date; in mild-winter regions, sow in late fall. You can also start seeds indoors (the preferred method where winter lows dip below −10°F/−23°C), but it's best to chill them for about 2 weeks in the refrigerator before planting. Then sow seeds in containers about 10 weeks before the last-frost date. Indoors or out, seeds may take up to 4 weeks to germinate.

MATTHIOLA
STOCK
Brassicaceae (Cruciferae)
COOL-SEASON ANNUALS
ZONES 1–45
FULL SUN OR LIGHT SHADE
REGULAR WATER
✿✿✿✿ FLOWERS IN LATE WINTER, SPRING, SUMMER

Matthiola incana

MOLUCCELLA laevis
BELLS-OF-IRELAND
Lamiaceae (Labiatae)
WARM-SEASON ANNUAL
ZONES 1–45; H1, H2
FULL SUN
REGULAR WATER
✿ FLOWERS IN SUMMER

Moluccella laevis

MONARDA

BEE BALM, WILD BERGAMOT
Lamiaceae (Labiatae)
PERENNIALS
ZONES A1–A3; 1–11, 14–17, 30–43
FULL SUN, EXCEPT AS NOTED
REGULAR WATER
✿ ❀ ✿ ✿ FLOWERS IN SUMMER

Monarda didyma

Monarda didyma
'Cambridge Scarlet'

Crush or rub the foliage, and you'll instantly recognize bee balm's kinship with mint. Spreading clumps of aromatic, lance-shaped, 6-inch-long leaves send up numerous leafy, branching stems crowned with one or two dense, shaggy-looking whorls of tubular, two-lipped flowers that are magnets for hummingbirds. Catalogs carry numerous named cultivars, usually selections of **M. didyma** or hybrids of it with the less showy *M. fistulosa.* **'Cambridge Scarlet'** and **'Croftway Pink'** are two old favorites that grow to 4 feet tall; **'Snow White'** is a white-blossomed 3-footer. *M. didyma* and the older cultivars are susceptible to powdery mildew, but many of the newer cultivars are at least partially resistant. Among these are **'Garden-view Scarlet'** and **'Raspberry Wine'**, both reaching 3 feet tall, and the 4-foot selections **'Jacob Kline'** (dark rosy red), **'Marshall's Delight'** (rose pink), and **'Violet Queen'**.

CULTURE. With good, organically enriched soil and regular watering, bee balm grows vigorously. Give full sun except in hotter regions, where partial shade is better. Overly dry soil and poor air circulation increase susceptibility to mildew, so be attentive to watering and make sure air circulation is good. Clumps spread rapidly and may even be invasive; divide them every 2 to 3 years in spring.

MYOSOTIS

FORGET-ME-NOT
Boraginaceae
PERENNIALS AND COOL-SEASON ANNUALS
ZONES A1–A3; 1–24, 32–45
PARTIAL SHADE
REGULAR TO AMPLE WATER
✿ ❀ ✿ FLOWERS IN LATE WINTER, SPRING

Myosotis sylvatica

In appearance, there's little difference between annual and perennial forget-me-nots. Both have bright green, lance-shaped leaves to about 4 inches long—hairy in annual *M. sylvatica*, glossy in perennial *M. scorpioides*. And both bear elongated, curving clusters of ¼- to ⅓-inch-wide, sparkling sky blue flowers. At bloom time, the blossoms form a cerulean cloud in lightly shaded and woodland plantings. *M. sylvatica* in particular is a favorite choice for underplanting spring-blooming bulbs such as daffodils and tulips.

Annual **M. sylvatica** reaches up to 1 foot high and spreads as wide as 2 feet. Its yellow-eyed blossoms appear in winter or early spring, depending on the severity of the winter, and continue to bloom as long as weather remains cool to mild. Variations include **'Rosylva'**, with pure pink flowers on a more compact plant; **'Blue Ball'**, with 6-inch, almost spherical plants well suited to containers; and the **Victoria** series, featuring blue, pink, and white blossoms.

Perennial **M. scorpioides** generally remains under a foot high but reaches 2 feet or more across, spreading by creeping roots. The blue springtime flowers typically have a yellow eye, though white- and pink-eyed forms exist. Named cultivars in white and various blue shades have been cataloged, but except for the long-blooming **'Mermaid'** (**'Semperflorens'**), they are not in general circulation.

CULTURE. As long as you can give them organically enriched soil and regular to ample water, forget-me-nots offer no cultural challenges. They'll even thrive in the always-moist soil beside a pond or stream. Both annual and perennial species look and perform best in cool weather and where summers are not excessively hot.

To increase plantings of *M. scorpioides*, divide clumps in early spring. Grow *M. sylvatica* from seed; it self-sows prolifically, so one planting can be a lifetime investment! Where winter lows hit 0°F/−18°C or below, sow outdoors several weeks before the last-frost date; or sow indoors 8 to 10 weeks before the last-frost date. In milder areas, sow seeds in fall for spring bloom (plants may overwinter to bloom a second year).

Planted at the edge of a path or border, the catmints provide a refreshing haze of cool color over a long period, beginning in midspring. Loose spikes of small (¼- to ½-inch), clustered blossoms cover billowy plants that usually are broader than tall; oval, slightly rough-textured, typically grayish leaves grow ¾ to 1½ inches long. Many of the catmints are as attractive to felines as catnip *(N. cataria)*; susceptible cats will roll frenziedly on the plants and nibble the foliage. Young plants usually need protection until they're large and tough enough to withstand such ardent attentions.

Most widely available is **N. × faassenii** (sometimes sold as **N. mussinii**). It forms a silvery gray-green mound about 2 feet wide and reaches 1 to 2 feet high in flower. The basic form bears loose spikes of soft lavender-blue blossoms; named selections include **'Porcelain'**, a 1½-foot plant with soft blue blossoms and blue-gray leaves, and white-flowered **'Snowflake'**. **'Dropmore'**, a 2-foot plant with longer spikes of rich blue flowers, may be sold as a *N. × faassenii* selection but is probably a hybrid. **'Six Hills Giant'**, to 2 to 3 feet high and 3 feet wide, is another probable *N. × faassenii* hybrid and looks like a larger version of it.

Husky **N. grandiflora** is an open, upright plant 2½ to 3 feet high and about 1½ feet wide; it has violet-blue flowers. Its cultivar **'Brandean'** bears lavender-blue blossoms emerging from purple calyxes; **'Dawn to Dusk'** has lilac-pink blossoms and purple calyxes. In both, the calyxes persist after flowers have finished.

Siberian catmint, **N. sibirica**, is another upright plant of about the same size as *N. grandiflora*, but its rich violet-blue blossoms are larger (to 1½ inches) and bloom later, appearing in summer. **'Souvenir d'André Chaudron'** (**'Blue Beauty'**) appears to be a *N. sibirica* hybrid and has the same plant size and flower color, but it blooms over a longer period.

CULTURE. All catmints are easy to grow, needing only well-drained soil and a warm, sunny location (or a lightly shaded spot, where summers are hot). To keep plants more compact and encourage repeat bloom later in summer, shear off spent flowering stems. To propagate, divide clumps in early spring or take stem cuttings in spring or summer. You also may find new plants from stems that self-layer where they touch the soil; dig and transplant these as desired.

Nepeta × faassenii

NEPETA

CATMINT

Lamiaceae (Labiatae)

PERENNIALS

ZONES 1–24, 30, 32–43

FULL SUN, EXCEPT AS NOTED

MODERATE WATER

✿ ✿ ❀ ✿ FLOWERS IN SPRING, SUMMER

Nepeta × faassenii

These tender tropical natives have been cherished by generations of gardeners for their easy-to-grow nature and colorful, often sweet-scented spring and summer blossoms. Though technically tender perennnials, they are grown as annuals everywhere—even in the frost-free regions where they can live from year to year. Plants are upright and narrow, with large, soft, oval leaves; both stems and leaves are slightly sticky to the touch. The flowers are narrow tubes that flare out into a star-shaped blossom about 2 inches across; many are notably fragrant, and all attract hummingbirds.

The most widely available plants are derived from **N. alata (N. affinis)**, sometimes known as flowering tobacco. The species reaches 2 to 4 feet or more tall, producing white blossoms that open as evening approaches, releasing a powerful perfume. Its hybrids, often cataloged as **N. × sanderae**, encompass a range of heights and colors. For guaranteed fragrance, choose white-blossomed **'Grandiflora'**, a night bloomer to 3 feet tall. For color variations (typically with reduced fragrance), you can choose from

NICOTIANA

Nyctaginaceae

PERENNIALS GROWN AS WARM-SEASON ANNUALS

ALL ZONES

FULL SUN, EXCEPT AS NOTED

REGULAR WATER

✿ ❀ ✿ ✿ ✿ FLOWERS IN SPRING, SUMMER

Nicotiana alata, Nicki strain

a number of day-blooming strains. Short plants (8 to 14 inches), good for containers and front-of-border plantings, include the mixed-color strains **Breakthrough, Domino, Havana,** and **Merlin.** The mixed-color **Nicki** strain grows to about 1½ feet; reaching the same height is red **'Crimson King'.** The **Daylight Sensation** strain produces flowers in white, lavender, purple, and pink on stems to 3 feet high. Taller still—to 3½ feet—is the **Heavenscent** series; this one offers strongly perfumed blossoms in white, pink, red, and purple.

Two 5-foot species make dramatic accents. *N. langsdorffii* is a branching, upright plant decorated with pendent clusters of bell-shaped flowers in bright green. Night-blooming *N. sylvestris* bears intensely fragrant, tubular white flowers in tiered clusters toward the tops of the plant.

CULTURE. Give nicotianas good, organically enriched, well-drained soil. They thrive in full sun except in hot-summer climates, where they appreciate dappled sun or light shade in the afternoon. Sow seeds indoors 6 to 8 weeks before the last-frost date. Where summers are fairly long, you can also sow seeds directly in the garden just after the last-frost date. In either case, merely press seeds into the soil without covering them; they need light to germinate. Deadhead spent blooms to prolong flowering.

NIGELLA damascena
LOVE-IN-A-MIST
Ranunculaceae
COOL-SEASON ANNUAL
ALL ZONES
FULL SUN OR PARTIAL SHADE
REGULAR WATER
✿ ✿ ✿ ✿ FLOWERS IN SPRING

Nigella damascena

An individual blossom of love-in-a-mist resembles the familiar bachelor's button *(Centaurea cyanus),* but it's framed in a ruff—a "mist"—of threadlike leaf segments. The same filigree foliage clothes the upright, 1½- to 2-foot-tall plant, giving it an airy, see-through appearance. The spring flowers are followed by conspicuous horned, papery-textured seed capsules that are decorative in the garden as well as in dried arrangements. Flowers come in blue, white, violet, and pink. The popular **Persian Jewels** strain features double blossoms in the complete range of colors. The **Miss Jekyll Hybrids** are a fine group with semidouble blossoms in bright blue, white, and pink. **'Mulberry Rose'** bears double blooms in rosy pink; **'Oxford Blue'** is taller than most (to 2½ feet), with double dark blue flowers and seedpods distinctly darker than those of the species.

CULTURE. Love-in-a-mist grows beautifully in average, well-drained soil. It is taprooted and does not transplant well, so it's best to sow seed directly where plants are to grow. Where winters are freezing to frosty, sow seeds outdoors 2 to 3 weeks before the last-frost date. In mild-winter regions, sow in fall for bloom in earliest spring—and if summers are also mild, you can sow every 4 weeks for continuous bloom until the plants are vanquished by heat. Love-in-a-mist self-sows readily, ensuring a good supply of replacement plants (if you're willing to take them wherever they happen to pop up).

OENOTHERA
EVENING PRIMROSE, SUNDROPS
Onagraceae
PERENNIALS
ZONES VARY
FULL SUN, EXCEPT AS NOTED
LITTLE TO MODERATE WATER
✿ ✿ ✿ FLOWERS IN SPRING, SUMMER

These adaptable, carefree plants provide a spring-and-summer bounty of silky, four-petaled flowers with a broad, flattened bowl shape. Some species bloom during the daylight hours, but others open in late afternoon and close the following morning.

Sundrops, *O. fruticosa,* grows in Zones 1–21, 30–45. A shrubby plant to 2 feet high and wide, it has shiny green leaves, reddish brown stems and buds, and clusters of 1- to 2-inch, bright yellow flowers that open during the day. Its form *O. f. glauca (O. tetragona)* bears light yellow blossoms on red stems. Cultivars of the basic species include **'Fireworks' ('Fyrverkeri'),** with red buds and purple-tinted foliage; **'Highlight' ('Hoheslicht'),** bearing slightly larger flowers; and **'Solstice' ('Sonnenwende'),** with leaves that turn red in summer, then darken to wine purple in fall.

Ozark sundrops, **O. macrocarpa (O. missouriensis),** is suited to Zones 1–24, 30, 33–37, 39–45. It forms a spreading plant to 2 feet across, the stem ends arching upward to about 6 inches; bright yellow, 3- to 5-inch blossoms open in the afternoon, set off against the backdrop of soft, velvety gray-green leaves. Conspicuous winged seed-pods follow the flowers.

Mexican evening primrose, **O. speciosa,** grows in Zones 2b–24, 29, 30, 33, 35, H1, H2. Rose pink, 2-inch-wide flowers with white centers darken with age; despite the plant's common name, they open in the daytime. Slender stems clothed in dark green foliage reach 10 to 15 inches tall on plants that can spread aggressively, colonizing large patches of ground. Selected cultivars include pure white **'Alba';** light pink **'Rosea'** (often incorrectly sold as **O. berlandieri** or **O. speciosa childsii**); shorter (and less aggressive) pink **'Siskiyou';** and **'Woodside White',** with green-centered white flowers that are pink tinged when they unfurl.

CULTURE. These plants tolerate drought and poor soil, but do best with average, well-drained soil and moderate water. They prefer full sun, though *O. speciosa* also performs well in light shade. To rejuvenate crowded plantings or obtain new plants, divide clumps in early spring; you also can take stem cuttings at this time.

TOP: *Oenothera fruticosa*
BOTTOM: *Oenothera speciosa*

ORNAMENTAL VEGETABLES

A number of edible plants can bring beauty to beds and borders. Unless otherwise noted, grow these plants in well-amended soil, in a full-sun location; water regularly.

Several kinds of amaranth (warm-season annual; Zones 1–45, H1, H2) have bright-colored foliage or flowers. Young, tender leaves can be cooked or added to salads. Showy, 4-foot-tall selections of **Amaranthus tricolor** include **'Aurora',** with dark green lower leaves and warm yellow upper ones, and **'Molten Fire',** with deep brownish red foliage. Sow seed in place in early summer; soil temperature must be above 70°F/21°C for germination. Or start seed indoors in spring.

Decorative cultivars of Swiss chard (**Beta vulgaris;** cool-season annual, all zones) include **'Rhubarb',** with dark green leaves and crimson stalks and leaf veins, and **'Bright Lights',** featuring leaves ranging from green to burgundy and leafstalks in white or various shades of yellow, orange, pink, red, purple, or green. Plants grow 1 to 2 feet high. Sow seed in place in the garden from early to midspring.

Flowering cabbage and flowering kale (**Brassica;** cool-season annuals, all zones) are grown for their highly ornamental, 10- to 14-inch-tall leaf

'Rhubarb' Swiss chard

rosettes in deep, rich colors. Flowering kale forms a looser head and has more heavily fringed leaves than flowering cabbage. In most varieties, outer leaves are deep blue green, while inner ones may be cream, pink, rose, or purple. Leaves are edible raw or cooked. Plant in very early spring; or plant in late summer for fall color. In mild-winter regions, plants are attractive throughout winter.

Bronze fennel, **Foeniculum vulgare 'Purpurascens',** is perennial in Zones 2b–11, 14–24, 29–41, H1, H2, but it is often grown everywhere as a biennial or annual. It features soft, ferny-looking, bronzy purple leaves on a 5- to 6-foot plant. Sow seed in its garden location in spring; give little to moderate water. This plant self-sows freely and can be invasive in mild-winter climates.

Shiso or beefsteak plant (**Perilla frutescens purpurascens;** warm season annual, all zones) has large, slightly fuzzy, deep red-purple leaves resembling those of coleus. The plant grows fast to 2 to 3 feet. Shiso leaves make an unusual vegetable or flavoring (they taste something like mint, something like cinnamon). Grow in full sun to part shade, in moist soil. Sow indoors 10 weeks before the last frost; or sow outdoors after the last frost. Removing the spikes of white flowers (which are not showy) helps control excessive self-sowing.

PAEONIA

PEONY

Paeoniaceae

PERENNIALS

ZONES A1–A3; 1–11, 14–20,
30–45

FULL SUN, EXCEPT AS NOTED

REGULAR WATER

🌸 ✿ ✿ ✿ FLOWERS IN LATE SPRING

TOP: *Paeonia* 'Chief Justice'
BOTTOM: *Paeonia* 'Largo'

Herbaceous peonies are old-fashioned favorites, cherished for their spectacular late-spring blossoms—and for foliage that is almost as beautiful as the flowers. Each year, new shoots rise from the ground in early spring and develop into rounded, shrubby clumps of large, handsome leaves divided into numerous segments. At bloom time, round buds at the stem ends open into fragrant, satiny blossoms that range in diameter from 4 to 10 inches.

Paeonia 'Festiva Maxima'

Such lovely and impressive flowers have naturally attracted the attention of breeders, and specialty catalogs now list multitudes of named hybrids in colors ranging from deep red through coral and all shades of pink to cream, white, and (more recently) yellow. These cultivars are classified by flower form and bloom time. Among forms, *double* peonies have countless petals, for a full, fluffy look. *Semidouble* types have a single row of petals and a center filled with stamens and smaller petals; *single* peonies also have just one row of petals, but they're centered with stamens only. *Japanese* (sometimes called bomb) peonies have a single row of petals and a large central mass of narrow, petal-like segments called staminodes. Bloom time is designated as early, midseason, or late; by choosing plants in each of these groups, you can enjoy flowers over a period of 4 to 6 weeks.

Because most peonies need definite winter chill to succeed, gardeners in the warmest of the zones listed above should look for varieties recommended for warmer-winter climates. In those areas, single or Japanese flower forms are generally more likely to turn in a good performance.

CULTURE. Planted the right way, in the right site, peonies can remain undisturbed indefinitely—good reason to pay careful attention to preparation. Choose a sunny but wind-sheltered spot; strong winds can break the blossom-heavy stems. (Where spring can be hot and dry, however, select only early-blooming kinds and plant in a location receiving light afternoon shade.) Be sure soil is well drained, and dig it deeply several days to several weeks before planting, adding plenty of organic matter. If soil is highly acid, incorporate lime when you prepare it.

Peony roots (technically rhizomes with tuberous roots) are usually planted in early fall, though in parts of the West they are also available for planting in early spring. Planting depth is critical, and it depends on your climate. In warm-winter regions, position the "eyes"—the growth buds at the top of the root—no deeper than 1 inch below the soil surface; this exposes the plant to as much winter cold as your climate offers. But where winter lows regularly reach 10°F/−12°C or lower, plant so that growth buds are 1½ to 2 inches beneath the soil. Be aware that, in any climate, planting too deeply reduces or eliminates flowering.

Peonies may not bloom the first spring after planting, but they'll start to hit their stride the following year. During periods of cool, humid weather, be on the alert for the fungal disease botrytis; symptoms include fuzzy, brown to gray spots on foliage and stems and buds that blacken and fail to open. To help prevent the problem, remove and discard dead or infected plant parts; clean up the planting area thoroughly in fall, disposing of all spent peony leaves and stems. As new growth emerges in spring, spray with a copper fungicide.

Though peonies can remain in the same place virtually forever, you can divide established clumps in early fall. Dig each clump carefully and hose off the roots; then divide it into rooted sections, making sure each has at least three growth buds. Replant divisions promptly.

Poppies are guaranteed attention getters, whether you choose the opulent Oriental type or the more modest Flanders Field poppies. The blossoms may be single or double, in bright or soft colors—but the petals are always silky and semitranslucent, with a pleated or crumpled texture. Single flowers are bowl shaped, often centered with a contrasting color; double blooms look like pompoms. The flowers are followed by decorative, nearly spherical (but flat-topped) seed capsules.

ANNUAL POPPIES

Flanders Field or Shirley poppy, *P. rhoeas* (Zones A1–A3; 1–24, 26, 28–45), blooms in spring and summer. In its wild form, this is the single bright red poppy of European fields. Modern versions, though, include a vast array of colors and combinations: white, soft blue, lilac, pink, salmon, red, orange, and bicolors. The single to double, 2- to 3-inch blossoms are carried on needle-thin, hairy, 2- to 3-foot-tall stems; leaves are pale green and deeply cut. The **Mother of Pearl** strain features mostly single flowers in muted, almost pearly-looking pastels and other colors; **Angels' Choir** offers a good array of colors and patterns in double flowers. **American Legion** and **Flanders Field** both bear brilliant scarlet blossoms with black centers.

Annual breadbox or opium poppy, *P. somniferum,* is a late-spring bloomer that succeeds in all zones. In its basic form, it's a striking plant with broad, jagged-edged gray-green leaves that clothe stems to 4 feet tall; the single, 4- to 5-inch blossoms are soft lilac pink. Thanks to selective breeding, however, colors now include not only pink shades but also white, red, plum, and blackish purple; flowers may be single, semidouble, or double. Spectacular double-flowered strains include **Frosted Salmon,** blackish maroon **Black Peony,** bright red **Oase,** and **White Cloud.** The large seed capsules of this poppy are the source of culinary poppy seed.

CULTURE. Sow seeds of annual poppies in well-drained, average to good soil. In areas where winter lows regularly drop below 10°F/−12°C, sow outdoors up to 4 weeks before the last-frost date. In warmer areas, sow in fall. The tiny seeds are difficult to distribute evenly; for best results, mix them with an equal amount of fine sand, then broadcast the mixture over the planting area. Barely cover the seeds with soil. In cool-summer climates, you can make successive sowings 6 weeks apart to get bloom over a long period. Remove spent flowers to prevent seed set; this will both prolong bloom and reduce the number of volunteer seedlings.

PERENNIAL POPPIES

Iceland poppy, *P. nudicaule,* grows as a summer-flowering perennial in Zones A2, A3, 1–6, 10, 32–45. But in mild-winter Zones 7–9, 12–24, 26 (upper half), 28, 31, it is grown as an annual for bloom in late winter and early spring. Clumps of blue-green, coarsely hairy, divided leaves send up thin stems bearing chalicelike blossoms 3 to 4 inches across. Colors include white, bright red, orange, and yellow, as well as softer shades of salmon, pink, and cream. Foot-tall **Champagne Bubbles** is a classic strain in pastel colors; **Partyfun** is the same size but includes many bright colors. **Wonderland** offers orange and pastel colors; its 10-inch stems are sturdier than most and resist wind. **Oregon Rainbows,** best adapted to the cool Pacific Northwest, features a full range of pastel colors on stems to 20 inches tall.

CULTURE. Plant Iceland poppies in well-drained, average soil. Where winter temperatures regularly drop below 10°F/−12°C, sow seeds outdoors for summer bloom as soon as soil can be worked; in milder regions, sow in fall for bloom in late winter or spring. If you're starting with young nursery-grown plants, set them out in fall in both cold- and mild-winter regions; they'll flower in summer or winter/spring, depending on climate.

Listing continues>

PAPAVER
POPPY
Papaveraceae
PERENNIALS AND WARM-SEASON ANNUALS
ZONES VARY
FULL SUN, EXCEPT AS NOTED
MODERATE TO REGULAR WATER
✿✿✿✿✿✿ FLOWERS IN SPRING
AND SUMMER, EXCEPT AS NOTED

Papaver rhoeas

Papaver orientale

Perennial Oriental poppy, **P. orientale,** is among the most spectacular of late-spring bloomers for Zones A1–A3, 1–11, 14–21, 30–45. Sumptuous, bowl-shaped blossoms to 8 inches wide (or wider) are carried on long, leafy stems that rise from clumps of finely divided, hairy green leaves. Foliage mounds grow about 2 feet high; stems can reach up to 4 feet, though height varies with the cultivar. The silken petals are tissue thin, with a crepe-paper texture; in many cultivars, they are black at the base, giving the flower a black center. The original Oriental poppies were neon orange or red, but the hundreds of cultivars sold today also offer blossoms in pastel shades, in white with colored edges, and with light rather than dark centers. The **Superpoppy** hybrids, with blossoms in red, pink, orange, and white, were developed to perform well in the mild-winter, hot-summer regions of the West Coast.

CULTURE. Oriental poppies perform best in zones with distinctly chilly winters. They need good drainage and will really flourish if you dig soil deeply and incorporate organic matter before planting. Choose a spot in full sun except in hot-summer areas, where light afternoon shade is better. Plant dormant roots in fall—3 inches deep in regions where soil freezes in winter, 1 inch deep in milder areas.

P. orientale and its various hybrids and strains all grow in spring, die down to the ground soon after flowering, send up new leaves in fall, and persist as small foliage tufts over winter. During growth and bloom, provide regular water; after bloom, moisture needs decrease (plants are fairly drought tolerant at that point). You can leave clumps in place for many years. If you need to divide for increase or to reduce crowding, do so in late summer. You also can take root cuttings in late summer; in fact, any cut roots left in the soil after digging may sprout.

PELARGONIUM
GERANIUM
Geraniaceae
PERENNIALS OFTEN GROWN AS
  WARM-SEASON ANNUALS
ZONES 8, 9, 12–24 AS PERENNIALS;
  ELSEWHERE AS ANNUALS
FULL SUN, EXCEPT AS NOTED
MODERATE TO REGULAR WATER
✿ ❀ ✿ ✿ ✿ FLOWERS IN SPRING, SUMMER

Pelargonium × domesticum

Bright and bountiful geraniums are mainstays of the summer garden, all-time favorites for pots and window boxes. Shrubby plants of various sizes, they are perennial in virtually frost-free, dry-summer climates—but they grow so fast and bloom so generously that they function as annuals in colder regions. Most have thick, almost succulent stems; long leafstalks carry rounded to heart-shaped leaves with edges that may be wavy, scalloped, toothed, or fluted. Five-petaled, somewhat to quite asymmetrical flowers are borne in large, rounded clusters.

Note: Though known by the common name "geranium," these plants should not be confused with the true or hardy geraniums described on page 124.

P. × domesticum goes by several names: Lady Washington pelargonium, Martha Washington geranium, regal geranium. Large, semiwoody plants 3 to 4 feet high and wide bear clusters of azalealike, 2- to 3-inch blossoms in white, lavender, pink shades, red, orange, or purple, usually with bright or velvety "thumbprints" in a darker color. Stiff dark green leaves are 2 to 4 inch inches across, with crinkled, sharp-toothed margins. Specialty growers offer many named cultivars.

Common or garden geranium, **P. × hortorum,** is the most widely grown of the tender geraniums, with the greatest available number of cultivars and strains. In frostless regions, plants grown in the ground may reach 3 to 4 feet high and wide, but compared to *P. × domesticum* they're soft—both in appearance and to the touch—rather than stiff. Leaves have scalloped margins and a covering of soft hairs; in shape, they range from nearly circular to somewhat maplelike. Many show a noticeable ring of darker color inward from the edge; this is most pronounced in the group known as zonal geraniums. Flowers are single or double and about 1 inch across, packed into dense clusters 4 to 6 inches in diameter; the color range includes white, violet, pink, red, orange, and coral.

Specialty growers carry a great many named cultivars. A few of the named zonal types are also available in the general nursery trade. Examples include 'Mrs. Pollock', with clusters of bright red-orange blossoms and green, cream-margined leaves with a maroon red zone; and 'Golden Ears' (perhaps identical to 'Vancouver Centennial'), bearing coral pink blossoms and deeply cut (nearly star-shaped) leaves in bronzy red with a chartreuse border. But much of the mass-market production for seasonal planting features multicolored seed-grown strains developed for compact growth and freedom of bloom. Prominent among these are Elite (fast-blooming, compact, 10-inch plants), Maverick (15-inch plants with zonal leaves, large blossom clusters), Multibloom (early-blooming, 10-inch plants), Orbit (14-inch plants with heavily zoned leaves, broad flower clusters), Sensation (shade-tolerant plants about 1 foot high), and Stardust (8- to 12-inch plants bearing deeply lobed leaves and star-shaped flowers with pointed petals).

Ivy geranium, *P. peltatum*, produces trailing, branching stems that are perfect for draping from window boxes and hanging baskets; in frost-free regions, it is an excellent ground cover. Glossy, five-lobed, ivylike leaves reach 3 inches across and are thick textured and succulent. Single or double flowers resemble those of *P. × hortorum* and come in white, pink shades, red, magenta, lavender, and various striped combinations. Many named cultivars exist, though in nurseries plants are often sold simply by color. White-flowered 'L'Elegante' is notable for its white-margined leaves. Summer Showers is a seed strain offering flowers in white, pink, red, maroon, and lavender.

CULTURE. All types grow best in well-drained soil. Set out plants as early as possible in spring but after all danger of frost is past. Choose a full-sun location except in hot-summer regions, where plants appreciate light shade in the afternoon. These geraniums perform best where summers are cool to mild and fairly dry; they dislike heat combined with humidity. If plants look like they're getting gangly, pinch stem tips periodically during the growing season to promote branching. Deadhead spent flower clusters both for neatness and to prevent seed set. Geranium budworm can ruin the flowers by eating buds before they open; see page 76 for controls.

New geraniums are easily started from stem cuttings taken in summer. To raise plants from seed, sow seeds indoors 14 to 16 weeks before the last-frost date. The plants will be killed by hard frosts, but you can overwinter potted specimens indoors or in a frost-free, well-lighted shelter.

Pelargonium × hortorum

Pelargonium × hortorum 'Golden Ears'

PENSTEMON
PENSTEMON, BEARD TONGUE
Scrophulariaceae
PERENNIALS SOMETIMES GROWN AS
   WARM-SEASON ANNUALS
ZONES VARY
FULL SUN, EXCEPT AS NOTED
WATER NEEDS VARY
✿ ✿ ❀ ✿ ✿ ✿ FLOWERS IN SPRING,
   SUMMER

The penstemons are noted for showy blossom spikes that appear over a long spring-and-summer bloom season—a show made even more exciting by the hummingbirds the flowers attract. The plants typically form clumps of upright stems bearing narrow, pointed leaves and spires of tubular to bell-shaped, five-lipped blooms. Most species come from arid or semiarid parts of the Midwest and West and are poorly adapted to humid climates and well-watered gardens. The species and hybrids described below, however, succeed in a wider range of climates and garden conditions.

Despite its Rocky Mountain origins, *P. barbatus* (Zones 1–20, 31–43) has a high tolerance for humid summers, but it does need some winter chill. The plant is a bit open, to 3 feet high and half as wide, with bright green, 2- to 6-inch-long leaves and narrow pink to red bells to 1½ inches long. 'Elfin Pink' has pure bright pink flowers on a 2-foot plant; dark pink 'Rose Elf' grows to 2½ feet. Two-foot-high 'Schooley's Yellow' offers an unusual color for a penstemon: soft lemon yellow. The seed-grown Rondo series has flowers in red, pink, lilac, and purple on plants to 16 inches high.

P. digitalis, native to the central and eastern U.S., is the best bet for humid-summer regions; it's adapted to Zones 1–9, 14–24, 29–43. Growing 3 to 5 feet tall, the plant has stems outfitted in leaves to 7 inches long and topped by clusters of white or pale pink, 1-inch bells. Its 2½- to 3-foot cultivar **'Husker Red'** has pinkish white blooms and rich maroon red foliage.

The showiest of these adaptable penstemons belong to the hybrid group designated ***P. × gloxinioides.*** Perennial in Zones 6–9, 12–24, these plants can be grown as annuals in other zones. They're compact, bushy growers 2 to 4 feet high, bearing 2-inch bells in almost all colors but orange and yellow; in many, the blossoms have white interiors. Among the many named selections are lavender **'Alice Hindley'**; deep purple **'Blackbird'** and **'Midnight'**; rosy pink **'Evelyn'**; dark scarlet **'Firebird'**; wine red **'Garnet'**; and pink-tinged **'Holly's White'**. **'Hopleys Variegated'** presents white-throated lilac-blue blossoms on plants with cream-margined leaves. The seed-grown **Kissed** series has flowers in various colors, all with white throats.

CULTURE. These penstemons grow easily in average soil as long as drainage is good; they won't tolerate saturated soil, especially in winter. *P. digitalis* takes regular watering. *P. barbatus* and *P. × gloxinioides* prefer moderate watering, though the latter will accept regular moisture if drainage is excellent. Where summers are hot, choose a site receiving a bit of shade during the heat of the day. After the first flush of flowers, cut plants back to encourage a second round of bloom.

Performance declines after 3 to 4 years. At that point, you can start replacement plants from stem cuttings taken in summer or by layering stems; some stems may even self-layer, providing replacement plants immediately.

Penstemon digitalis

Penstemon × gloxinioides 'Firebird'

PEROVSKIA
RUSSIAN SAGE
Lamiaceae (Labiatae)
PERENNIAL
ZONES 2–24, 28–43
FULL SUN
LITTLE TO MODERATE WATER
✿ FLOWERS IN SUMMER

In the shimmering heat of midsummer, Russian sage's cool blue haze of bloom is especially welcome. Many gray-white stems clothed in gray-green foliage form a shrubby, upright clump 3 to 4 feet high and wide. Along the lower parts of the stems, leaves are 2 to 3 inches long and deeply cut; higher up, they become smaller and are toothed rather than cut. Each stem terminates in a long, branching spray of small, tubular lavender-blue blossoms that seem to float over the foliage.

Though Russian sage is usually sold as ***P. atriplicifolia,*** the plants in general circulation are thought to be hybrids between that species and *P. abrotanoides.* Widely grown **'Blue Spire'** (sometimes sold as *P. atriplicifolia* 'Superba' or *P.* 'Longin') has deep violet-blue blossoms on distinctly upright, 2-foot stems. Lighter blue choices include **'Blue Mist'**, which comes into flower earlier than other cultivars, and **'Blue Haze'**. **'Filigran'** is denser and more compact than the others, with light blue flowers held above silvery, filigreelike foliage. Lavender-blue **'Little Spire'** is a relatively dwarf cultivar reaching only about 2 feet high.

CULTURE. Russian sage will grow in almost any soil—poor to rich—as long as drainage is good. To keep the plants as bushy as possible, cut them nearly to the ground in early spring, leaving just one or two pairs of growth buds on each vigorous stem. Especially in lighter soils, established plants often will spread by underground stems to form colonies. Plants can remain in place indefinitely, but if you want to increase a planting, you can dig and transplant rooted stems from the clump's perimeter. Or take stem cuttings in summer.

Perovskia

In any contest for favorite annual, petunias would be top contenders. They're easy to grow, even in poor, sandy soil, and can produce color virtually nonstop from shortly after planting until stopped by frost. In the mildest areas, they'll live through the winter and grow as perennials, though their second-year performance seldom equals the first-year show. Flowers are pleasantly fragrant, single or double, ranging in size from under 1 inch to 6 inches across. Single flowers are shaped like trumpets; double types are so full and fluffy they look like carnations. You'll find a broad range of colors, and possible patterns vary widely, too. Blossoms may be solid colored, edged in white, marked with contrasting veins, or centered in a contrasting dark or light color; star-patterned bicolors sport a dark center and dark stripes radiating out onto each lobe of the flower.

Most petunias sold today fall into the four categories described below. Some are designated F_1—short for first-generation hybrids. These plants are more vigorous and more uniform in character than F_2 plants.

Hybrid Grandiflora. As the name suggests, these have the largest flowers among petunias. Plants reach 15 to 27 inches high and can spread to 3 feet. The majority have single flowers to $4\frac{1}{2}$ inches across, with ruffled or fringed edges; colors include pink shades, red, blue, white, yellow, and striped combinations. **Double Hybrid Grandifloras,** with heavily ruffled flowers, come in all of those colors but yellow. Many strains are available. Among these, **Fluffy Ruffles** produces ultra-large flowers—up to 6 inches across. **Magic** and **Supermagic** are compact plants with 4- to 5-inch blooms in just white, pink, red, and blue. **Dream** and **Storm** hold up better in rainy weather than most Hybrid Grandifloras; **Aladdin** reaches blooming size from seed more quickly than most. **Hula-hoop** and **Frost** have colored flowers with white picotee edges; the **Daddy** series features flowers with a network of darker veins on the petals. **'Prism Sunshine'** is a soft but bright yellow. **Cascade, Countdown,** and **Supercascade** have trailing stems.

Hybrid Multiflora (Floribunda). Plants of these strains resemble Hybrid Grandifloras, but they bloom much more profusely and tend to be denser and more compact. Blossoms are smaller (about 2 inches wide), single or double, with smooth petal edges. **Celebrity** and **Primetime** are two strains that offer a wide array of color choices, including yellow; plants of **Merlin** are profusely branched.

Hybrid Milliflora. Dwarf plants grow just 6 to 8 inches high and wide, forming neat mounds that stay compact without pinching or cutting back. Flowers are 1 to $1\frac{1}{2}$ inches across. The **Fantasy** series offers flowers in white, blue, pink, and red.

Trailing petunias. Plants are low and wide spreading, suitable for containers as well as small-scale ground cover. The seed-grown, heavy-blooming **Wave** series bears flowers in pink shades and purple; plants reach just 6 inches high but can spread to 5 feet across. Cutting-grown types are available only as started plants. Among these, **Cascadias** have $1\frac{1}{2}$-inch flowers in an extensive color range; **Surfinias** are similar but come only in white, pink, and bluish purple shades. **Petitunias** have the smallest flowers (just $\frac{3}{4}$ inch across); **Supertunias** have the largest, at $2\frac{1}{2}$ inches wide.

CULTURE. Plant petunias in average to good, well-drained soil. To raise plants from seed, sow indoors 8 to 10 weeks before the last-frost date; simply press seeds into soil, since they need light in order to germinate. Plant outdoors after all danger of frost is past. After plants are established, pinch them back about halfway to promote compact growth. Fertilize monthly; deadhead to prevent seed set and promote continued flowering. As plants become leggy or straggly, cut them back to restore compactness; new growth will quickly fill in. The fungal disease botrytis can damage flowers and foliage in humid weather; geranium budworm can ruin the flowers. See pages 75 and 76 for controls. Smog can cause spots on leaves of young plants, especially those with white flowers.

PETUNIA × hybrida

Solanaceae

PERENNIAL GROWN AS
   WARM-SEASON ANNUAL
ALL ZONES
FULL SUN
REGULAR WATER
✿ ✿ ❀ ✿ ✿ FLOWERS IN SPRING,
   SUMMER, FALL

Petunia × hybrida, Daddy series

Petunia × hybrida 'Purple Wave'

PHLOMIS

Lamiaceae (Labiatae)

PERENNIALS

ZONES 2–24, 31–41, EXCEPT AS NOTED

FULL SUN, EXCEPT AS NOTED

LITTLE TO MODERATE WATER

✿❀✿✿✿ FLOWERS IN SPRING, SUMMER

Phlomis russeliana

These Mediterranean natives never fail to perform, even when given just a meager diet. All have the same basic appearance: upright stems are clothed with opposite pairs of hairy to furry, roughly arrow-shaped leaves and carry nearly ball-shaped whorls of tubular, two-lipped blossoms in their upper reaches.

P. russeliana, with furry olive green leaves to 8 inches long, spreads to form a low, ground-covering patch. Flower stems rise 2 to 3 feet tall in early summer, offering tiered whorls of soft yellow blossoms that age to cream. After the flowers fade, the dried stalks remain attractive until or even throughout winter. **P. samia** also forms a low-growing foliage mat; its scallop-edged, 4- to 8-inch-long leaves are medium green on top, white and woolly beneath. Flowers come all through summer on 2- to 3-foot stems; the standard colors are purple and dark lilac, but forms exist with white and nearly green blossoms.

Tuberous-rooted **P. tuberosa** (Zones A1–A3; 1–24, 31–45) forms a rosette of deep green, finely hairy leaves to 10 inches long; clumps remain discrete and do not spread widely. In late spring and early summer, flower stems rise 3 to 6 feet high, bearing tiered whorls of purple or lilac-pink flowers.

CULTURE. These plants are not particular about soil quality, but they must have good drainage. Give them full sun; *P. russeliana* will also succeed in light shade. All tolerate drought but look and perform better with moderate watering, especially where summers are hot and dry. To increase plantings, divide clumps in early spring; or remove and replant rooted pieces from a clump's perimeter.

PHLOX

Polemoniaceae

PERENNIALS AND COOL-SEASON ANNUALS

ZONES VARY

EXPOSURE NEEDS VARY

REGULAR WATER

✿✿❀✿✿✿ FLOWERS IN SPRING, SUMMER

Phlox drummondii, Phlox of Sheep strain

Ranging from low, spreading annual and perennial plants to taller, upright classics for the perennial border, the many phloxes are reliable sources of bright, pure color. All have blossoms that are quite similar in shape: a slender tube flares out to a flat, five-segmented flower that's circular in outline. In some of the low-growing sorts, the segments may be separate, giving the blossom the look of a star or pinwheel; in the tall kinds, the segments are usually overlapping, so that each blossom resembles an unbroken circle.

Annual phlox, **P. drummondii** (Zones A2, A3; 1–45; H1), blooms in spring and summer, bearing dense clusters of sweet-scented, ½- to 1-inch-wide flowers. It spreads to about a foot and grows from 6 to 18 inches high, depending on the strain; stems are somewhat sticky, clothed in nearly oval leaves 1 to 3 inches long. Flowers come in blue, purple, white, yellow, orange, red, and pink; some have a central eye, either in white or a darker shade of the blossom color. Annual phlox is excellent for borders, in containers, even as a small-scale ground cover. Many mixed-color strains are sold, including **Dolly, Beauty,** and **Globe** (all 6 inches); **Cecily** and **Fantasy** (8 inches); and 15-inch **Grandiflora. Phlox of Sheep** (1 foot) and **Unique** (10 inches) offer a mix of soft pastels; **Twinkle** (6 inches) has star-shaped flowers.

Perennial phloxes fall into two fairly distinct groups. One contains several low-growing, mostly spring-flowering species; these are spreading plants, good for foreground plantings or ground cover. The second group contains the summer-blooming sorts, typified by border phlox *(P. paniculata);* they grow 2 to 4 feet tall and bear showy flowers in dense terminal clusters.

Belonging to the first group, sweet William phlox, **P. divaricata** (Zones 1–17, 28–43), reaches about 1 foot high and spreads by creeping rhizomes. Its leafy stems are clothed in oval, 1- to 2-inch-long leaves; fragrant lavender-blue blossoms appear in open clusters at stem ends. Selections include icy blue 'Clouds of Perfume' and 'Dirigo Ice'; 'Eco Texas Purple', with maroon-centered blue flowers; and white 'Fuller's White' and 'White Perfume'. The variant form **P. d. laphamii** reaches

1½ feet and offers bright blue blossoms (purple in the selection **‘Louisiana Purple’**); its hybrid **‘Chattahoochee’** has maroon-eyed lavender flowers on a 10-inch-high plant.

Another low grower is creeping phlox, ***P. stolonifera*** (Zones A2, A3; 1–17, 28–45). It mounds 6 to 8 inches high and spreads by stolons; stems are clothed in narrow leaves to 1½ inches long. Bloom time brings a lavish show of lavender, inch-wide flowers in small clusters. Named selections include **‘Bruce’s White’**; lavender-blue **‘Blue Ridge’**; deep lavender **‘Sherwood Purple’**; and **‘Melrose’**, **‘Pink Ridge’**, and **‘Spring Delight’**, all with pink flowers.

Phlox subulata

Moss pink, ***P. subulata*** (Zones 1–17, 28–45), is a favorite for growing on banks and in rock gardens. Creeping stems clothed in needlelike, ½-inch leaves form a 6-inch-high mat that is transformed into a sheet of brilliant color in late spring or early summer. The ¾-inch flowers range from white through lavender blue, violet, and magenta to some fairly neon shades of pink. Many named selections are available; the unusual **‘Candy Stripe’** has deep pink blossoms margined in white.

The second perennial group—the tall, summer-blooming phloxes—is dominated by two species that produce large flower clusters atop lofty stems. Thick-leaf phlox, ***P. maculata*** (Zones 1–14, 18–23, 31–45), blooms in early summer, bearing ¾-inch flowers in elongated to nearly cylindrical clusters to 15 inches long. Colors include white and all shades of pink (from pale pink to magenta), often with a contrasting central eye. The plant reaches 3 to 4 feet high and has shiny green, lance-shaped, 2- to 4-inch leaves that resist powdery mildew. Nurseries offer named selections, including rose pink **‘Alpha’**, pink-and-white **‘Natascha’**, lavender-eyed white **‘Omega’**, and deep lilac-pink **‘Rosalinde’**. Classic pure white **‘Miss Lingard’** may be a selection or a hybrid with a similar species, *P. carolina*.

Phlox maculata ‘Alpha’

Blooming in midsummer, border or summer phlox, ***P. paniculata*** (Zones 1–14, 18–21, 27–43), boasts fragrant flowers in dome-shaped to pyramidal clusters up to 8 inches across. Colors include white, lavender, and soft pink as well as intense shades of salmon orange, magenta, red, maroon, and purple; many feature a contrasting eye. Plants reach 2 to 4 feet in bloom, depending on the cultivar. Leaves are a bit larger and duller than those of *P. carolina* and *P. maculata* and are notoriously susceptible to powdery mildew in late summer. Of the numerous available cultivars, some are resistant (but not immune) to mildew. These include **‘Bright Eyes’**, with crimson-eyed pale pink flowers; white **‘David’** and **‘Fujiyama’** (**‘Mount Fujiyama’**); red-eyed pink **‘Eva Cullum’**; and lilac-pink **‘Franz Schubert’**.

CULTURE. *P. drummondii* prefers a sunny spot and fairly light, well-drained soil, thoroughly amended with organic matter. Sow seeds so that plants will flower during cool to mild weather, since heat—especially in combination with humidity—puts an end to performance. In mild-winter areas, you can sow seeds as early as fall for bloom in early spring; plants will continue flowering into summer if temperatures remain mild. Where winters are definitely cold and summers are hot, you can sow seeds outdoors 2 to 3 weeks before the last-frost date or indoors 6 to 8 weeks before that date. In cool-summer areas, sow indoors or outdoors, at the times just stated; plants should bloom throughout summer.

Among perennial phloxes, low-growing *P. divaricata* and *P. stolonifera* prefer light shade in most climates, but in cool-summer regions, they’ll also prosper in full sun. *P. subulata* prefers full sun in all but the hottest climates. Plant all three of these species in well-drained, organically enriched soil. To increase your plantings, you can divide plants in early spring.

The tall phloxes need regular attention to remain healthy and attractive. They’re at their best where summers are cool to mild and will take full sun there; in hot-summer regions, they fare better with more shade and a mulch to help retain moisture around

Phlox paniculata ‘Franz Schubert’

Phlox paniculata

the roots. Plant in well-prepared soil enriched with plenty of organic matter; water regularly throughout the growing season. To lessen problems with powdery mildew on *P. paniculata*, look for resistant cultivars and locate them where air circulation is good (away from walls and hedges), being sure not to crowd plants. Each clump will send up numerous stems; for the best display, cut out all but the strongest four to six of these. During bloom time, deadhead regularly. Besides encouraging a second flowering from side shoots, this will prevent seed set and a resultant crop of volunteer seedlings—which tend to produce purplish pink flowers, regardless of the parent's color. To maintain vigor, divide clumps every 2 to 4 years in early spring.

PHORMIUM
NEW ZEALAND FLAX

Agavaceae

PERENNIALS

ZONES 7–9, 14–28, H1, H2; PLANTS REGROW AFTER FREEZES IN ZONES 5, 6

FULL SUN OR PARTIAL SHADE

LITTLE TO MODERATE WATER, EXCEPT AS NOTED

❀ ❀ FLOWERS IN LATE SPRING, EARLY SUMMER; MOST ARE GROWN PRIMARILY FOR FOLIAGE IN SHADES OF GREEN, CREAM, BRONZE, RED, AND PURPLE, OFTEN IN MULTICOLORED COMBINATIONS

Dramatic accents for garden beds and containers alike, these striking evergreen perennials form irislike fans of sword-shaped leaves; established clumps are foliage fountains that look like grasses with very broad leaves. Multibranched spikes of tubular flowers come in late spring to early summer. Two species and a group of hybrids between the two offer a considerable choice of plant sizes and foliage colors.

P. cookianum (P. colensoi), forming clumps up to 5 feet high and 10 feet across, has gracefully arching, medium green, droopy-tipped leaves up to 3 inches wide and 5 feet long. Yellow flowers come on stems barely taller than the foliage. 'Dwarf', as the name implies, is a smaller-growing selection—just 3 feet high and 5 to 6 feet across. Leaves of *P. c. hookeri* 'Tricolor' are green with cream stripes and a thin red edge; in its sport 'Cream Delight', leaves feature a creamy yellow central stripe and a narrow green margin edged in dark red. Both cultivars will reach about 3 feet high and twice as wide.

P. tenax is a larger, bolder plant with bronzy green, stiffly upright leaves that can reach 5 inches wide and 9 feet long; mature clumps have a spread equal to or slightly greater than their height. Erect reddish brown stalks to 10 feet high develop a "hat rack" of branches holding many dull red to reddish orange blossoms. 'Variegatum', reaching 8 feet high and wide, has narrower leaves than the species, in grayish green with a cream margin. Two smaller versions of the same thing are 1-foot 'Tiny Tiger' ('Aurea Nana') and 2-foot 'Toney Tiger'. Other variegated cultivars include 6-foot 'Veitchianum' ('Radiance', 'Williamsii Variegatum'), with green leaves sporting a yellow central stripe, and 5-foot 'Pink Stripe' ('Pink Edge'), with purple-tinted gray-green leaves narrowly edged in bright pink.

Bronze- to purple-leafed selections to 8 feet high and wide are variously labeled 'Atropurpureum', 'Bronze', 'Purpureum', and 'Rubrum'; these are usually raised from seed, so there's some variation in leaf color regardless of the particular name. Smaller reddish- to bronze-leafed cultivars include 5-foot 'Atropurpureum Compactum' ('Monrovia Red'); 3-foot-tall 'Bronze Baby'; and brown, 5-foot 'Chocolate'. Two 1½-footers with red-brown foliage are 'Jack Spratt' (with twisting leaves) and 'Thumbelina' (with upright leaves). For other colors, try 6-foot 'Dusky Chief', with wine red leaves edged in coral, and purple-black 'Morticia', to 4 feet.

Many other cultivars noted for brightly colored foliage have been developed from *P. cookianum* and *P. tenax*. They're smaller than *P. tenax* and tend to be less tolerant of cold and heat than either parent; damage is likely at temperatures below 20°F/−7°C. This sampling is representative of the sizes and colors available. Three 3-foot-tall choices are 'Apricot Queen', forming a dense clump of yellowish green, apricot-blushed leaves with a green edge and hairline-thin red margin; 'Dazzler', with narrow, arching, twisting leaves in maroon striped with bright red; and 'Gold Sword', an upright grower with bright yellow leaves edged in green. 'Dark Delight' forms a 4-foot-tall clump of arching, bronzed red-purple leaves with an orange midrib. 'Yellow

Phormium tenax 'Jack Spratt'

Wave', reaching 4 to 5 feet high, has broad chartreuse leaves with a lime green margin. **'Maori Chief'** and **'Sundowner'** are both upright 6-footers with leaves in green shades, striped or margined in pink. Four-foot **'Maori Maiden'** reverses the color scheme: it has salmon pink leaves (fading to cream) with a narrow olive green margin. **'Rainbow Warrior'** is similar but darker; its leaves turn nearly blood red in winter.

CULTURE. Plant in well-drained, average soil. New Zealand flaxes do best where summers are cool to mild; in these climates, they'll grow in full sun to light shade and prosper with little to moderate water. In hot-summer areas, they need light shade during the hottest hours of the day (this is particularly true of hybrid cultivars) and moderate watering—even regular watering if soil is light. Where winters are too cold for these plants to survive in the ground, grow them in containers and move to a cool greenhouse over winter. Clumps can remain in place indefinitely with no need for division. However, to increase a particular plant, you can divide it in spring (or dig and transplant rooted pieces from the clump's perimeter).

Phormium 'Yellow Wave'

Physostegia virginiana 'Variegata'

Blossoms that resemble those of snapdragon *(Antirrhinum)* explain one of this plant's common names. The second name, "obedient plant," refers to a curious trait: the flowers will remain in place if twisted or pushed out of position. The plant forms a spreading clump, sending up 3- to 4-foot stems clothed in toothed, lance-shaped leaves to 5 inches long. In summer or early fall, each stem is topped by a tapering spike of inch-long flowers. The typical blossom color is bright bluish pink, but named cultivars offer other choices. **'Bouquet Rose'** has rose pink blossoms, while **'Red Beauty'** offers deeper rose blooms; both grow about 3 feet tall. Three 2-foot cultivars are **'Summer Snow'**, with pure white flowers; rose pink **'Vivid'**; and **'Variegata'**, bearing pink blossoms set off by foliage strikingly variegated in creamy white.

CULTURE. False dragonhead grows best with good soil and plenty of moisture. Under these conditions, it spreads rapidly and will require dividing and replanting every 2 to 3 years in spring.

PHYSOSTEGIA virginiana
FALSE DRAGONHEAD,
OBEDIENT PLANT
Lamiaceae (Labiatae)
PERENNIAL
ZONES A3; 1–9, 14–24, 26–45
FULL SUN TO PARTIAL SHADE
REGULAR WATER
❀ ✿ FLOWERS IN SUMMER, EARLY FALL

Physostegia virginiana

Balloonlike, nearly spherical buds open to star-shaped, 2-inch summer flowers like wide-open campanulas. Typically blue violet with purple veining, the blossoms are carried on slender stalks at the ends of upright, 3-foot stems clothed in broadly oval, 3-inch leaves. Named cultivars offer variations in plant size and flower color. White-blossomed **'Fuji White'** grows to 2 feet tall; **'Hakone Blue'**, with double bright blue flowers, and **'Shell Pink'** both reach 1½ to 2 feet high. Still shorter are two cultivars bearing blooms in the basic blue violet: **'Mariesii'** (1 to 1½ feet tall) and **'Sentimental Blue'** (just 10 inches high).

CULTURE. Balloon flower grows best in well-prepared, well-drained, fairly light soil. Give it full sun except in hot-summer regions, where light shade or filtered sunlight is

PLATYCODON grandiflorus
BALLOON FLOWER
Campanulaceae (Lobeliaceae)
PERENNIAL
ZONES 1–10, 14–24, 26, 28–45
FULL SUN, EXCEPT AS NOTED
REGULAR WATER
✿ ✿ ❀ ✿ FLOWERS IN SUMMER

preferable. If gophers are a problem in your garden, protect the plants' roots from them. Flowering will continue for 2 months or more if you regularly remove the spent blossoms (do so carefully, to keep from damaging new buds growing nearby along the stem). Plants die back completely in fall and new growth appears quite late the following spring, so mark locations carefully to avoid digging up roots by accident. Plants are a bit slow to establish and don't need division to maintain vigor—but if you want more plants, divide in spring, taking plenty of soil along with the deep roots.

Platycodon grandiflorus

POLYGONATUM
SOLOMON'S SEAL
Liliaceae
PERENNIALS
ZONES A1–A3; 1–9, 14–17, 28–45
PARTIAL TO FULL SHADE
REGULAR WATER
❀ FLOWERS IN SPRING

Polygonatum biflorum

Studies in elegance, these plants form gradually spreading clumps, sending up stems that grow upright for a distance and then arch outward. Broadly oval leaves are set on both sides of the stems, arranged in nearly horizontal planes. Where leaves join the stems, small, bell-shaped white blossoms are suspended on threadlike stalks; small blue-black berries may follow the flowers. In fall, leaves and stems turn bright yellow, then die back.

Sometimes called small Solomon's seal, *P. biflorum* has 4-inch leaves on stems to 3 feet tall; flowers come in twos or threes. The plant known as great Solomon's seal was once designated *P. commutatum* or *P. canaliculatum*, but it is now regarded simply as a large form of *P. biflorum*. Its stems can reach 5 feet tall, its leaves 7 inches long; flowers appear in groups of two to ten.

P. odoratum '**Variegatum**' bears 4-inch leaves neatly margined in creamy white on 2- to 3-foot stems that are dark red until fully grown. Blossoms appear individually or in pairs.

CULTURE. These plants grow best in the moist, organically rich soil typical of woodlands, but they perform reasonably well in drier soils—even in competition with tree roots. Clumps can remain in place indefinitely, with no need for division. If you want to increase a planting, however, do so in early spring: remove rhizomes (each with at least one growth bud) from the clump's edge and replant immediately.

PORTULACA
Portulacaceae
WARM-SEASON ANNUALS
ALL ZONES
FULL SUN
MODERATE WATER
❀❀❀❀❀ FLOWERS IN SPRING, SUMMER, FALL

Flaunting silky-sheened blossoms in neon-bright colors, these plants add a definite sparkle to foreground plantings and containers. They have succulent leaves and stems and are at their best in warm weather, unfazed even by summer heat that stops many other plants in their tracks.

Old-fashioned favorite *P. grandiflora*, rose moss, is a spreading, trailing plant with reddish stems and narrow, virtually cylindrical, inch-long leaves. It blooms from spring into autumn, bearing single to double flowers that resemble inch-wide roses; they typically open in the morning and close by midafternoon. The mixed-color **Margarita** strain offers larger blossoms (to 1½ inches); deep pink '**Margarita Rosita**' is sold separately. Also available in a wide palette of both single and mixed colors (including some bicolors) is the **Sundial** strain, with still larger (2-inch) blooms that remain open later into the afternoon. The **Passion Fruit** strain contains flowers in cream and in fuchsia shades, irregularly marked and splashed with contrasting color.

Another portulaca resembles edible purslane *(P. oleracea)* and is widely known by the same common name, though in fact it's a different plant. Thick stems hug the ground and spread to 2 feet, bearing fleshy, oval leaves about 1 inch long; single, 1-inch-wide flowers last just a day but are produced over a long period in late spring and summer. Belonging to these "purslanes" are the **Wildfire** hybrids, which come in the full range of portulaca colors. Also included here is the **Duet** strain, offering several selections with yellow, pink, or white flowers with petal margins irregularly marked in another color.

CULTURE. These plants revel in hot weather and plenty of sunshine. Though they'll take more luxurious conditions, they perform brilliantly with just average soil (of any type) and moderate water. They're good choices for exposed, hard-to-water locations such as parking strips and hillsides. Both *P. grandiflora* and the purslanes are fine choices for containers and hanging baskets.

Sow seeds outdoors after the danger of frost is past; or sow indoors 6 to 8 weeks before the last-frost date. Just press seeds into soil, but do not cover them; they need light in order to germinate. All will self-sow readily, though seedlings tend not to show as wide a color range as the parents.

Portulaca grandiflora 'Sundial Peppermint'

Whether planted along a shaded path, in a border, or near a pond or stream, primroses provide an air of woodland or country-garden charm. Foliage rosettes send up stems bearing circular, five-petaled flowers, each petal notched or indented at its apex; blossoms may be borne individually, in clusters at the stem tips, or in tiered clusters along the stem. Primroses often are considered a symbol of spring, and most are in fact spring blooming—but some start flowering in mid- to late winter in mild climates, and a few bloom in early summer. The genus is a complex one, comprising hundreds of species and hybrids. The primroses described here are relatively common and relatively easy to grow, as long as they receive the conditions they need.

Fairy primrose, *P. malacoides,* will grow as a perennial in Zones 8, 9, 12–24, but even in those zones it is usually treated as an annual—as it must be in Zones 1–7, 31–41. Long-stalked, soft-textured leaves are pale green ovals to 3 inches long, with blunt-toothed margins. Stems reach 10 to 18 inches high, bearing tiered, loosely packed whorls of ½-inch flowers in white, lavender, pink, or rosy red. Depending on the mildness of winter, bloom can come at any time from midwinter to late spring. Fairy primrose is usually seen as a container plant, though in mild-winter areas it can be massed for an ephemeral flowering ground cover, looking especially fetching beneath early-flowering deciduous trees and with early-blooming daffodils.

Sometimes called drumstick primrose, perennial *P. denticulata* (Zones A2, A3; 1–6, 34–43) carries its dense, ball-shaped clusters of ½-inch flowers atop stout, foot-high stems. Colors run from blue to lavender to violet; there are white and lilac-pink forms as well. At bloom time in early spring, the medium green, spatula-shaped leaves are about 6 inches long; they later lengthen to about 1 foot. Polyanthus primrose, *P.* × *polyantha* (Zones 1–24, 32–41), is generally regarded as the most adaptable primrose. This hybrid group forms clumps of fresh green, tongue-shaped leaves to about 8 inches long; yellow-centered, 1- to 2-inch-wide flowers appear from winter to early or midspring, in an array of colors including everything but true green and black. The showy blossoms are carried in terminal clusters on stocky, 8- to 12-inch stems. Many strains are available, usually in mixed colors, though the **Gold Laced** strain has mahogany blossoms with yellow centers and edges.

P. sieboldii (Zones A2, A3; 2–7, 14–17, 34, 36–40) has downy, wrinkled, arrow-shaped light green leaves with scalloped margins. Each leaf is 2 to 4 inches long, carried on a slender leafstalk. In late spring, slender 4- to 8-inch stems bear clusters of

PRIMULA
PRIMROSE
Primulaceae
PERENNIALS, SOME GROWN AS
    COOL-SEASON ANNUALS
ZONES VARY
PARTIAL TO FULL SHADE, EXCEPT AS NOTED
REGULAR WATER, EXCEPT AS NOTED
✿ ✿ ❀ ✿ ✿ ✿ ✿ FLOWERS IN WINTER,
    SPRING, SUMMER

Primula denticulata

Primula × polyantha

1- to 1½-inch-wide lavender flowers with a white eye. Named selections come in pure white as well as in purple shades ranging from lavender to wine violet. Leaves die back after flowering, helping this primrose endure hotter, drier summers more successfully than other species.

English primrose, ***P. vulgaris*** (***P. acaulis;*** Zones A3, 2–6, 14–17, 21–24, 32–41), resembles *P. × polyantha* in general appearance, though it's a bit smaller. Bright green, wrinkled, 10-inch-long leaves shaped like canoe paddles form clumps to 8 inches high; in early spring, light yellow, fragrant, 1¼-inch flowers appear on individual stems just barely taller than the foliage. Garden strains may have two or three flowers per stem, in colors including white, yellow, red, blue, bronze, and wine red. The **Sweetheart** series has double flowers.

Though all primroses like regular watering, some are real moisture lovers, suited to boggy soil and even shallow water. These include the so-called Candelabra types, with tiered flower clusters on stems taller than those of other primroses. The most widely available of these is ***P. japonica***, successful in Zones A3, 2–6, 15–17, 32 (cooler parts), 34, 36–40. During its bloom period in late spring to early summer, blossom stalks rise to as high as 2½ feet above clumps of tongue-shaped light green leaves to 9 inches long. The 1½-inch flowers typically come in purple, red, pink, and white; **'Miller's Crimson'** is a standard dark red cultivar, while **'Potsford White'** is a superior white selection with larger-than-usual blossoms. The skyscraper of these moisture lovers is ***P. florindae*** (Zones A2, A3; 3–6, 15–17). Stems to 3 feet tall carry nodding terminal clusters of up to 60 bell-shaped, ¾-inch, fragrant yellow flowers. Glossy, broadly oval medium green leaves are about 9 inches long, carried on long leafstalks.

CULTURE. Primrose species are native to woodlands and moist meadows, in cool, humid climates. They like the same conditions in gardens: organically enriched soil and a cool, moist atmosphere. In cool-summer areas, especially where foggy, overcast conditions are common, you can plant primroses in nearly full-sun locations. Elsewhere, plant them in full or part shade (be sure they receive protection from afternoon sun). Most of the primroses profiled above do best with regular watering, but the last two described—*P. japonica* and *P. florindae*—prefer even more moisture, thriving in squashy, marshy soil as well as in very shallow (even moving) water.

Primrose plants form tight clumps; when performance eventually declines, divide the clumps right after flowering finishes.

Primula vulgaris

PULMONARIA
LUNGWORT
Boraginaceae
PERENNIALS
ZONES 1–9, 14–17, 32–43
PARTIAL TO FULL SHADE
REGULAR WATER
✿ ✿ ✿ ✿ ✿ FLOWERS IN SPRING

These charming woodland plants are decorative in both leaf and blossom, and their low stature and dense growth make them ideal for pathway edgings or even small-scale ground covers. Hairy, broadly oval to lance-shaped leaves form rosettes or clumps; in many kinds, the foliage is attractively dappled with gray or silver. Smaller leaves appear on the flowering stems, just beneath the clusters of nodding funnel- or trumpet-shaped flowers. The blossoms open just before or just as new growth emerges in spring. After bloom ends, the plants produce more foliage; with regular watering, they'll stay attractive throughout summer.

Blue lungwort, ***P. angustifolia***, has bright blue flowers opening from pink buds; plants reach 8 to 12 inches high and have dark green, unspotted leaves to a foot long. Selected forms include **'Blaues Meer'**, with larger, brighter blue flowers than the species, and sky blue ***P. a. azurea***. Silver-spotted dark green, slightly floppy leaves to 20 inches long distinguish ***P. longifolia***. Its purplish blue flowers, borne on 8- to 12-inch stalks, bloom later in spring than those of other species. Its selection **'Bertram Anderson'** has vivid deep blue blossoms and fairly upright-growing foliage.

P. rubra, one of the earliest-blooming lungworts, has coral red flowers on 16-inch stems and pale green, unspotted, 6-inch leaves. **'Bowles' Red'** is an especially fine selection; **'Barfield Pink'** has brick red blossoms edged and veined in white. **'David Ward'** features coral-colored flowers and olive green foliage margined in cream.

Blue-flowered Bethlehem sage, *P. saccharata,* presents foot-long, beautifully spotted leaves on plants growing 1 to 1½ feet high. More widely available than the species are various choice selections, among them **'Margery Fish'** and **'Mrs. Moon'**, with pink buds opening to blue flowers; **'Janet Fisk'**, with similar flowers carried above heavily marbled leaves; **'Pierre's Pure Pink'**, salmon pink in both bud and open blossom; and **'Reginald Kaye'**, with rose pink buds that unfurl to violet blooms.

Many hybrid lungworts are also sold, most featuring especially beautiful foliage. **'Excalibur'** has violet-blue flowers and striking silvery white leaves margined in dark green. The sky blue blossoms of **'Roy Davidson'** are set off against long, narrow deep green leaves evenly marked with silver. **'Spilled Milk'** features foliage of an almost solid silver white, margined and sparsely flecked in dark green; blue flowers open from pink buds. Blue-flowered **'Golden Haze'** is named for its foliage: each leaf is irregularly edged in gold, and a golden overlay covers the entire leaf.

CULTURE. Lungworts need soil that's well drained but always moist. Incorporate plenty of organic matter before planting. Choose a spot in partial to full shade; even with moist soil, leaves tend to wilt in full sun. After a number of years, clumps will become crowded and require division. Do the job in early fall; be sure to keep the newly planted divisions well watered.

TOP: *Pulmonaria longifolia*
BOTTOM: *Pulmonaria* 'Excalibur'

RICINUS communis

CASTOR BEAN
Euphorbiaceae
WARM-SEASON ANNUAL
ZONES 1–45; H1, H2
FULL SUN
MODERATE TO REGULAR WATER
❀ FLOWERS IN SUMMER; GROWN PRIMARILY
  FOR FOLIAGE

Fast-growing castor bean is a dramatic accent for the summer garden—not for its flowers, which are inconsequential, but for the large leaves that lend a tropical air to any planting. Carried on long stalks, the leaves have 5 to 11 pointed lobes and can reach 1½ feet across (or even more) on young plants; foliage size decreases as the plant gets older and larger. Clusters of tiny white flowers come on foot-high stalks in summer, followed by conspicuous prickly reddish husks that contain attractively marked (and poisonous) seeds about the size of lima beans. In frost-free regions, castor bean lives from year to year, becoming treelike and woody. In colder areas, its annual bulk and height depend on the length of the growing season; expect it to grow anywhere from 6 to 15 feet tall and about half as wide.

A number of named cultivars exist, among them **'Carmencita'**, with reddish bronze foliage; **'Carmencita Pink'**, with pink seeds husks instead of the usual red ones; and **'Zanzibarensis'**, with green leaves that can reach 3 feet across. **'Dwarf Red Spire'** has bronzy red leaves on plants just to 6 feet high.

Note that the seeds ("beans") of castor bean are toxic if ingested.

CULTURE. Castor bean grows best in a sunny location with average to good soil and moderate to regular water. In all but frostless regions, you'll need to push it along quickly, with attentive watering and feeding, to get the maximum impact within a single growing season. To keep leaves from becoming tattered, choose a windless location; stake plants if they start to lean. In regions with a fairly long growing season, sow seeds outdoors after the last-frost date (to hasten germination, soak them in lukewarm water overnight before planting). Where the growing season is shorter, plant seeds indoors (in individual pots) 6 to 8 weeks before the last-frost date; plant seedlings outdoors when all danger of frost is past.

Ricinus communis 'Carmencita'

RODGERSIA

Saxifragaceae
PERENNIALS
ZONES 2–9, 14–17, 32–41
PARTIAL SHADE, EXCEPT AS NOTED
AMPLE WATER
❀ ✿ ✿ FLOWERS IN SUMMER

Rodgersia pinnata 'Superba'

Reminiscent of oversize astilbes, rodgersias form large mounds of handsome foliage that are decorative throughout the growing season; the airy summertime flower plumes are a bonus. Leafstalks rise directly from clumps of intertwined rhizomes, bearing leaves composed of jagged-edged leaflets. The flower stalks rise above the foliage, carrying tiny blossoms in many-branched spikes. Leaves usually take on bronze tones by fall, then disappear entirely over the winter.

The largest species is *R. aesculifolia*, bearing five- to seven-leafleted leaves to 2 feet across that resemble those of horsechestnut *(Aesculus)*. It can reach as high as 6 feet in bloom, when pyramidal spikes of white flowers appear. *R. pinnata* is a bit smaller overall, with leaves to 16 inches across and reddish, 3- to 4-foot flower stems. Red is the usual flower color, but there are variations, including white 'Alba'; creamy pink 'Elegans'; and dark pink 'Superba', which grows somewhat taller than the species and has bronzy foliage.

Each leaf of *R. podophylla* consists of five 10-inch leaflets that radiate from a central point; the foliage is bronze when new, maturing to green by summer. Flower stems can reach 5 feet, bearing nodding clusters of creamy white blossoms. *R. sambucifolia* differs from the others in foliage: its leaves have narrow leaflets arranged opposite one another in feather fashion (as many as five pairs of leaflets, plus a single terminal leaflet). Flat-topped plumes of creamy white flowers come on 3-foot stalks.

CULTURE. Rich soil and constant moisture are the secrets to success with rodgersias. They won't grow in standing water, but they're right at home in the marshy soil alongside a stream or pond. In the garden, provide the best and most retentive soil possible; liberally amend it with organic matter. Except in cool- and very mild-summer areas, where they'll take full sun, give these plants afternoon shade—or even light shade all day. The thick rhizomes form slowly spreading clumps that can remain in place indefinitely. If you want to increase your plantings, remove rhizomes from a clump's edge in late winter or early spring and replant immediately.

RUDBECKIA

CONEFLOWER
Asteraceae (Compositae)
PERENNIALS AND BIENNIALS
ZONES 1–24, 28–43, EXCEPT AS NOTED
FULL SUN
MODERATE TO REGULAR WATER
✿ ✿ ✿ FLOWERS IN SUMMER, FALL

Rudbeckia hirta
'Marmalade'

Showy, carefree plants for the summer and fall garden, these yellow daisies are descendants of North American species. They are more compact and longer blooming than their ancestors, but they retain the original flower form: the common name "coneflower" refers to the raised, typically dark cone in the center of each blossom.

Gloriosa daisy or black-eyed Susan, *R. hirta*, is by nature a biennial or even a short-lived perennial—but because it flowers the first summer from seed sown in early spring, it is often treated as an annual. Branching, 4-foot-tall plants are narrowly upright, with sandpapery stems and lance-shaped, 4-inch leaves. In the most basic form, flowers are 2 to 4 inches wide, with a row of orange-yellow petals surrounding a black-purple cone; seed strains offer variations in plant size and flower form and color, including double blossoms and bicolor patterns. 'Indian Summer', to 3½ feet tall, bears golden yellow, single to semidouble blossoms 6 to 9 inches across. Three-foot 'Kelvedon Star' has single yellow flowers with striking dark petal bases. 'Irish Eyes' ('Green Eyes'), reaching 2½ feet, has the usual yellow petals, but they surround a light green cone that turns brown with age. Two-foot 'Marmalade' has orange-yellow petals and a dark brown cone. For a mixture of colors—yellow, orange, bronze, and bicolors—try the **Gloriosa Daisy** strain, with single flowers to 6 inches across on 2½- to 3-foot stems. The **Gloriosa Double Daisy** strain produces double, 4½-inch blossoms in a more limited color range (just yellow and orange). At the short end of the scale are 20-inch 'Goldilocks', with double, 4-inch yellow blossoms; 16-inch 'Sonora', bearing 5- to 6-inch yellow-and-mahogany blooms; 10-inch 'Toto', with semidouble, 4-inch yellow flowers; and the **Becky** strain, also 10 inches tall, bearing 4- to 6-inch-wide blossoms in yellow shades and bicolors.

Most widely grown of the perennial coneflowers is ***R. fulgida sullivantii* 'Goldsturm'**. From midsummer through fall, clumps of lance-shaped, 4-inch leaves send up branching, 2- to 2½-foot stems bearing 3-inch, single yellow flowers with a black center. The **Goldsturm** seed strain has similar flowers, but plants may be taller.

R. laciniata is a bulky, 10-foot plant with deeply lobed, 4-inch leaves. Better suited to gardens, though, is its smaller selection **'Hortensia' ('Golden Glow')**, with double, 2- to 3½-inch blossoms on a 6- to 7-foot plant that can spread widely and quite aggressively. The hybrid **'Goldquelle'** has similar flowers, but it grows just 3 feet high and forms clumps that remain more compact. ***R. nitida*** (Zones 2−9, 14−24, 28−35, 37−41) looks like a shorter (6-foot) version of *R. laciniata*. More widely grown than the species is its selection (or possibly hybrid) **'Herbstsonne' ('Autumn Sun')**, a slender, 6-foot plant bearing 4- to 5-inch, single yellow flowers with a bright green central cone that ages to yellow.

CULTURE. All these plants are easy to grow, needing only average to good soil and moderate to regular watering. To raise *R. hirta* from seed, sow outdoors 2 weeks before the last frost; where the growing season is short, sow indoors 6 to 8 weeks before the last-frost date. Simply press seeds into the soil without covering them; they need light to germinate. To keep perennial types looking good, divide clumps in spring every 2 to 4 years. Curb the spread of *R. laciniata* 'Hortensia' as needed, either by division or by cutting away the edges of the clump.

Rudbeckia fulgida sullivantii 'Goldsturm'

Painted tongue looks like a high-class, really dolled-up petunia, offering trumpet-shaped, 2- to 2½-inch flowers that feature an unusual combination of velvety texture, rich yet muted color, and delicate veining. The plant grows upright, carrying its exotic blossoms in clusters atop 2- to 3-foot stems. Both the stems and the narrow, oblong, 4-inch leaves are sticky. In most areas, bloom comes in late spring and early summer, but where summers are cool, the show will continue until frost if you remove spent blossoms regularly.

Several mixed-color strains are shorter than the species. Reaching 1½ to 2 feet are **Bolero,** bearing gold-veined flowers, and **Casino,** with low-branching plants that are bushier than most. **Royale,** just 15 to 20 inches high, is the best bet for growing in containers.

Salpiglossis sinuata,
Casino series

SALPIGLOSSIS sinuata
PAINTED TONGUE
Solanaceae
COOL-SEASON ANNUAL
ZONES 1–45
FULL SUN, EXCEPT AS NOTED
REGULAR WATER
✿ ✿ ✿ ✿ ✿ FLOWERS IN SPRING AND
EARLY SUMMER, EXCEPT AS NOTED

CULTURE. Germination can be spotty, so in-ground sowing inevitably results in a planting with gaps. To avoid this problem, start seeds indoors in containers; sow 8 to 10 weeks before the last-frost date and keep pots at 70 to 75°F/21 to 24°C. Simply press the seeds into the potting mix without covering them, since they need light to sprout. Plant out seedlings a week or so before the last-frost date, being sure to harden them off first (see page 79). Give plants good, organically enriched soil. A sunny spot is best except in hot-summer regions, where light afternoon shade is preferable (and will prolong the bloom period).

SALVIA

SAGE, SALVIA

Lamiaceae (Labiatae)

PERENNIALS, BIENNIALS, AND
    WARM-SEASON ANNUALS

ZONES VARY

FULL SUN, EXCEPT AS NOTED

REGULAR WATER

✿ ✿ ❀ ✿ ✿ FLOWERS IN SPRING,
    SUMMER, FALL

Salvia coccinea 'Lady in Red'

Salvia coccinea 'Coral Nymph'

Sages are a large and useful group of garden plants—and gardeners' choices are expanding each year, as new species and hybrids are offered for planting in the milder West and Southwest. The plants presented here are the more widely adapted sorts, tried and true annual and perennial performers in both cold- and warm-winter regions. All have the characteristic two-lipped flowers of the mint family; some have colorful calyxes that add to the display. A number of sages are appreciated for aromatic foliage, and many offer that rarest of flower colors: true blue.

Annual clary, **S. viridis** (**S. horminum;** all zones), grows quickly to 1½ to 2 feet high and has 2-inch-long, oval medium green leaves. Bloom is in early summer, but the actual flowers are insignificant; the decorative elements are the 1½-inch, dark-veined bracts beneath each blossom, which are showy both fresh and dried. The **Claryssa** strain includes plants with bracts in white, blue, and pink; these colors also are available separately.

Several other sages are commonly grown as annuals everywhere, though most can be perennial in certain mild zones. Tropical sage, **S. coccinea,** is one of these—a short-lived perennial in Zones 12–24, 26–30, H1, H2. The bushy, upright plant grows to 3 feet tall and nearly as wide, clothed in hairy, oval dark green leaves to 2½ inches long. Spikes of 1-inch summer flowers come in white, pink shades, orange to red, and bicolors. Named seed-grown selections include **'Lady in Red'**; salmon **'Brenthurst'** (**'Lady in Pink'**); white **'Lactea'** (**'Lady in White'**) and **'White Nymph'**; and white-and-coral **'Coral Nymph'** (**'Cherry Blossom'**). Mealycup sage or Texas violet, **S. farinacea** (perennial in Zones 7–10, 12–24, 26–29; H1, H2), is a rounded, shrubby plant that grows quickly to 3 feet high. The narrow, pointed, 3-inch-long leaves are smooth gray green above, woolly and white beneath. From late spring to frost, ³⁄₄- to 1-inch blossoms appear on stems to about a foot long; colors run from deep violet blue through lighter blue shades to white. A number of shorter, more compact strains have been developed for bedding and container use. These include foot-tall **'Strata'**, bearing blue flowers with woolly, silver-white calyxes; 14-inch-high **'Cirrus'** (white) and **'Rhea'** (deep blue); and 20-inch-tall **'Victoria'**, with violet-blue blooms, and its white counterpart **'Victoria White'**.

Scarlet sage, **S. splendens** (perennial in Zones 21–25, 27; H2), has long been a mainstay of summer annual plantings. It's a bushy, 3- to 4-foot tall plant with bright green, 2- to 4-inch, heart-shaped leaves and spikes of fire engine red, 1½-inch flowers. Selections offer shorter plants (8 inches to 2 feet high) in a wider color range that includes some less assertive hues. You'll find flowers in orange, pink shades, purple, lavender, white, and bicolors that combine white with another color.

Two attractive sages grow as biennials or short-lived perennials. While most sages are planted for their colorful flowers, silver sage, **S. argentea** (Zones 1–24, 26, 28–45), is a striking foliage plant as well. It spends its first year developing into a 2-foot-wide clump of triangular, gray-green, 8-inch leaves covered with silvery hairs. In the summer of its second year, it produces multibranched, 3-foot stems carrying 1½-inch white flowers with silvery calyxes. If you let the plant set seed, it will usually die but leave you with volunteer seedlings; if you cut out the flowering stems after blooms fade, the clump may live for another year.

Clary sage, **S. sclarea** (Zones 2–24, 27–41), forms a handsome foliage clump 2 to 3 feet across, composed of wrinkled, oval to lance-shaped gray-green leaves to 1½ feet long. Multibranched, 3- to 4-foot flower spikes come in late spring to early summer of the second year; each 6- to 12-inch branch bears whorls of 1¼-inch lavender-blue blossoms with a white lower lip, and conspicuous purplish pink bracts continue the color show after the flowers fade. **'Alba'** has white flowers and bracts.

'Turkestanica' *(S. s. sclarea, S. s. turkestanica)* is a particularly vigorous form to 5 feet tall, with pink flowers and lilac bracts. Plants usually die after bloom, but volunteer seedlings provide replacement plants.

Reliably perennial sages are among the best sources of blue and purple for the summer and fall garden. Prairie or pitcher sage, *S. azurea grandiflora (S. pitcheri)*, grows in Zones 1–24, 26 (northern part), 27–43. Each clump sends up multiple stems that need support to remain upright. Stems are set with narrow, 4-inch leaves and grow to 5 feet high, displaying foot-long spikes of sky blue flowers from summer until frost.

Salvia farinacea

Three other species are similar enough to have created some name confusion in the nursery trade over the years; in fact, several of the named cultivars have been listed under more than one of these species. All three grow in Zones 2–10, 14–24, 30–41. *S. nemorosa* spreads by rhizomes, forming a 2- to 3-foot-wide clump of lance-shaped dull green leaves to 4 inches long. Upright, branched stems rise 1½ to 3 feet in summer and fall, bearing tiered, 3- to 6-inch clusters of ½-inch flowers. Nurseries offer named selections, including **'Lubecca'**, with gray-green leaves and violet flowers, and **'Ostfriesland' ('East Friesland')**, with blue-violet flowers and pinkish purple bracts. Both reach about 1½ feet high. *S. × superba* is found in nurseries as the cultivar **'Superba'**, but be aware that some plants sold by that name are not the genuine article (though they do resemble it). The plant is much like *S. nemorosa*, but it has green leaves with scalloped edges. From midspring until autumn, many-branched, 3-foot stems bear closely clustered, 6- to 8-inch tiers of violet-blue, ½-inch blossoms with red-purple bracts (the identifying feature) that persist long after flowers drop. *S. × sylvestris (S. deserta)* also resembles *S. nemorosa* but has wrinkled, medium green, slightly shorter leaves with scalloped edges. Flower stems have few or no branches and can reach 1 to 2½ feet, depending on cultivar; from spring through fall, ½-inch blossoms appear along the top 6 to 8 inches of the stem. Two taller cultivars are **'Blauhügel' ('Blue Hill')**, with medium blue flowers on 2-foot stems, and **'Mainacht' ('May Night')**, which starts flowering in midspring and has indigo, ¾-inch flowers on 2- to 2½-foot stems. In the 1- to 1½-foot range are **'Rosakönigin' ('Rose Queen')**, bearing purplish pink flowers with red bracts, and **'Schneehügel' ('Snow Hill')**, with green-bracted white blossoms.

Whorled clary, *S. verticillata*, is suited to Zones 2–10, 14–24, 30–41. The plant is a fine leafy presence in the garden, forming a clump to 2½ feet wide. The medium green, wavy-margined, softly hairy leaves are more or less oval, to 6 inches long. Leafy flower stems rise to 3 feet, carrying ½-inch blossoms in dense, widely spaced whorls. The flowers are typically violet to lavender, with conspicuous violet calyxes; with regular deadheading, they'll bloom from early summer through fall. **'Alba'** has white flowers and calyxes; 2-foot **'Purple Rain'** is particularly showy, with blossoms and calyxes in rich purple.

TOP: *Salvia nemorosa* 'Ostfriesland'
BOTTOM: *Salvia verticillata* 'Purple Rain'

CULTURE. The sages need good drainage and moderately fertile soil; those described here require regular water (though *S. argentea* is particularly sensitive to overly moist soil in winter). In hot-summer areas, plants appreciate some shade in the afternoon. All perennial types (including those grown as annuals) can be propagated from stem cuttings taken in spring or summer. Those that form clumps can be divided in spring— and should be when performance starts to decline from overcrowding. For annual *S. viridis*, the perennials grown as annuals, and the biennial species *S. sclarea* and *S. argentea*, you can set out transplants in spring (after frost danger is past) or start from seed. Where winters are frost free or just slightly frosty, sow outdoors after the last-frost date; in colder regions, sow indoors 6 to 8 weeks before the last-frost date. Just press seeds into the soil, since they need light to germinate.

SANVITALIA procumbens
CREEPING ZINNIA
Asteraceae (Compositae)
WARM-SEASON ANNUAL
ZONES 1–45
FULL SUN
MODERATE TO REGULAR WATER
✿ ✿ FLOWERS IN SUMMER, FALL

As the common name indicates, this colorful annual could easily pass for a zinnia in flower and foliage. Leaves are sandpapery, to 2 inches long; the summer-into-fall blossoms are inch-wide yellow daisies with dark centers. The plant reaches just 4 to 6 inches high but spreads to 1½ feet or wider. For variations on the species, try **'Mandarin Orange'**, with orange flowers; **'Yellow Carpet'**, bearing blooms of a softer lemon yellow; or fully double **'Gold Braid'**, with blossoms showing no dark center. Creeping zinnia makes a showy small-scale ground cover and will spill attractively from pots, hanging baskets, and window boxes.

Sanvitalia procumbens

CULTURE. Sow seeds in light-textured, well-drained soil; just press them in, since light aids germination. Where frost is light or absent, you can sow seeds outdoors in fall; where winters are chilly but the growing season is fairly long, sow outdoors around the last-frost date. In colder areas, sow indoors 6 to 8 weeks before the last-frost date.

SCABIOSA
PINCUSHION FLOWER
Dipsacaceae
PERENNIALS AND WARM-SEASON ANNUALS
ZONES VARY
FULL SUN, EXCEPT AS NOTED
MODERATE TO REGULAR WATER
✿ ✿ ❀ ✿ ✿ FLOWERS IN SPRING AND
   SUMMER, EXCEPT AS NOTED

The blossoms' protruding stamens look something like pins bristling from a pincushion—hence these plants' common name. Each flower head is composed of countless tiny, closely packed tubular blooms. In the annual species, all of them are about the same size; in perennial types, the outer flowers are larger, giving the effect of a ring of petals around a central "cushion." Stems are smooth and knitting-needle thin.

Annual **S. atropurpurea** (Zones 1–45; H1, H2) may persist as a short-lived perennial where winters are mild. Clumps of oblong, coarsely toothed leaves send up numerous stems to 3 feet high, each bearing a 2- to 3-inch, sweetly fragrant flower; colors run from nearly black through dark red to pink shades, violet, lavender, and white. Mixed-color strains offering the full range of blossom colors include **Double Mixed** (to 3 feet), **Dwarf Double Mixed** (to 1½ feet), and **Sweet Scabious** (to 2½ feet). **'QIS Scarlet'**, **'Salmon Queen'**, and deep maroon **'Ace of Spades'** are 3-foot-tall, single-color seed strains.

Among perennial species, **S. caucasica** (Zones 1–10, 14–24, 32–43) forms clumps of long, narrow leaves that vary from smooth edged to finely cut. Flexible, 2-foot stems bear 3-inch flowers in blue or white; selected cultivars include lavender-blue **'Blue Perfection'**, darker blue **'Moerheim Blue'**, white **'Perfecta Alba'** (with 15-inch stems), and **'Bressingham White'**. Among seed strains, **'Fama'** produces lavender-blue flowers on 20-inch stems; **House's Mix (House's Novelty Mix)** grows to 2½ feet, with flowers in white and shades of blue and lavender.

Finely cut gray-green leaves distinguish **S. columbaria** (Zones 2–11, 14–24, 32–35). In spring and summer—or almost year-round in the mildest regions—2-foot stems bear 2-inch flowers in blue shades, white, and pink. Named cultivars include deep lavender-blue **'Butterfly Blue'** and soft pink **'Pink Mist'**.

CULTURE. All pincushion flowers do best in sandy to loam soil enriched with organic matter (and amended with lime, if the soil is acid). Good drainage is essential; perennial species are particularly sensitive to wet soil in winter. To start annual *S. atropurpurea*, sow seeds indoors about 5 weeks before the last-frost date, or sow outdoors just after that date. Among perennials, *S. caucasica* is best suited to regions with cool to mild summers, where it can grow in full sun; in warmer regions, it performs better with light shade during the afternoon. For hot-summer regions, *S. columbaria* is the better choice. To get additional plants, divide clumps or take basal cuttings in spring. With both annual and perennial types, regularly remove spent flowers to prolong bloom.

Scabiosa columbaria 'Pink Mist'

These undemanding perennials are succulents that bear large clusters of many tiny, star-shaped flowers. You'll find a multitude of ground-hugging sorts for rock gardens and for use as ground cover—but the plants profiled here are larger sorts, better suited to beds and borders. All form dense clumps that start the year as growth buds at ground level, develop into mounds of fleshy, rubbery foliage, and then send up leafy stems that terminate in nearly flat-topped flower clusters. After bloom ends, the stems die but dry out and remain standing until beaten down by rain or snow (or picked for dried arrangements). Botanists have reclassified all the following plants into the genus *Hylotelephium*, but catalogers and nurseries are still likely to list them under *Sedum*.

Sedum spectabile 'Brilliant'

S. spectabile (Hylotelephium spectabile) is suited to Zones 1–24, 28–43. Reaching about 1½ feet high, the erect to slightly spreading stems are set with oval, 3-inch blue-green leaves. Dense, 6-inch clusters of pink flowers open in late summer and gradually age to brownish maroon. Cultivars with different blossom colors include deep rose-red **'Brilliant'**, soft rose **'Carmen'**, pure white **'Iceberg'** (with lime-green leaves), coppery red **'Indian Chief'**, and carmine red **'Meteor'**.

S. telephium (Hylotelephium telephium; Zones 1–24, 29–43) resembles *S. spectabile* in general appearance but has narrower, oblong gray-green leaves and taller stems (to 2 feet); its blossoms open purplish pink in late summer, then turn maroon brown with age. Most cultivars differ from the species in foliage color. **'Arthur Branch'** has purplish bronze leaves, wine red stems, and deep pink blooms; pink-flowered **'Matrona'** has red stems and red-blushed, pink-margined foliage; **'Munstead Red'** carries its deep rose flowers over purplish green leaves. Cultivars of ***S. telephium maximum*** include **'Atropurpureum'** (dusty pink flowers, burgundy leaves) and **'Gooseberry Fool'** (creamy green flowers, purple stems, purple-flushed foliage).

Ever-popular ***S. 'Autumn Joy'*** (Zones 1–10, 14–24, 29–43), reaching 1½ to 2 feet, is probably a hybrid between *S. spectabile* and *S. telephium*. It has blue-green, 2- to 3-inch leaves and bears broad, rounded clusters of pink flowers that age to coppery pink, then to rusty bronze. Another presumed hybrid, 1½- to 2-foot **'Frosty Morn'**, has white-margined grayish green leaves and pale pink blossoms.

CULTURE. Stonecrops need well-drained soil but are not fussy about fertility. The *S. spectabile* cultivars will take moderate to regular watering, but all the others do better with a regular supply. When floppy stems and decreased bloom indicate overcrowding, divide clumps in early spring. To increase a favorite kind, dig out a rooted chunk from a clump's edge in early spring; or take stem cuttings in late spring and early summer.

From mid- or late summer into fall, goldenrods *(Solidago)* brighten the garden with large, branching clusters of small yellow flowers carried on leafy stems that rise from tough, woody, spreading rootstocks. For all their flamboyant color and ease of care, they are not as widely planted as they deserve, largely because their pollen is incorrectly thought to cause hay fever. (The actual culprit is usually ragweed, which blooms at the same time.) Gardeners in the Midwest and East may also dismiss these plants as mere rangy roadside weeds—but a number of named cultivars are shorter and more compact than some of the wild forms, entirely suitable for cultivated gardens.

Listing continues>

SEDUM
STONECROP
Crassulaceae
PERENNIALS
ZONES VARY
FULL SUN
REGULAR WATER, EXCEPT AS NOTED
❀ ✿ ✿ ✿ FLOWERS IN SUMMER, FALL

Sedum 'Autumn Joy'

SOLIDAGO (and ✕ SOLIDASTER)
Asteraceae (Compositae)
PERENNIALS
ZONES 1–11, 14–23, 28–45
FULL SUN TO LIGHT SHADE
MODERATE WATER
✿ FLOWERS IN SUMMER, FALL

Solidago sphacelata 'Golden Fleece'

Solidago rugosa can reach 5 feet tall, bearing glowing gold fall flowers on arching, widely branching stems. Its cultivar **'Fireworks'** is a better garden bet: it grows to 3 feet tall and wide, with fluffy golden flower sprays on near-horizontal branches. For a foreground position, try 1½- to 2-foot **S. sphacelata 'Golden Fleece'**, an arching, mounding clump that comes alive in late summer with sprays of golden yellow blossoms. You can use it as an individual accent or mass it for a fast-growing ground cover.

For a striking departure from other goldenrods, look for 2- to 3½-foot **S. flexicaulis 'Variegata'**, with leaves brightly splashed in yellow. Narrow spikes of yellow flowers bloom in late summer.

A number of hybrid goldenrods are available in the short to medium height range. **'Cloth of Gold'**, just 1½ feet high, has a long bloom season that begins as early as midsummer. **'Crown of Rays' ('Strahlenkrone')** is a 2-footer with wide, flat, branched flower clusters. **'Goldenmosa'** bears mimosalike blossom clusters on stems to about 2½ feet tall. **'Goldkind' ('Golden Baby')** is another 2-foot plant; its flowers come in plumelike clusters.

× **Solidaster luteus** is a hybrid between *Solidago* and a hardy aster. It resembles goldenrod in habit, but the late-summer flowers are larger, reminiscent of small, primrose yellow asters. Plants grow to 2 feet high; unlike the generally self-supporting goldenrods, they require staking.

CULTURE. These undemanding plants grow as well in semiwild gardens as they do in highly cultivated ones. All they need is average soil and moderate watering. To rejuvenate clumps and control spreading, divide every 3 to 4 years in early spring.

STACHYS
Lamiaceae (Labiatae)
PERENNIALS
ZONES VARY
FULL SUN TO LIGHT SHADE
MODERATE WATER
✿ ❀ ✿ ✿ FLOWERS IN LATE SPRING, SUMMER, FALL

Stachys byzantina 'Silver Carpet'

Certain common features link these plants—square stems and aromatic foliage, for example—but beyond that they differ considerably.

Mexican native **S. albotomentosa** grows in Zones 7–10, 12–24, 29, 30. Its selected form **'Hidalgo'** has white, woolly stems and heavily veined, somewhat heart-shaped green leaves with white undersides; it reaches 2½ feet high and sprawls to as much as 5 to 6 feet across. Spikes of small summer flowers open salmon pink and age to brick red.

Old favorite lamb's ears, **S. byzantina (S. lanata, S. olympica;** Zones 1–24, 29–43), is a classic foreground plant and small-scale ground cover. The thick, soft, 4- to 6-inch-long, elliptical leaves do indeed resemble gray-white, furry lamb's or rabbit's ears. The plant increases rapidly, a single foliage rosette spreading into a clump as the stems root where they touch soil. In the basic species, upright, 1- to 1½-foot flower stems rise above the foliage in late spring or early summer, bearing small leaves and whorls of small purple blossoms. Massed plantings may become patchy after bloom. Cultivars vary significantly from the species. **'Big Ears' ('Countess Helene von Stein')** boasts leaves about twice as large as those of *S. byzantina;* it flowers only sparsely. **'Cotton Boll'** has the standard foliage, but in place of flowers, it produces wads of white, cottonlike fluff spaced along the stems. Sparse-flowering **'Primrose Heron'** has foliage covered in the usual white wool, but its leaves are yellow in spring, turning to chartreuse and then to gray green by summer. **'Silver Carpet'** blooms only rarely and forms a foliage cover that retains a solid, gap-free appearance for considerably longer than plantings of the flowering forms.

Scarlet hedge nettle, **S. coccinea** (Zones 7–10, 12–24, 29, 30), is a Southwestern native that forms a semishrubby clump to 1½ feet high and wide. The oval, 3-inch green leaves are heavily veined and wrinkled; spikes of small, brilliant red flowers appear in midsummer and continue into fall.

S. macrantha (***S. grandiflora;*** Zones 1–24, 29–45) makes a dense, foot-high clump of long-stalked, heart-shaped dark green leaves with scalloped edges; wrinkled and roughly hairy, they reach 3 inches long. Slender stems rise above the foliage to 1½ to 2 feet, bearing smaller leaves and tiered whorls of showy purplish pink blossoms in late spring and summer. Available cultivars include white-flowered **'Alba'; 'Hummelo'**, with semiglossy leaves and rosy lavender flowers on 1½-foot stems; **'Robusta'**, earlier to bloom and a bit larger in all parts; and **'Superba'**, with violet flowers. A similar species, ***S. officinalis***, also grows in Zones 1–24, 29–45; it differs primarily in having elongated rather than heart-shaped leaves and small lilac-pink flowers in more closely spaced whorls. It too has a white-blossomed cultivar **'Alba'**.

CULTURE. These are easy-to-grow plants, content with average, well-drained soil and moderate watering. *S. albotomentosa* and *S. coccinea* need full sun. The others will grow in full sun to partial shade—and may need some afternoon shade in hot-summer regions. When vigor declines or plantings show bare spots, divide and replant in spring. *S. byzantina* will need division more frequently than the others.

Stachys macrantha

With their warm, bright colors, marigolds just seem to say "summer." They light up the garden, growing quickly and easily and producing masses of bloom over several months; and their wide height range assures you of finding a marigold for any sunny garden (or container) location. Today's gardeners can also choose from an array of colors and flower types. In addition to the traditional yellow and orange, you'll find blooms in cream, near-white, bronzy red, maroon, and bicolors; forms vary from basic single daisies to double, drumstick-like pompoms. All types make long-lasting cut flowers.The finely cut, dark green foliage is typically strongly aromatic—some people like the fragrance, others emphatically do not.

Tagetes erecta,
Jubilee strain

Despite the nativities suggested by their common names, all marigolds are descended from New World species. So-called African marigold, ***T. erecta,*** was originally a 3- to 4-foot plant used strictly for middle and background planting—but breeders have developed a number of lovely strains in more useful heights that run from around 1 to 2½ feet. All have double flowers 3 to 5 inches across. Examples of taller mixed-color strains include **Climax** (2½ to 3 feet high) and **Odorless** (to 2½ feet, with scentless foliage and flowers). In the 16- to 20-inch range are mixed-color **Galore, Inca, Lady,** and **Perfection,** plus cream **Sweet Cream.** Mixed-color **Jubilee** is a bit taller at 1½ to 2 feet. Shortest of all are 16-inch **Antigua** and foot-tall **Discovery** and **Guys and Dolls.**

French marigold, ***T. patula,*** is the traditional small-flowered, front-of-the-border marigold, with single to double flowers in yellow, orange, copper, mahogany, and bicolors on plants that range from 6 to 18 inches high. Mixed-color, double-blossomed strains include 8-inch **Janie** (1¾-inch flowers), **Bonanza** (2-inch flowers), and the following foot-tall choices, all with 2- to 2½-inch blooms: **Aurora, Hero,** and **Sophia.** Two single-flowered strains are **Disco** (to about 1 foot) and 1- to 1½-foot **Mr. Majestic,** with blooms featuring a striking gold-and-mahogany pinwheel pattern.

Listing continues>

TAGETES
MARIGOLD
Asteraceae (Compositae)
WARM-SEASON ANNUALS
ALL ZONES
FULL SUN
REGULAR WATER
❀ ❁ ❁ ❁ FLOWERS IN LATE SPRING, SUMMER, FALL

Tagetes patula, Hero strain

Tagetes tenuifolia 'Lemon Gem'

Triploid hybrids are an especially vigorous group derived from crosses between *T. erecta* and *T. patula*. In plant and blossom, they resemble *T. patula*, with 2½- to 3-inch flowers on foot-tall plants; because they are sterile, you don't need to remove spent blossoms to prevent seed set. Mixed-color strains are **Nugget, Trinity,** and **Zenith.**

Signet marigold, ***T. tenuifolia (T. signata),*** produces 1-inch single flowers in amazing profusion on bushy plants to about 1 foot high. **Gem** and **Starfire** are mixed-color strains.

CULTURE. Given a sunny spot and average garden soil, marigolds are virtually foolproof (rich soil or overfertilization will encourage plants to produce leaves at the expense of flowers). In areas with a long growing season, sow seeds outdoors after the last-frost date. Where the growing season is shorter and winters are colder, start seeds indoors 6 to 8 weeks before the last-frost date. The tallest *T. erecta* types are likely to need staking. To make them sturdier—possibly strong enough to stand on their own—set them deep. Strip off any leaves from the lower 1 to 3 inches of stem, then plant so the stripped portion is below the soil line. Pinch taller types to promote bushy growth. During the bloom season, regularly deadhead all but the triploid hybrids to prevent seed set and prolong flowering.

THALICTRUM
MEADOW RUE
Ranunculaceae
PERENNIALS
ZONES 2–10, 14–17, 32–41,
   EXCEPT AS NOTED
LIGHT SHADE, EXCEPT AS NOTED
REGULAR WATER
✿ ❀ ✿ FLOWERS IN LATE SPRING, SUMMER

With their graceful, fernlike leaves and branching, open blossom clusters, airy-looking meadow rues are choice perennials for a shaded border or the edge of a wooded spot. Their foliage is similar to that of columbine *(Aquilegia),* to which they are related, but they're generally much larger plants with leafy flower stems rising 2 to 6 feet high. Flower shape is different, too: the profuse small, petal-less blossoms have four sepals and a prominent cluster of stamens. Bloom comes in late spring and summer.

Thalictrum aquilegifolium

Earliest to bloom each year is ***T. aquilegifolium,*** a 2- to 3-foot-high clump with blue-tinted foliage. Flowers consist of clouds of rosy lilac, fluffy stamens carried just above the leaves; later, attractive seed heads develop. Forms featuring other colors include **'Thundercloud'**, with particularly large purple flower heads, and ***T. a. album,*** with white blooms. Chinese meadow rue, ***T. delavayi (T. dipterocarpum;*** Zones 2–10, 14–17, 31–41) forms large clumps of especially delicate green leaves. From these rise dark purple, 3- to 6-foot stems bearing flowers that consist of lavender to violet sepals and yellow stamens. Blossoms of **'Hewitt's Double'** look double due to extra sepals and petal-like stamens; individual flowers are long-lasting, and the total display can go on for 2 months.

Light yellow flowers set ***T. flavum glaucum (T. speciosissimum)*** apart from the other meadow rues. Upright plants reach 5 feet when in flower, their fluffy pale yellow flower heads combining beautifully with the fernlike blue-green foliage. ***T. rochebrunianum*** has intricately branched flower stems that can grow to about 6 feet, bearing blossoms composed of lilac sepals and yellow stamens. Leaves are green.

CULTURE. Meadow rues thrive in good, well-drained, organically enriched soil. They do well anywhere in dappled sunlight or light shade; in cool-summer regions, they'll also grow in full sun. Flower stems may require staking to remain upright, especially in the case of *T. delavayi* and *T. flavum glaucum.* You'll need to divide clumps every 4 to 5 years in early spring.

Thalictrum aquilegifolium

Tithonia rotundifolia 'Fiesta del Sol'

Big and brassy, Mexican sunflower is impossible to overlook. The upright, bushy plant quickly grows to 6 feet high, blazing in summer and fall with 3- to 4-inch single, yellow-centered red-orange daisies. The largest leaves can reach 1 foot long; they are more or less oval, sometimes with several lobes. Thanks to its size and density, this plant makes a good annual hedge or background screen when set out in groups. **'Torch'** is an especially fine form. **'Goldfinger'** is a shorter plant, just 2½ to 3½ feet tall; compact **'Fiesta del Sol'** is shorter still (to about 2 feet) and comes into bloom earlier. Four-foot **'Aztec Sun'** has golden blossoms tinged with apricot; the **Arcadian Blend** strain, also to 4 feet, produces flowers in yellow, gold, and orange.

CULTURE. Well-drained, average soil suits Mexican sunflower. Where winters are fairly mild and the growing season is long, sow seeds outdoors after the last frost. Where the growing season is shorter, sow seeds indoors 6 to 8 weeks before the last-frost date. This plant is at its best in hot-summer regions. Stems are hollow, prone to bend or break in windy areas and when weighed down by overhead watering or rainfall; staking is a good idea, especially for the taller kinds. Remove spent flowers regularly to prevent seed set and keep bloom going.

TITHONIA rotundifolia
MEXICAN SUNFLOWER
Asteraceae (Compositae)
WARM-SEASON ANNUAL
ALL ZONES
FULL SUN
REGULAR WATER
✿ ✿ FLOWERS IN SUMMER, FALL

Tropaeolum majus

Fans of crayon-bright nasturtiums can choose between the familiar vining type (page 181) and the bushy, dwarf plants described here, good for foreground plantings and containers. The light green leaves are nearly circular, from 2 to 7 inches across, set off-center at the ends of long leafstalks; both leaves and immature seeds are edible and add a watercress-like tang to salads. The blossoms are nearly symmetrical five-lobed trumpets to 2½ inches across, with a spur projecting from the back. Nasturtiums' usual flowering season is spring, but in desert areas gardeners plant them for winter bloom.

A number of seed strains are available, in mixed as well as separate colors. Two strains to 1 foot high and wide are **Jewel**, offering the full range of colors as well as some bicolors, and **Whirlybird**, in separate and mixed colors. The mixed-color **Tom Thumb** strain is shorter—just 6 to 9 inches. The **Alaska** strain, with mixed colors on plants to 15 inches, is notable for its foliage: leaves are smaller than the usual and strikingly marbled in creamy white. **'Empress of India'** is a rather lax plant to 2 feet high and wide, with dark orange-scarlet flowers and dark green, purple-tinted foliage.

CULTURE. Well-drained soil is a must—preferably sandy soil of limited fertility (too-rich soil produces foliage at the expense of flowers). This plant does best in cool weather, dislikes warm, humid conditions, and literally burns out in summer heat.

Where summers are hot, sow seeds as early as possible for bloom in the cooler springtime; in the low desert and in virtually frost-free areas, sow in fall for bloom beginning in winter. It's best to sow outdoors, but where the growing season is fairly short, you can sow indoors 4 to 5 weeks before the last frost. Plant just one or two seeds in each small pot; plants resent disturbance, so this makes transplanting simpler. In mild-winter regions, plants may live over into a second year, and you are likely to get volunteer seedlings.

TROPAEOLUM majus
NASTURTIUM
Tropaeolaceae
COOL-SEASON ANNUAL
ALL ZONES
FULL SUN OR LIGHT SHADE
REGULAR WATER
✿ ✿ ✿ ✿ FLOWERS IN SPRING,
   EXCEPT AS NOTED

Tropaeolum majus, Alaska strain

VERBASCUM
MULLEIN
Scrophulariaceae
PERENNIALS
ZONES VARY
FULL SUN
MODERATE WATER
✿❀✿✿ FLOWERS IN LATE SPRING,
SUMMER

Verbascum chaixii

Like delphinium and foxglove *(Digitalis)*, the mulleins are valuable for vertical accents in the landscape. Plants form rosettes of large, broad leaves (woolly in some species), above which rise 1- to 6-foot-tall spikes closely set with five-petaled, circular, nearly flat flowers about an inch across. Many mulleins—including the striking roadside weed *V. thapsus*—are biennial, but those presented here are reliably perennial.

Sometimes called nettle-leaved mullein, *V. chaixii* (Zones 2–11, 14–24, 31–41) forms a 2-foot-wide rosette of hairy green or slightly gray foliage. In late spring, flower spikes (branched, in older plants) rise to 3 feet, bearing red-centered yellow blossoms. '**Album**' bears white flowers with purple centers. Imposing *V. olympicum* (Zones 3–10, 14–24, 32–34, 39) produces a 3-foot-wide rosette of white leaves covered in soft, downy hairs. Branching stems appear in summer, growing as tall as 5 feet and carrying bright yellow flowers. Purple mullein, *V. phoeniceum* (Zones 1–10, 14–24, 32–43), forms a 1½-foot-wide rosette of dark green leaves that are smooth on top, hairy beneath. Slender, 2- to 4-foot spikes appear in spring; the usual flower color is purple, though rose, white, and yellow are also possible.

A number of hybrid mulleins (Zones 3–10, 14–24, 32–34, 39) offer 1- to 1½-inch flowers in the standard colors as well as appealing melon tints. The **Benary Hybrids** and **Cotswold Hybrids** are derived from *V. phoeniceum* and resemble it in general aspect. Coppery pink '**Cotswold Queen**' and rose pink '**Pink Domino**' reach 3 to 3½ feet tall; peach pink '**Helen Johnson**' grows about 2 feet high. '**Jackie**' has cantaloupe orange blossoms on 1½-foot stems.

CULTURE. Tough and undemanding, the mulleins do well with well-drained, average to fairly poor soil and just moderate watering. Regularly cut off spent flower spikes—both to induce a second round of bloom from new stems and to prevent seed setting, which can result in numerous volunteer seedlings (difficult to remove because of their taproots). To increase a planting, it's simplest to let just a few plants produce seeds; keep in mind, though, that seedlings of hybrid selections won't replicate the parent plant. To propagate hybrids (or any other mullein, for that matter), take root cuttings in early spring or separate and transplant rooted young rosettes from the clump.

Verbascum
'Helen Johnson'

VERBENA
Verbenaceae
PERENNIALS, SOME GROWN AS
    WARM-SEASON ANNUALS
ZONES VARY
FULL SUN
MODERATE WATER, EXCEPT AS NOTED
✿❀✿ FLOWERS IN SPRING,
    SUMMER, FALL

Easy to grow, reveling in sunshine and warmth, and bearing colorful flowers throughout much of the growing period, verbenas are understandably one of the mainstays of the warm-season garden. And offering a multitude of choices in blues, purples, and white, they provide a refreshing counterpoint to the yellows and oranges of many other warm-weather favorites. Strictly speaking, all are perennials—but many of the more tender types grow and bloom so quickly that they are almost always grown as annuals, even where they can survive the winter.

Garden verbena, *V.* × *hybrida (V. hortensis)*, is usually treated as an annual but can be a short-lived perennial in Zones 8–29, H1, H2. Plants in this hybrid group are freely branching and rather bushy, varying from 6 to 12 inches high and 1 to 3 feet across. Bright green, oblong leaves to 4 inches long form a dense backdrop for flat,

3-inch clusters of flowers that may be white, blue, purple, pink, or red; the colored forms often have a white eye. Mixed-color seed strains include 6-inch **Romance,** 9-inch **Sandy,** 10-inch **Quartz,** and 1-foot **Showtime.** As the name implies, pastel '**Peaches and Cream**' has blossoms in a blend of soft peach and cream on a plant to 9 inches high and about a foot wide. '**Blue Lagoon**', an upright grower to about 10 inches high and wide, bears flowers in pure bright blue.

V. peruviana (V. chamaedrifolia) is also typically grown as an annual, though it can be perennial in Zones 8–24, 29, 30. The species is a ground-hugging mat of spreading stems set with small dark green leaves and clusters of white-centered scarlet flowers. Nurseries usually offer named cultivars (usually hybrids of the species) that make a higher cover, up to about 6 inches. Widely grown '**Starfire**' has red blossoms; pink choices include '**Appleblossom**', '**Cherry Pink**', '**Little Pinkie**', '**Princess Gloria**', '**Raspberry Rose**', and '**St. Paul**'. Moss verbena, *V. pulchella gracilior (V. tenuisecta),* is still another species that can be grown as an annual, though it is perennial in Zones 7–9, 14–24, 28–31. Finely divided dark green leaves cover a plant that may reach 6 inches high and spread as ground cover to as much as 5 feet. Clusters of blue, violet, or purple flowers appear from spring through fall in the mildest regions. '**Alba**' is a white-blossomed selection.

Hardy perennial verbenas include drought-tolerant *V. bipinnatifida* (Zones 1–24, northern part of 26, 27–43). It's a spreading plant to 16 inches high, 1½ to 2 feet wide, bearing clusters of blue blossoms over finely divided, lightly hairy green leaves. Among perennial hybrids is well-known *V.* '**Homestead Purple**' (Zones 2–24, 28–41), a dense, bushy grower 1 to 2 feet high and up to 3 feet wide, with dark green, deeply scallop-edged, 2-inch-long leaves and a lavish show of clustered bright purple blossoms from summer into fall. Other popular hybrids are the **Tapien** and **Temari** hybrids (Zones 4–9, 12–24, 28–31; H1, H2), both with dark green leaves. The former, growing 4 inches high and up to 1½ feet wide, has finely cut foliage and flowers in blue, purple, lavender, pink, and red. The latter has broadly oval leaves on plants to 3 inches high and 2½ feet wide; blossom colors are purple, wine red, and pink.

Two other perennial verbenas are quite different in appearance from the preceding. South American native *V. bonariensis* (Zones 8–24, 28–31, warmer parts of 32) is a large, dramatic-looking plant that sends up slender, branching, lightly leafy, 3- to 6-foot stems at bloom time; these rise above coarse, 2- to 4-inch leaves growing in a low clump. Each stem tip bears a cluster of small purple flowers that almost seem to float in the air; a clump of stems forms a see-through "fishnet." This species grows from a stout rootstock and increases by prolific seeding. It has naturalized in warmer regions of the U.S.—as has another South American native, *V. rigida* (*V. venosa;* Zones 3–24, 28–33). Stems reach 10 to 20 inches high, the clumps spreading into patches or colonies by means of underground shoots. Sandpapery, strongly toothed gray-green leaves to 4 inches long ascend stems that end in clusters of small purple flowers. Pale lilac '**Lilacina**', lavender-blue '**Polaris**', and scarlet '**Flame**' are selected forms.

CULTURE. All verbenas need average soil, good drainage (especially important in winter), and a location with good air circulation (to discourage powdery mildew). Moderate watering suits most; 'Homestead Purple' and the Tapien and Temari hybrids, however, are best with regular watering. To start any verbena from seed, sow indoors 8 to 10 weeks before the last-frost date; in warm-winter regions, you can also sow outdoors as soon as frost danger is past. You can start new plants of the low-growing and spreading types from stem cuttings in spring and summer (and from sections of stem that have rooted where they touch the soil). *V. bonariensis* readily self-sows, giving you a constant supply of new plants. To increase *V. rigida,* you can remove rooted shoots from the outside of a clump.

TOP: *Verbena × hybrida* 'Quartz Burgundy'
BOTTOM: *Verbena bonariensis*

VERONICA

SPEEDWELL

Scrophulariaceae

PERENNIALS

ZONES 1–9, 14–21, 32–43,
EXCEPT AS NOTED

FULL SUN, EXCEPT AS NOTED

REGULAR WATER

✿ ✿ ❀ ✿ FLOWERS IN SUMMER,
EXCEPT AS NOTED

Veronica austriaca teucrium 'Crater Lake Blue'

The speedwells are an invaluable summertime source of cool, soothing blue shades and white. A number of species are small-scale ground covers. The plants discussed below, however, are more upright, their tiny, starlike flowers held aloft in tapering spikes that rise like candles above shrubby clumps of narrow, pointed leaves. Shopping for these plants can be confusing. A few species may be listed under two (or more) names, and named cultivars are not always assigned to the same species. If the catalog descriptions—or the actual plants!—you see don't agree with the descriptions given here, don't worry. From the gardener's standpoint, it's easiest to make choices based simply on a plant's stated height and the color of its flowers and foliage.

V. austriaca teucrium '**Crater Lake Blue**', to 12 to 15 inches high and wide, bears dark green, 1½-inch leaves and short spikes of vivid medium blue flowers. Appropriately named *V. longifolia* has 3-inch leaves on a plant to around 2½ feet high. The basic blossom color is deep blue; selections include white-flowered '**Alba**' and bushy '**Blauriesin**' ('**Blue Giantess**'), with bright blue blooms. Old favorite *V. spicata* (Zones A2, A3; 1–9, 14–21, 28, 31–43) blooms over a long summer period, producing spikes of blue flowers that rise to 2 feet above rounded clumps of glossy green, 1- to 2-inch leaves. Two widely sold cultivars (both a bit shorter than 2 feet) are white '**Icicle**' and deep rose '**Rotfuchs**' ('**Red Fox**').

Several hybrid speedwells appear to be derived from *V. spicata* and resemble it in general habit. One popular choice is '**Sunny Border Blue**', to 2 feet high; it has crinkled dark green leaves and bears deep blue-violet blossoms in late spring to early summer, depending on climate. Three other hybrids, all successful in Zones 1–7, 14–17, 32–43, are 2-foot '**Blue Charm**', with lavender-blue flowers; foot-tall '**Goodness Grows**', a long-blooming plant (late spring to fall) with intense violet-blue blooms; and 1½-foot '**Noah Williams**', which resembles *V. spicata* 'Icicle' but has white-edged leaves.

CULTURE. Speedwells appreciate average soil with good drainage. In most climates, they prefer a full-sun location, but where summers are hot they do better with a little afternoon shade. Remove spent blossom spikes to encourage new flowering growth. When clumps decline in vigor, dig and divide them in early spring. You also can increase plants from stem cuttings taken in spring and summer.

VIOLA

Violaceae

PERENNIALS, SOME GROWN AS
COOL-SEASON ANNUALS

ZONES VARY

EXPOSURE NEEDS VARY

REGULAR WATER

✿ ✿ ❀ ✿ ✿ ✿ FLOWERS IN WINTER,
SPRING, SUMMER

Pansies, violets, and violas have been cherished by generations of gardeners for their jewel-like colors and, in the case of violets, for their sweet, distinctive perfume as well. Though all are perennials, pansies and most violas are grown as cool-season annuals. All have five-petaled flowers borne singly at the tips of slender stems. In pansies and many violas, the petals are nearly equal in size and shape, forming a flat blossom with a circular outline. In violets, however, petals differ in both shape and size, and the blossoms have an asymmetrical look.

Viola cornuta, Sorbet series

Viola or tufted pansy, *V. cornuta*, grows in Zones A2, A3, 1–24, 29–45 as an annual; perennial cultivars grow in Zones 1–10, 14–24, 29–43. Numerous seed-raised strains are available, featuring 1- to 2-inch flowers and broadly oval to elliptical, wavy-edged leaves on bushy plants to about 8 inches high and wide. Many solid colors are available—white, blue, purple, pink, red, orange, yellow; you'll also find numerous bicolor combinations, some of them with contrasting "whisker" patterns. The **Sorbet** series is particularly cold resistant, making it a good bet in zones where violas can be grown for winter color; plants also last longer into hot weather than most.

Specialty nurseries carry reliably perennial cultivars and hybrids of *V. cornuta* that form larger mounds than the species, growing about 2 feet wide. Among plants listed as hybrid violas are khaki-colored **'Irish Molly'** and virtually black **'Molly Sanderson'**. Another group of hybrids, the violettas, includes **'Raven'** (deep purple with orange eye), **'Rebecca'** (cream with violet-flecked margins), and creamy yellow, purple-whiskered **'Whiskers'**.

Pansy, *V. × wittrockiana,* grows in all zones. Plants look like slightly larger violas, reaching 10 to 12 inches high and wide, with broadly oval to heart-shaped leaves. Flowers, though, are notably larger—2 to 4 inches across—and come in an even more dazzling array of colors and patterns. The basic colors include white, blue, purple, lavender, pink, red, mahogany, brown, orange, apricot, yellow, and pink; you can find essentially solid-colored individuals, but far more widely grown are bi- and multicolored sorts. In many, the lower three petals are marked with dark, velvety blotches: the familiar pansy "face." Strains are too numerous to mention in detail, and new ones enter the market constantly. A few offer unmistakable, even startling flowers. **'Jolly Joker'** has a Halloween color scheme: bright orange lower petals, black-purple upper ones. The **Joker** series offers bicolored blooms in a variety of sharply contrasting colors. **'Padparadja'** is a solid tangerine scarlet; **'Springtime Black'** is a lustrous, velvety black. **'Brunig'** and **'Rippling Waters'** have dark flowers with striking petal edges: mahogany blooms with a yellow edge in the former, purplish black flowers edged with white in the latter.

Sweet violet, *V. odorata* (Zones 1–24, 29–43), grows just 4 to 8 inches high. An individual plant consists of a clump of long-stalked, nearly circular leaves—but one plant will spread in strawberry fashion, sending out long runners that root to produce new plants. Sweet-scented, ¾- to 1-inch flowers come in late winter to early spring, carried on stems just long enough to rise to the top of the foliage or barely above it; when bloom is at its peak, a violet patch is a sheet of color. Purple (or violet) is the color associated with these flowers, and **'Royal Robe'** is a widely sold example. But you'll also find violets in white, pink, lilac, and light to dark blue, and a few cultivars have double flowers. A small group of hybrids, the **Parma Violets** (Zones 4–9, 14–24, 29–31), features smaller, very double, highly fragrant flowers on plants that resemble a typical *V. odorata* but are less vigorous and spread more slowly. Named representatives include deep violet **'Marie Louise'** and lavender **'Duchesse de Parme'**.

CULTURE. Pansies and violas need good, organically enriched, well-drained soil and a location in sun or partial shade. In mild-winter regions, set out nursery plants in fall for winter-to-spring bloom; in cold-winter regions, set out plants as early as possible in spring for summer bloom. If you are starting from seed, timing depends on amount of winter cold. In mild-winter regions, sow seeds in late summer for planting out in fall; you'll get flowers in winter and spring. In colder areas, sow seeds indoors 10 to 12 weeks before the last-frost date for flowers by early summer. During the bloom period, remove spent flowers on pansies and violas to prevent seed set and prolong bloom. As weather warms, and particularly as night temperatures rise, performance declines; plants become ragged, unsightly, and start to fail at some point in summer in all but the coolest regions. In these cool-summer areas, you can cut back plants lightly in summer to control legginess; this can result in a passable display into fall.

Violets, too, appreciate good, organically enriched, well-drained soil, but they'll also thrive in fairly average soil with casual care. Give them partial to full shade, though in cool-summer regions they'll also grow in full sun. Set out plants in winter (in mild-winter regions) to spring (in colder areas). You can dig and divide for increase in early spring; or just dig rooted portions from a clump's perimeter.

Viola × wittrockiana 'Joker Poker Face'

Viola odorata 'White Czar'

ANNUAL VINES

A number of all-time favorite vines are annuals—and no wonder. Starting from seeds planted early in the year, these plants grow quickly to flowering size, giving you both color and bountiful foliage over a long season. Grow them on trellises, posts, walls, or fences; the largest ones can even cover an arbor. A few are also useful as fast-growing temporary ground covers. Unless otherwise noted, all do best in a sunny location. With a few exceptions (noted below), you should start seeds of these vines indoors in early spring; transplant seedlings to the garden after the weather has warmed. If you plan to train the vines on a temporary trellis or fence, be sure to set it up before setting out plants in the garden (or sowing seed in place); that way, you'll avoid damaging tender young growth.

Asarina scandens

Known as climbing snapdragon or chickabiddy, members of the genus ***Asarina*** (a tender perennial grown as an annual in Zones 1–45) have tubular flowers that resemble bell-shaped ("snapless") snapdragon (*Antirrhinum*) blooms. The twining stems, clothed in triangular to oval green leaves, will climb string, wire, or sticks, clamber over the ground, or spill over a retaining wall or the edges of a hanging basket. Largest is ***A. barclaiana,*** growing to 12 feet and bearing 2- to 3-inch flowers in white, pink, or purple. The same colors are available in the somewhat smaller-flowered ***A. scandens,*** which reaches just 4 to 8 feet. These plants require well-drained soil and prefer a location where their roots will be in shade, their tops in sun. They may live over winter and become perennials in Zones 17–27.

Cup-and-saucer vine, ***Cobaea scandens*** (a tender perennial grown as an annual in Zones 3–41), is extremely vigorous, reaching as much as 25 feet in a single season. The "cup and saucer" of the common name refer to the look of the flowers: the petals form a broad-based, 2-inch-long "cup," which rests on a circular, saucer-like, green calyx (the "saucer"). The cup is green at first, turning violet or rosy purple as it ages; '**Alba**' has white cups. Leaves are divided into two or three pairs of oval, 4-inch leaflets. At the end of each leaflet are curling tendrils that enable the vine to cling to string,

Ipomoea nil,
Early Call strain

wire, or rough surfaces. In cool-summer regions, flowering begins in late summer. In mild-winter areas (Zones 24–27; H1, H2), vines are perennial; they bloom in midsummer the first year from seed, from spring into fall in subsequent years.

Hyacinth bean (***Dolichos lablab,*** sometimes sold as ***Lablab purpurescens;*** all zones) grows quickly to 10 feet. It has purple stems and leaves composed of three broadly oval, 3- to 6-inch-long leaflets with purple veins. In late summer and early autumn, sweet pea–shaped purple flowers stand out from the vine on long stems; these are followed by edible, velvety magenta purple beans to 2½ inches long. Grow these plants

Dolichos lablab

as you would string beans, planting seeds in place in the garden after the last frost, in soil enriched with organic matter.

The genus ***Ipomoea*** includes several popular summer-blooming annual vines successful in all zones. They are related to dwarf morning glory (*Convolvulus tricolor,* described on page 111). The old-fashioned favorite vining morning glory, ***I. tricolor,*** twines vigorously to 10 to 15 feet, bearing heart-shaped leaves and the familiar funnel-shaped flowers 3 to 4 inches across. The traditional variety with sky-blue flowers is '**Heavenly Blue**'; '**Pearly Gates**' has white flowers, while '**Crimson Rambler**' features blossoms in an intense magenta. There are also mixed-color strains including pink, purple, and lavender blooms. On sunny days, flowers open in the morning and close by afternoon; when weather is overcast, they'll remain open all day.

I. nil, also called morning glory, looks much like *I. tricolor* in plant and blossom. Selections include rosy red **'Scarlett O'Hara'** and pale red-brown **'Chocolate'.** The **Early Call** strain, featuring mixed colors of pink, magenta, blue, white, and lavender, blooms earlier than other members of the *I. nil* group, making it a good choice for short-summer regions.

The seed coat (outer covering) of morning glories is very hard, preventing the seed from absorbing moisture. Nicking each seed with a sharp knife or soaking seeds overnight in warm water before planting will improve germination. Where the growing season is long, seeds can be sown outdoors where the plants are to grow, 2 weeks after the last frost date.

Sweet pea, *Lathyrus odoratus* (all zones), is one of the best-known garden flowers, offering a delightful combination of beauty, color, and fragrance. Climbing to 5 feet or taller, it bears upright, long-stemmed clusters of flowers in cream, white, blue, purple, violet, red, and pink; there are also bicolor combinations featuring one of the usual colors plus white or cream. Seed companies offer a number of strains and varieties. For best success, plant seeds directly in the garden, in the spot where the vines are to grow.

Unlike many other annual vines, sweet peas are at their best in cool to mild weather; hot temperatures end their productivity. The planting time and variety best for you depend on your climate. In mild-winter, hot-summer areas, early-flowering strains will bloom in winter from seed sown in late summer; spring-flowering strains planted from October to early January will bloom from spring until hot weather arrives. In regions with cool winters and warm to hot summers, plant seeds of spring-flowering strains as soon as soil is workable in early spring. Summer-flowering strains are best for

Lathyrus odoratus

regions with cold winters and warm (but not hot) and/or short summers.

Like morning glories, sweet peas have a very hard seed coat (outer covering). To improve germination, pretreat the seeds as directed at left for morning glories. Plant in good, well-amended soil; keep soil moist but not saturated. To prolong bloom, remove all spent flower clusters.

Black-eyed Susan vine, *Thunbergia alata* (a tender perennial grown as an annual in all zones), reaches 10 feet tall, climbing by twining stems. The bright green, triangular leaves are about 3 inches long. Slender, 1-inch, tubular orange flowers with black throats bloom all summer; yellow- and white-flowered varieties are also available. In Zones 23–27 and H2, vines may live from year to year as perennials.

Thunbergia alata

Garden favorites everywhere, nasturtiums, *Tropaeolum majus* (all zones), are fast growing and easy to raise from seed. Vining types climb to about 6 feet, gripping their supports with coiling leafstalks; without support, they can serve as colorful ground covers. (See page 175 for information on dwarf, nonclimbing varieties.) The round bright green leaves grow on long stalks; the long-spurred flowers, blooming from summer into fall, reach 2½ inches across and have a refreshing fragrance. Orange is the traditional color, but choices also include creamy white, yellow, red brown, and maroon. Young leaves, flowers, and unripe seedpods have a peppery tang and are used in salads. In early spring, sow seed in place in the garden, in well-drained, average soil. The plants grow quickly and often reseed.

Canary bird flower, *T. peregrinum* (tender perennial grown as an annual in all zones), reaches 10 to 15 feet. Each leaf is deeply divided into five lobes. The inch-wide, canary yellow flowers have fringed petals and curved green spurs; they appear throughout summer until frost. Plant in light shade, in well-drained soil. Plants may become perennial in Zones 24–27, H1, H2.

Tropaeolum peregrinum

ZAUSCHNERIA
(Epilobium)
CALIFORNIA FUCHSIA
Onagraceae
PERENNIALS
ZONES 2–11, 14–24, EXCEPT AS NOTED
FULL SUN, EXCEPT AS NOTED
LITTLE TO MODERATE WATER,
    EXCEPT AS NOTED
❀ ✿ ✿ ☆ FLOWERS IN SUMMER, FALL

Zauschneria californica latifolia

ZINNIA
Asteraceae (Compositae)
WARM-SEASON ANNUALS
ZONES 1–45; H1, H2
FULL SUN
REGULAR WATER
✿ ❀ ✿ ✿ ✿ ☆ FLOWERS IN SUMMER

These plants are distantly related to true fuchsia and have somewhat similar blooms—hence the common name. However, the 1- to 2-inch, typically red or orange blossoms aren't pendent, but are instead carried in an almost horizontal position. Blossoms consist of a tube that flares out into an unequally lobed trumpet; leaves are narrow, ½ to 1½ inches long, and often gray or silvery in color. Growth varies from upright and almost shrublike to low and spreading. Thriving in hot, sunny locations, these natives of western North America typically grow best in areas of low humidity and sparse summer rainfall. They spread by underground stems and can be considered mildly invasive in manicured gardens; they excel in naturalistic plantings, on banks, and at the fringes of cultivated areas.

Botanists have recently reclassified these plants from *Zauschneria* to *Epilobium;* in nurseries and catalogs, you may find them listed under either name.

Z. californica (Epilobium canum canum) is the tallest species, with upright or arching growth to 2 feet. The leaves usually are grayish, the blossoms orange to scarlet. Selected forms include upright **'Bowman'**, semitrailing **'Calistoga'**, mounding **'Cloverdale'**, and compact **'Dublin'**; a white-flowered form is also occasionally sold. Leaves of **'Catalina'** are silvery white; **'Solidarity Pink'** has light pink blossoms. **'Etteri'**, forming a low mat of silvery foliage, is probably a hybrid with *Z. septentrionalis.*

The geographic variant **Z. c. garrettii (Epilobium canum garrettii)** is represented in nurseries by its selection **'Orange Carpet'**. A significant departure from the species, this is a low, compact plant to about 4 inches high and 16 inches wide. Another geographic variant, **Z. c. latifolia (Epilobium canum latifolium),** grows 1 to 1½ feet tall, its stems clothed in broadly elliptic green leaves. Its selection **'Arizonica' (Z. arizonica)** presents its bright orange flowers on stems to 3 feet high.

Humboldt County fuchsia, **Z. septentrionalis (Epilobium septentrionale;** Zones 5–7, 14–17, 19–24), is a mat-forming spreader to 8 inches high, with screaming scarlet flowers that stand in striking contrast to the gray-green to silvery leaves. **'Wayne's Silver'** has especially silvery leaves on a particularly dense plant.

CULTURE. California fuchsias usually flourish in poor, even rocky soil, though most also do well in more standard garden soil if drainage is good. Most prefer full sun and get along with little water. Exceptions are *Z. californica* 'Etteri', which requires moderate watering; *Z. californica garrettii* 'Orange Carpet', which does best with light afternoon shade and regular water; and *Z. septentrionalis*, which needs light afternoon shade and moderate water in hot-summer areas.

To curb a clump's spread, simply remove sections from the perimeter—and to increase a planting, transplant those sections to another location.

Hot stuff! With their showy blossoms in bright, pure, unshaded colors, zinnias are the perfect embodiment of their Latin American origins, enlivening the garden with bold brushstrokes straight from a Diego Rivera mural. True to their roots, they languish in cool, damp conditions but come alive in hot weather. Single-flowered individuals sport the basic daisy: a circular center surrounded by ray petals. Standard garden zinnias, however, are primarily semidouble- to double-flowered numbers resembling slightly shaggy pompoms.

Zinnia angustifolia 'Star White'

Looking like a domesticated wildflower, *Z. angustifolia* produces inch-wide single flowers; each bright orange petal is marked with a pale longitudinal stripe. Linear leaves to 2½ inches long cover a mounding, branching plant to 16 inches high and wide. **'Classic'** has 1½-inch blossoms on a plant to 1 foot high and 2 feet wide. White selections include **'Star White'** and **'Tropical Snow'** (both with 2-inch flowers) and **'Crystal White'** (with 1½-inch blooms). The **Star** series bears 2-inch flowers in orange, yellow, and white.

Zinnia elegans 'Whirligig'

The most familiar zinnia, *Z. elegans,* includes plants from under a foot high to 4 feet tall, with flowers from less than an inch to as much as 5 inches across. This group offers a zinnia for every conceivable sunny garden spot, containers included. Plants are upright but branching, bearing oval to lance-shaped leaves with a rough surface; leaf size is proportional to plant height and can reach 5 inches long in the tallest kinds. Flower forms include full double, cactus flowered (double with quilled petals), and crested (blossoms have a cushionlike center surrounded by rows of broad petals). Colors include white, lavender, purple, pink, red, orange, yellow, cream, and lime green (in the cultivar **'Envy'**), as well as bicolors and striped combinations.

Zinnia elegans, Candy Cane Mix

The tallest strains, all double flowered, are 4-foot **Benary's Giants** (also sold as **Blue Point** and **Park's Picks**), with 4- to 5-inch flowers; **Oklahoma,** with 1½-inch flowers on plants to 3½ feet tall; 3-foot **Dahlia-flowered Mix,** with 4- to 5-inch flowers; and 3-foot **'Big Red Hybrid',** with 5- to 6-inch blossoms. Strains of intermediate size (double flowered, unless otherwise noted) include 1½-foot **Candy Cane Mix,** with 4-inch white flowers striped in pink, rose, or red; the similar **Candy Stripe,** to 2 feet tall; 2- to 3-foot **Giant Cactus-flowered Mix** (semidouble, 4- to 5-inch flowers); 2½-foot **Ruffles Hybrids** (3½-inch flowers with ruffled petals); 2½-foot **Sun Hybrids** (flowers to 5 inches across); and **'Whirligig',** with 3- to 4½-inch bicolored blooms on 20-inch plants. Strains with plants to 1 foot tall and double flowers to 3 inches wide are **Dasher Hybrid Mixed, Parasol Mixed, Peter Pan Hybrid Improved,** and mildew-resistant **Small World.** The **Lilliput** and **Pompon** series reach 1½ feet tall and bear 1½-inch double blossoms.

Hybrids between *Z. elegans* and *Z. angustifolia* look like a slightly larger version of the *Z. angustifolia* parent, growing about 1½ feet high and wide and bearing narrow leaves and 2-inch flowers. The **Profusion** series comes in orange and cherry red, the flowers containing a second row of petals.

Upright-growing *Z. haageana* reaches 2 feet tall and has narrow, 3-inch leaves. Available strains bear double, 2-inch-wide flowers in yellow, orange, and mahogany red; all three colors are sometimes present in a single blossom. Foot-tall **Persian Carpet** and 16-inch **Old Mexico** are two popular choices.

CULTURE. Give zinnias a full-sun location with average to good, well-drained soil. These are hot-weather plants, and there's no point setting them out in cool weather: they won't start growing until temperatures are warm. In mild-winter regions, you can sow outdoors after the danger of frost is past and soil has warmed; in colder areas, sow indoors 6 to 8 weeks before the last-frost date. Powdery mildew is a potential problem in foggy regions, where plants are given overhead watering, and where nights are cool; it can also crop up in all areas as nights turn longer and cooler heading into fall.

Zinnia, Profusion series

SUNSET'S GARDEN CLIMATE ZONES

A plant's performance is governed by the total climate: length of growing season, timing and amount of rainfall, winter lows, summer highs, humidity. *Sunset*'s climate zone maps take all these factors into account—unlike the familiar hardiness zone maps devised by the U.S. Department of Agriculture, which divide the U.S. and Canada into zones based strictly on winter lows. The U.S.D.A. maps tell you only where a plant may survive the winter; our climate zone maps let you see where that plant will thrive year-round. Below and on page 188 are brief descriptions of the zones illustrated on the maps on pages 186–188. For more information, consult *Sunset*'s regional garden books.

ZONE 1A. Coldest Mountain and Intermountain Areas in the West

All zone is west of Continental Divide. Growing season mid-June to early September, with mild days, chilly nights. Average lows to –0°F/–18°C, extreme lows to –40F/–40C; snow cover (or winter mulch) key to perennials success.

ZONE 1B. Coldest Eastern Rockies and Plains Climate

All zone is east of Continental Divide. Growing season mid-May to late September: warm days, warmer nights than 1A. Summer rainfall present, wind a constant. Winter Arctic cold fronts create sudden temperature shifts; average lows to 0°F/–18°C, extreme lows to –50°F/–46°C.

ZONE 2A. Cold Mountain and Intermountain Areas

Growing season mid-May to mid-September. Occurs at lower elevation than Zone 1A; summers are mild, winters to 10°F/–12°C (extremes to –30°F/–34°C) with snow. The coldest zone for growing sweet cherries, hardiest apples.

ZONE 2B. Warmer-Summer Intermountain Climate

Growing season mid-May to October. Premier fruit- and grain-growing climate with long, warm to hot summers. Winters to 12°F/–11°C (extremes to –20°F/–23°C) with snow.

ZONE 3A. Mild Areas of Mountain and Intermountain Climates

Growing season May to mid-October. Long, dry, warm summers favor a variety of warm-season crops, deciduous fruits, many ornamentals. Occurs at higher elevation the farther south it is found. Winter temperatures drop to 15°F/–9°C with extremes to –18°F/–28°C; snow is possible.

ZONE 3B. Mildest Areas on Intermountain Climates

Growing season early April to late October. Compared to Zone 3A, summers are warmer, winters milder: to 19°F/-7°C with extremes to –15°F/–26°C. Snow is possible. Excellent climate for vegetables, also a wide variety of ornamentals that prefer dry atmosphere.

ZONE 4. Cold-winter Western Washington and British Columbia

Growing season: early May to early Oct. Summers are cool, thanks to ocean influence; chilly winters (19° to –7°F/–7° to –22°C) result from elevation, influence of continental air mass, or both. Coolness, ample rain suit many perennials and bulbs.

ZONE 5. Ocean-influenced Northwest Coast and Puget Sound

Growing season: mid-April to Nov., typically with cool temperatures throughout. Less rain falls here than in Zone 4; winter lows range from 28° to 1°F/–2° to –17°C. This "English garden" climate is ideal for rhododendrons and many rock garden plants.

ZONE 6. Oregon's Willamette Valley

Growing season: mid-Mar. to mid-Nov., with somewhat warmer temperatures than in Zone 5. Ocean influence keeps winter lows about the same as in Zone 5. Climate suits all but tender plants and those needing hot or dry summers.

ZONE 7. Oregon's Rogue River Valley, California's High Foothills

Growing season: May to early Oct. Summers are hot and dry; typical winter lows run from 23° to 9°F/–5° to –13°C. The summer-winter contrast suits plants that need dry, hot summers and moist, only moderately cold winters.

ZONE 8. Cold-air Basins of California's Central Valley

Growing season: mid-Feb. through Nov. This is a valley floor with no maritime influence. Summers are hot; winter lows range from 29° to 13°F/–2° to –11°C. Rain comes in the cooler months, covering just the early part of the growing season.

ZONE 9. Thermal Belts of California's Central Valley

Growing season: late Feb. through Dec. Zone 9 is located in the higher elevations around Zone 8, but its summers are just as hot; its winter lows are slightly higher (temperatures range from 28° to 18°F/–2° to –8°C). Rainfall pattern is the same as in Zone 8.

ZONE 10. High Desert Areas of Arizona, New Mexico, West Texas, Oklahoma Panhandle, and Southwest Kansas

Growing season: April to early Nov. Chilly (even snow-dusted) weather rules from late Nov. through Feb., with lows from 31° to 24°F/–1° to –4°C. Rain comes in summer as well as in the cooler seasons.

ZONE 11. Medium to High Desert of California and Southern Nevada

Growing season: early April to late Oct. Summers are sizzling, with 110 days above 90°F/32°C. Balancing this is a 3½-month winter, with 85 nights below freezing and lows from 11° to 0°F/–12° to –18°C. Scant rainfall comes in winter.

ZONE 12. Arizona's Intermediate Desert

Growing season: mid-Mar. to late Nov., with scorching midsummer heat. Compared to Zone 13, this region has harder frosts; record low is 6°F/–14°C. Rains come in summer and winter.

ZONE 13. Low or Subtropical Desert

Growing season: mid-Feb. through Nov., interrupted by nearly 3 months of incandescent, growth-stopping summer heat. Most frosts are light (record lows run from 19° to 13°F/–17° to –11°C); scant rain comes in summer and winter.

ZONE 14. Inland Northern and Central California with Some Ocean Influence

Growing season: early Mar. to mid-Nov., with rain coming in the remaining months. Periodic intrusions of marine air temper summer heat and winter cold (lows run from 26° to 16°F/–3° to –9°C). Mediterranean-climate plants are at home here.

ZONE 15. Northern and Central California's Chilly-winter Coast-influenced Areas

Growing season: Mar. to Dec. Rain comes from fall through winter. Typical winter lows range from 28° to 21°F/–2° to –6°C. Maritime air influences the zone much of the time, giving it cooler, moister summers than Zone 14.

ZONE 16. Northern and Central California Coast Range Thermal Belts

Growing season: late Feb. to late Nov. With cold air draining to lower elevations, winter lows typically run from 32° to 19°F/0° to –7°C. Like Zone 15, this region is dominated by maritime air, but its winters are milder on average.

ZONE 17. Oceanside Northern and Central California and Southernmost Oregon

Growing season: late Feb. to early Dec. Coolness and fog are hallmarks; summer highs seldom top 75°F/24°C, while winter lows run from 36° to 23°F/2° to –5°C. Heat-loving plants disappoint or dwindle here.

ZONE 18. Hilltops and Valley Floors of Interior Southern California

Growing season: mid-Mar. through late Nov. Summers are hot and dry; rain comes in winter, when lows reach 28° to 10°F/−2° to −12°C. Plants from the Mediterranean and Near Eastern regions thrive here.

ZONE 19. Thermal belts around Southern California's Interior Valleys

Growing season: early Mar. through Nov. As in Zone 18, rainy winters and hot, dry summers are the norm—but here, winter lows dip only to 27° to 22°F/−3° to −6°C, allowing some tender evergreen plants to grow outdoors with protection.

ZONE 20. Hilltops and Valley Floors of Ocean-influenced Inland Southern California

Growing season: late Mar. to late Nov.—but fairly mild winters (lows of 28° to 23°F/−2° to −5°C) allow gardening through much of the year. Cool and moist maritime influence alternates with hot, dry interior air.

ZONE 21. Thermal Belts around Southern California's Ocean-influenced Interior Valleys

Growing season: early Mar. to early Dec., with same tradeoff of oceanic and interior influence as in Zone 20. During winter rainy season, lows range from 36° to 23°F/2° to −5°C—warmer than Zone 20, since colder air drains to the valleys.

ZONE 22. Colder-winter Parts of Southern California's Coastal Region

Growing season: Mar. to early Dec. Winter lows seldom fall below 28°F/−2°C (records are around 21°F/−6°C), though colder air sinks to this zone from Zone 23. Summers are warm; rain comes in winter. Climate here is largely oceanic.

ZONE 23. Thermal Belts of Southern California's Coastal Region

Growing season: almost year-round (all but first half of Jan.). Rain comes in winter. Reliable ocean influence keeps summers mild (except when hot Santa Ana winds come from inland), frosts negligible; 23°F/−5°C is the record low.

ZONE 24. Marine-dominated Southern California Coast

Growing season: all year, but periodic freezes have dramatic effects (record lows are 33° to 20°F/1° to −7°C). Climate here is oceanic (but warmer than oceanic Zone 17), with cool summers, mild winters. Subtropical plants thrive.

ZONE 25. South Florida and the Keys

Growing season: all year. Add ample year-round rainfall (least in Dec. through Mar.), high humidity, and overall warmth, and you have a near-tropical climate. The Keys are frost-free; winter lows elsewhere run from 40° to 25°F/4° to −4°C.

ZONE 26. Central and Interior Florida

Growing season: early Feb. to late Dec., with typically humid, warm to hot weather. Rain is plentiful all year, heaviest in summer and early fall. Lows range from 15°F/−9°C in the north to 27°F/−3°C in the south; arctic air brings periodic hard freezes.

ZONE 27. Lower Rio Grande Valley

Growing season: early Mar. to mid-Dec.. Summers are hot and humid; winter lows only rarely dip below freezing. Many plants from tropical and subtropical Africa and South America are well adapted here.

ZONE 28. Gulf Coast, North Florida, Atlantic Coast to Charleston

Growing season: mid-Mar. to early Dec. Humidity and rainfall are year-round phenomena; summers are hot, winters virtually frostless but subject to periodic invasions by frigid arctic air. Azaleas, camellias, many subtropicals flourish.

ZONE 29. Interior Plains of South Texas

Growing season: mid-Mar. through Nov. Moderate rainfall (to 25" annually) comes year-round. Summers are hot. Winter lows can dip to 26°F/−3°C, with occasional arctic freezes bringing much lower readings.

ZONE 30. Hill Country of Central Texas

Growing season: mid-Mar. through Nov. Zone 30 has higher annual rainfall than Zone 29 (to 35") and lower winter temperatures, normally to around 20°F/−7°C. Seasonal variations favor many fruit crops, perennials.

ZONE 31. Interior Plains of Gulf Coast and Coastal Southeast

Growing season: mid-Mar. to early Nov. In this extensive east-west zone, hot and sticky summers contrast with chilly winters (record low temperatures are 7° to 0°F/−14° to −18°C). There's rain all year (an annual average of 50"), with the least falling in Oct.

ZONE 32. Interior Plains of Mid-Atlantic States; Chesapeake Bay, Southeastern Pennsylvania, Southern New Jersey

Growing season: late Mar. to early Nov. Rain falls year-round (40" to 50" annually); winter lows (moving through the zone from south to north) are 30° to 20°F/ −1° to −7°C. Humidity is less oppressive here than in Zone 31.

ZONE 33. North-Central Texas and Oklahoma Eastward to the Appalachian Foothills

Growing season: mid-April through Oct. Warm Gulf Coast air and colder continental/arctic fronts both play a role; their unpredictable interplay results in a wide range in annual rainfall (22" to 52") and winter lows (20° to 0°F/−7° to −18°C). Summers are muggy and warm to hot.

ZONE 34. Lowlands and Coast from Gettysburg to North of Boston

Growing season: late April to late Oct. Ample rainfall and humid summers are the norm. Winters are variable—typically fairly mild (around 20°F/−7°C), but with lows down to −3° to −22°F/−19° to −30°C if arctic air swoops in.

ZONE 35. Ouachita Mountains, Northern Oklahoma and Arkansas, Southern Kansas to North-Central Kentucky and Southern Ohio

Growing season: late April to late Oct. Rain comes in all seasons. Summers can be truly hot and humid. Without arctic fronts, winter lows are around 18°F/−8°C; with them, the coldest weather may bring lows of −20°F/−29°C.

ZONE 36. Appalachian Mountains

Growing season: May to late Oct. Thanks to greater elevation, summers are cooler and less humid, winters colder (0° to −20°F/−18° to −29°C) than in adjacent, lower zones. Rain comes all year (heaviest in spring). Late frosts are common.

ZONE 37. Hudson Valley and Appalachian Plateau

Growing season: May to mid-Oct., with rainfall throughout. Lower in elevation than neighboring Zone 42, with warmer winters: lows are 0° to −5°F/−18° to −21°C, unless arctic air moves in. Summer is warm to hot, humid.

ZONE 38. New England Interior and Lowland Maine

Growing season: May to early Oct. Summers feature reliable rainfall and lack oppressive humidity of lower-elevation, more southerly areas. Winter lows dip to −10° to −20°F/−23° to −29°C, with periodic colder temperatures due to influxes of arctic air.

ZONE 39. Shoreline Regions of the Great Lakes

Growing season: early May to early Oct. Springs and summers are cooler here, autumns milder than in areas farther from the lakes. Southeast lakeshores get the heaviest snowfalls. Lows reach 0° to −10°F/−18° to −23°C.

ZONE 40. Inland Plains of Lake Erie and Lake Ontario

Growing season: mid-May to mid-Sept., with rainy, warm, variably humid weather. The lakes help moderate winter lows; temperatures typically range from −10° to −20°F/−23° to −29°C, with occasional colder readings when arctic fronts rush through.

Continued on page 188

Sunset's Garden Climate Zones

Climate Zones		1A	1B	2A	2B	3A	3B	4	5	6	7	8	9	10	11	12	13	14	15	16	17	18	19	20	21	22

James Bay

ONTARIO

QUÉBEC

NEW BRUNSWICK

45

45

45

Lake of the Woods

Lake Superior

43

43

43

43

MINNESOTA

45

Québec ●

Presque Isle ●

43

42

Duluth ●

35

MICHIGAN

43

MAINE

Bangor ●

38

94

Minneapolis ●

94

WISCONSIN

43

MICHIGAN

43

Montréal ●

Ottawa ●

St. Lawrence River

VERMONT

95

Portland ●

43

90

43

Lake Huron

75

41

43

Burlington ●

42

NEW HAMPSHIRE

38

43

Lake Michigan

94

43

Lake Michigan

Milwaukee ●

39

80

94

39

Detroit ●

Lake Erie

Toronto ●

43

40

39

Buffalo ●

90

NEW YORK

81

90

40

44

87

39

42

91

Albany ●

87

Boston ●

MASSACHUSETTS

34

RHODE ISLAND

CONNECTICUT

34

35

Dubuque ●

41

Chicago ●

80

Cleveland ●

90

80

79

PENNSYLVANIA

80

Newark ●

New York ●

78

95

37

81

IOWA

90

74

80

55

57

65

INDIANA

94

69

75

71

OHIO

77

Akron ●

Pittsburgh ●

76

Philadelphia ●

NEW JERSEY

32

Des Moines ●

80

Indianapolis ●

70

41

Columbus ●

70

DELAWARE

34

29

41

ILLINOIS

71

Cincinnati ●

79

36

66

Washington, D.C. ●

MARYLAND

35

Springfield ●

70

WEST VIRGINIA

95

64

55

35

65

Louisville ●

35

Charleston ●

Richmond ●

Kansas City ●

70

St. Louis ●

70

57

Ohio River

64

VIRGINIA

32

85

31

MISSOURI

44

65

KENTUCKY

81

95

35

36

77

Raleigh ●

44

Nashville ●

40

85

NORTH CAROLINA

40

TENNESSEE

24

75

40

ARKANSAS

40

33

32

SOUTH CAROLINA

31

Memphis ●

65

85

32

Columbia ●

95

Arkansas River

35

Little Rock ●

40

59

Atlanta ●

26

20

30

33

GEORGIA

16

Red River

30

55

Birmingham ●

59

85

Savannah ●

Shreveport ●

20

MISSISSIPPI

ALABAMA

31

LOUISIANA

31

Jackson ●

59

75

49

65

28

Jacksonville ●

Mobile ●

10

75

10

Lake Pontchartrain

10

95

Houston ●

10

28

New Orleans ●

FLORIDA

45

Orlando ●

Gulf of Mexico

4

Tampa ●

26

75

Lake Okeechobee

25

Miami ●

Atlantic Ocean

0   100   200   300 miles

© 2001 Sunset Books Inc. All rights reserved.

| 23 | 24 | 25 | 26 | 27 | 28 | 29 | 30 | 31 | 32 | 33 | 34 | 35 | 36 | 37 | 38 | 39 | 40 | 41 | 42 | 43 | 44 | 45 | Climate Zones |

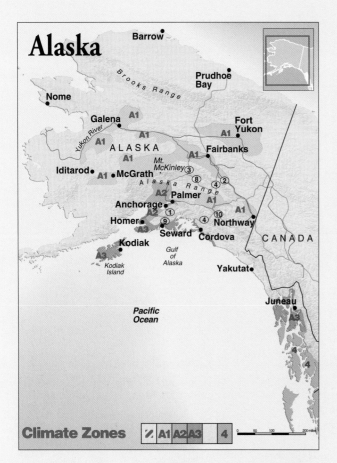

Alaska

Climate Zones ▨ A1 A2 A3 4   0 50 100 200 miles

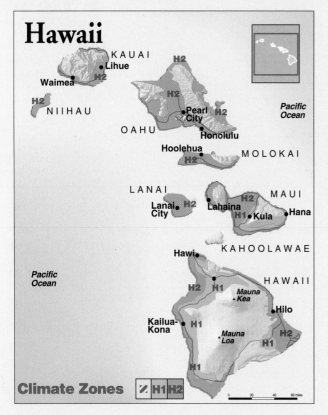

Hawaii

Climate Zones ▨ H1 H2   0 20 40 60 miles

ZONE 41. Northeast Kansas and Southeast Nebraska to Northern Illinois and Indiana, Southeast Wisconsin, Michigan, Northern Ohio

Growing season: early May to early Oct. Winter brings average lows of −11° to −20°F/−23° to −29°C. Summers in this zone are hotter and longer west of the Mississippi, cooler and shorter nearer the Great Lakes; summer rainfall increases in the same west-to-east direction.

ZONE 42. Interior Pennsylvania and New York; St. Lawrence Valley

Growing season: late May to late Sept. This zone's elevation gives it colder winters than surrounding zones: lows range from −20° to −40°F/−29° to −40°C, with the colder readings coming in the Canadian portion of the zone. Summers are humid, rainy.

ZONE 43. Upper Mississippi Valley, Upper Michigan, Southern Ontario and Quebec

Growing season: late May to mid-Sept. The climate is humid from spring through early fall; summer rains are usually dependable. Arctic air dominates in winter, with lows typically from −20° to −30°F/−29° to −34°C.

ZONE 44. Mountains of New England and Southeastern Quebec

Growing season: June to mid-Sept. Latitude and elevation give fairly cool, rainy summers, cold winters with lows of −20° to −40°F/−29° to −40°C. Choose short-season, low heat-requirement annuals and vegetables.

ZONE 45. Northern Parts of Minnesota and Wisconsin, Eastern Manitoba through Interior Quebec

Growing season: mid-June through Aug., with rain throughout; rainfall (and humidity) are least in zone's western part, greatest in eastern reaches. Winters are frigid (−30° to −40°F/−34° to −40°C), with snow cover, deeply frozen soil.

ZONE A1. Alaska's Coldest Climate—Fairbanks and the Interior

Growing season mid-May to early September. Summer days are long, mild to warm; permafrost usually recedes below root zone. Winter offers reliable snow cover. Season extenders include planting in south and west exposures, boosting soil temperature with mulches or IRT plastic sheeting. Winter lows drop to −20°F/−29°C, with occasional extremes to −60°F/−51°C.

ZONE A2. The Intermediate Climate of Anchorage and Cook Inlet

Growing season mid-May to mid-September. Climate is moderated by mountains to the north and south, also by water of Cook Inlet. Microclimates reign supreme: winter lows may be 5°F/−15°C but with extremes of −40°F/−40°C possible. Summer days are cool to mild and frequently cloudy.

ZONE A3. Mild Southern Maritime Climate from Kodiak to Juneau

Growing season mid-May to October. Summers are cool and cloudy, winters rainy and windy. Typical lows are to 18°F/−8°C with extremes to −18°F/−28°C. Winter-spring freeze-thaw cycles damage plants that break growth early. Cool-weather plants revel in climate but annual types mature more slowly than usual.

ZONE H1. Cooler Volcanic Slopes from 2,000 to 5,000 Feet Elevation

Found only on Hawaii and Maui, this zone offers cooler air (and cooler nights) than lower Zone H2; temperatures here are better for low-chill fruits (especially at higher elevations) and many non-tropical ornamentals. Warm-season highs reach 65° to 80°F/19° to 27°C; cool-season lows drop to around 45°F/7°C.

ZONE H2. Sea Level to 2,000 Feet: the Coconut Palm Belt

The most heavily populated region in the islands, this has tepid climate with high temperatures in the 80° to 90°F/27° to 32°C range, low temperatures only to about 65°F/18°C. Rainiest period is November through March, the remaining months, on leeward sides, being relatively dry. Windward sides of islands get more precipitation than leeward sides from passing storms and year-round tradewind showers.

Sources

In most areas, local nurseries offer increasingly wide selections of annual and perennial plants and seeds. However, mail-order suppliers often remain the only source for unusual, newly introduced, and hard-to-find varieties. Listed here are some of the growers who publish catalogs offering plants and seeds (some charge a small fee for their catalogs).

ANDRÉ VIETTE FARM AND NURSERY
P. O. Box 1109
Fishersville, VA 22939
(540) 943-2315
www.viette.com

BLUESTONE PERENNIALS
7211 Middle Ridge Road
Madison, OH 44057
(800) 852-5243
www.bluestoneperennials.com

BUSSE GARDENS
17160 245th Avenue
Big Lake, MN 55309
(800) 544-3192

CARROLL GARDENS
444 East Main Street
Westminster, MD 21157
(800) 638-6334
www.carrollgardens.com

THE CROWNSVILLE NURSERY
P.O. Box 797
Crownsville, MD 21032
(410) 849-3143
www.crownsvillenursery.com

DIGGING DOG NURSERY
P.O. Box 471
Albion, CA 95410
(707) 937-1130
www.diggingdog.com

FORESTFARM
990 Tetherow Road
Williams, OR 97544-9599
(541) 846-7269
www.forestfarm.com

GARDEN PLACE, INC.
6780 Heisley Road
Mentor, OH 44061-0388
(440) 255-3059
www.springbrookgardens.com

HERONSWOOD NURSERY
7530 NE 288th Street
Kingston, WA 98346-9502
(360) 297-4172
www.heronswood.com

HIGH COUNTRY GARDENS
2902 Rufina Street
Santa Fe, NM 87505-2929
(800) 925-9387
www.highcountrygardens.com

NICHE GARDENS
1111 Dawson Road
Chapel Hill, NC 27516
(919) 967-0078
www.nichegardens.com

SHADY OAKS NURSERY
1101 South State Street
P.O. Box 708
Waseca, MN 56093-0708
(800) 504-8006
www.shadyoaks.com

WAYSIDE GARDENS
1 Garden Lane
Hodges, SC 29695-0001
(800) 845-1124
www.waysidegardens.com

WHITE FLOWER FARM
P. O. Box 50
Litchfield, CT 06759-0050
(800) 503-9624
www.whiteflowerfarm.com

MAIL-ORDER SOURCES
FOR SEEDS OF ANNUALS
AND PERENNIALS

W. ATLEE BURPEE AND CO.
300 Park Avenue
Warminster, PA 18991-0001
(800) 888-1447
www.burpee.com

J. L. HUDSON, SEEDSMAN
Star Route 2, P. O. Box 337
La Honda, CA 94020

JOHNNY'S SELECTED SEEDS
Foss Hill Road
RR1, Box 2580
Albion, ME 04910-9731
www.johnnyseeds.com

PARK SEED
1 Parkton Avenue
Greenwood, SC 29647-0001
www.parkseed.com

SELECT SEEDS ANTIQUE FLOWERS
180 Stickney Hill Road
Union, CT 06076-4617
(860) 684-9310
www.selectseeds.com

THOMPSON & MORGAN
P. O. Box 1308
Jackson, NJ 08527-0308
(800) 274-7333
www.thompson-morgan.com

SUBJECT INDEX

Acid soil, 63
Alkaline soil, 63
Annuals
    caring for, 70–73
    defined, 6
    designing with, 18–23, 25, 26–27
    mail-order sources for, 189
    planting, 67, 68–69, 78–79
    pruning, 72
    selecting, 66
    when to plant, 66
Annual vines, 180–181
Aphids, 76
Assassin bugs, 74

Bare-root perennials, 67
Basal cuttings, 83
Beds, planting, 64–65
Beetles, 74, 76
Biennials, 7
    when to plant, 66
Birds, plants that attract, 40, 57
Botrytis, 75
Butterflies, plants that attract, 41, 57

Clay, 62
Climate, 12
Climate zones, 184–188
Cold frames, 82
Cold hardiness and planting sites, 13, 66, 73
Color
    combinations, 28–31
    designing with, 28–31
    flower, by season, 32–37
Composting, 62–63
Containers
    garden plan using, 59
    growing plants in, 68–69
    planting from, 67
    plants for, 42–43
Contrasting color schemes, 30
Cool colors, 28
Cool-season annuals, 66
Cottage gardens, plans for, 51, 54
Cut flowers, plants for, 38
Cutting back, 72

Cuttings, starting plants from, 82–83
Cutworms, 76

Damsel bugs, 74
Deadheading, 72
Diseases, 74–75
Division, 81
Drainage, 62
Drought-tolerant garden, plan for, 56
Drought-tolerant plants, 16

Exposure, 12

Fertilizing, 70–71
    container-grown plants, 68
Flowers
    to attract birds and butterflies, 40–41, 57
    colorful, by season, 32–37
    for cutting, 38
    fragrant, 39
    size and presentation of, 21
Foliage
    colorful, 20, 26–27
    using in garden design, 20, 24–27
Form and size of plants, using in garden design, 18–21
Fragrant plants, 39
Frost and freeze protection, 73

Garden plans, 45–59
Geranium budworms, 76
Gray mold, 75
Gray, using in garden design, 31

Hanging baskets, 69
Harmonious color schemes, 29

Insect pests, 74–76
Insects, beneficial, 74

Lacewings, 74
Lady beetles, 74
Landscape fabrics, 77
Leaf miners, 76
Loam, 62

Mail-order sources for plants and seeds, 189
Mites, 76
Moist soil, plants for, 17
Monochromatic color schemes, 29
Mulching, 67, 70

Nitrogen, 64, 70–71

Organic matter, 62, 64

Perennials
    caring for, 70–73
    defined, 6
    designing with, 18–27
    dividing, 81
    mail-order sources for, 189
    planting, 67, 68, 78–79
    pruning, 72
    selecting, 66
    when to plant, 66
    winter protection for, 73
Pests, 74–76
pH, soil, 63
Phosphorus, 64, 70–71
Pinching, 72
Plans, garden, 45–59
    for attracting birds and butterflies, 57
    autumn assembly, 53
    breath of spring, 51
    for containers, 59
    cool summer island, 48
    cottage-garden border, 54
    creating, 46
    with ornamental grasses, 58
    shady perennial, 55
    summer opulence, 52
    unthirsty island, 56
    warm-season sizzler, 50
    white, 49
Planting, 66–69
    bare-root, 67
    from containers, 67
    in containers, 68–69
    spacing, 67, 68
    when to plant, 66
    wildflowers, 80
Planting beds, preparing, 64–65
Potassium, 64, 70–71
Powdery mildew, 75

Propagation, 78–83
    from cuttings, 82–83
    dividing, 81
    from seeds, 78–79, 80
Pruning, 72

Raised beds, 65
Root cuttings, 82
Root rot, 75
Rust, 75

Sand, 62
Seedlings, transplanting, 79
Seeds
    mail-order sources for, 189
    starting plants from, 78–79, 80
Shade garden, plan for, 55
Shade, plants for, 14
Size and form of plants, using in garden design, 18–21
Slugs, 76
Snails, 76
Soil
    amending, 62–63, 64, 65
    for containers, 68
    drainage, testing, 62
    pH of, 63
    and planting sites, 13
    types of, 62
Staking plants, 73
Stem cuttings, 83
Syrphid flies, 74

Thinning, 72
Thrips, 76
Tobacco budworms, 76

Warm colors, 28
Warm-season annuals, 66
Watering, 13, 68, 70
Water-loving plants, 17
Weed control, 77
White
    garden (planting plan), 49
    using in the garden, 31
Whiteflies, 76
Wildflowers, growing from seed, 80
Window boxes
    installing, 68
    plants for, 69
Winter protection, 73

PLANT INDEX

Acanthus, 84
Achillea, 85
Aconite *(Aconitum),* 85
Aconitum, 85
Adenophora, 86
Agapanthus, 86
Agastache, 87
Ageratum houstonianum, 87
Alcea rosea, 88
Alchemilla mollis, 89
Alstroemeria, 89
Althaea rosea. See Alcea rosea, 88
Alum root *(Heuchera),* 134
Alyssum saxatile. See Aurinia saxatilis, 96

Amaranth *(Amaranthus tricolor),* 151
Amaranthus tricolor, 151
Amsonia, 90
Anchusa, 90
Anemone, 91
Antirrhinum majus, 91
Aquilegia, 92
Artemisia, 93
Aruncus, 94
Asarina, 180
Asclepias tuberosa, 94
Aster, 95
Astilbe, 96
Aurinia saxatilis, 96

Baby's breath *(Gypsophila paniculata),* 130
Bachelor's button *(Centaurea cyanus),* 104
Balloon flower *(Platycodon grandiflorus),* 161
Baptisia, 97
Basket-of-gold *(Aurinia saxatilis),* 96
Beard tongue *(Penstemon),* 155
Bear's breech *(Acanthus),* 84
Bee balm *(Monarda),* 148
Beefsteak plant *(Perilla frutescens purpurascens),* 151
Begonia, 97
Bellflower *(Campanula),* 100

Bells-of-Ireland *(Moluccella laevis),* 147
Bergenia, 98
Beta vulgaris, 151
Bethelem sage *(Pulmonaria saccharata),* 165
Blanket flower *(Gaillardia),* 123
Bleeding heart *(Dicentra),* 116
Blue oat grass *(Helictotrichon sempervirens),* 128
Blue star flower *(Amsonia),* 90
Brassica, 151
Briza maxima, 126
Bronze fennel *(Foeniculum vulgare 'Purpurascens'),* 151
Brunnera macrophylla, 98

PHOTOGRAPHY CREDITS

Em Ahart: 70 top; **Max Badgley:** 74 top right; **Paul Bousquet:** 24 bottom; **Marion Brenner:** 9 middle left, 22 center, 40 bottom right, 85 bottom, 92 bottom, 101 top, 117 bottom, 122 bottom, 151 middle, 174 bottom left; **Rob Cardillo:** 25 bottom left, 26 top left, 27 top, 29 top left, 34 top, middle, 38 bottom left, 40 bottom left, 87 bottom, 90 top left, 91 top, 92 top, 97 bottom, 104 top left, 111, 112 middle, 122 top, 123 bottom, 132 right, 139 top, 173 middle, 181 bottom left, back cover right; **David Cavagnaro:** 7 top right, 15 bottom left, 17 bottom left, 35 bottom, 86 top left, 87 top, 89 top, 93 middle, 93 bottom, 94 bottom, 95 bottom, 96 middle, 101 bottom, 104 bottom left, 108 bottom, 121 bottom, 125 bottom left, 126 left, 127 top right, 128 bottom right, 151 top right, 156 top left, 165 top, 169 bottom, 173 top, 176 left, 178 left, 180 bottom, 181 top right; **Peter Christiansen:** 77 right; **Richard Cowles:** 77 left; **Rosalind Creasy:** 8 top right, bottom right, 9 top left, 80, 88 bottom left, 105 bottom, 106 bottom, 151 bottom, 153; **Claire Curran:** 36 bottom right, 38 top right, 114 right; **Robin B. Cushman:** 6 top left, 12 top, 30 bottom, 41 top right, 65 top right, 149 right; **Janet Davis:** 13 bottom; **R. Todd Davis:** 21 top right, 109 top, 145 top, 148 top right; **Alan & Linda Detrick:** 15 bottom right, 18 top, 20 bottom right, 23 top left, 25 bottom right, 30 top, 37 middle right, 96

top right, 97 top, 103 bottom, 118 top, 119 top, 128 bottom left, 130 top, 137 top, 143 right, 148 bottom, 161 left, 165 middle, 167 top, 170 bottom, 177 top, bottom, 178 right, 179 top, 183 top right, back cover top left; **William Dewey:** 160 bottom; **Ken Druse:** 68 top; **Philip Edinger:** 141 top; **Derek Fell:** 7 top left, 90 bottom left, 127 middle right, 146 bottom; **Roger Foley:** 17 top, 20 bottom left, 170 top; **Steven W. George:** 110 bottom; **David Goldberg:** 75 center left, 135 top, 148 top left, 159 bottom; **Goldsmith Seeds:** 33 top; **Steven Gunther:** 43 bottom, 99 bottom; **Jamie Hadley:** 81; **Lynne Harrison:** 89 bottom, 98 middle left, 107 middle, 120, 123 top, 130 bottom, 131 bottom, 133 top, 137 middle, 140 top, 164 bottom, 171 top, 176 right; **Jessie M. Harrison:** 136 top; **Philip Harvey:** 46 bottom, 62; **Saxon Holt:** 16 bottom right, 17 bottom center, 18 bottom, 27 bottom, 29 top right, 34 bottom, 69, 71, 86 middle right, 107 bottom, 116 bottom left, 128 top left, 129 top right, 131 top, middle, 135 bottom, 140 bottom, 143 left, 158 top, 159 middle, 160 top, 161 top right, bottom right, 164 top, 169 middle, 183 bottom right; **Dency Kane:** 88 top left, 129 bottom left, 150 bottom; **Janet Loughrey:** 19, 25 top, 40 top, 142 bottom, 154 bottom; **Mary-Kate MacKay:** 39 bottom; **Allan Mandell:** 3 top left, 4, 8 bottom left, 9 bottom left, 21 top left, 126 center

back cover bottom left; **Charles Mann:** 12 bottom left, 16 top left, 26 bottom left, 31 bottom, 37 bottom left, 53, 85 top, 93 top, 94 top, 104 right, 112 bottom, 113 top, 117 bottom, 118 top, 125 top right, 127 left, 129 top left, 133 bottom, 138 bottom, 141 bottom, 146 top, 149 left, 152 top left, 162 bottom, 182 left; **Mayer/Le Scanff, The Garden Picture Library:** 20 top left; **David McDonald:** 116 right, 174 top left, 181 bottom right; **Baldassare Mineo:** 124 top; **Jerry Pavia:** 3 bottom left, 33 middle, 84, 90 top right, 105 bottom, 106 top, 107 top, 108 top, 112 bottom, 119 bottom, 121 top, 127 bottom right, 132 left, 137 bottom, 138 top, 152 bottom, 157 top, bottom, 166 top, 169 top, 172 top, 174 right, 175 bottom right, 180 top right; **Joanne Pavia:** 22 right, 31 top left, 55; **Pam Peirce:** 75 left; **Norman A. Plate:** 6 right, 9 top center, bottom right, 30 middle, 38 bottom right, 42 top, bottom, 43 top left, top right, 46 top, 63 top, 65 top left, 66, 68 bottom, 79 all, 82, 99 top, 100 top, 110 top, 139 bottom, 155 bottom, 182 right, 183 top left; **Rob Proctor:** 7 bottom right; **Howard Rice, The Garden Picture Library:** 145 bottom; **John Rizzo:** 171 bottom; **Susan A. Roth:** 3 top right, middle, bottom right, 6 middle left, bottom left, 8 top left, 10, 12 bottom right, 14 top, 15 top, 16 bottom right, 21 bottom right, 22 left, 23 top right, 24 bottom left, top right, 26 bottom right, 27

middle, 28 top, 29 bottom right, 31 top right, 36 middle left, 39 top, 41 top left, 44, 60, 98 top left, 102 bottom, 103 top, 105 middle, 109 bottom, 113 bottom, 126 right, 128 middle left, 134 top, 144 top, 150 top, 158 bottom, 163 top, 165 bottom, 168 top, 175 top, 179 bottom, 180 top left; **Mark Rutherford:** 33 bottom, 91 bottom; **Richard Shiell:** 36 top left, 88 right, 100 bottom, 115 all, 134 bottom, 139 middle, 142 top, 147 bottom, 152 top right, 155 top, 159 bottom, 173 bottom; **Malcolm C. Shurtleff:** 75 center right; **Chad Slattery:** 23 bottom, 134 middle; **Lauren Springer:** 1; **Randy & Kara Stephens-Flemming:** 116 top left, 129 top center; **J. G. Strauch, Jr.:** 75 right; **Thomas J. Story:** 39 middle left, middle right; **Michael S. Thompson:** 17 bottom right, 28 bottom left, 35 top, 36 bottom left, 37 bottom right, 41 bottom, 51, 70 bottom, 95 top, 96 bottom right, 98 bottom right, 102 top, 114 left, 124 bottom, 125 bottom right, 128 top right, 136 bottom, 144 bottom, 154 top, 156 bottom, 162 bottom, 163 bottom, 168 bottom, 172 bottom; **Ron West/Nature Photography:** 74 top left, center left, center right, bottom left, bottom right, 76 all; **Rick Wetherbee:** 167 bottom; **Didier Willery, The Garden Picture Library:** 147 bottom; **Doug Wilson:** 37 top right, 56; **Tom Woodward:** 14 bottom, 86 bottom, 166 bottom, 175 middle; **Cynthia Woodyard:** 13 top, 57, 156 top right.